Maritime Asia vs.
Continental Asia

Published in association with the
Japan Publishing Industry Foundation for Culture

Maritime Asia

vs.

Continental Asia

National Strategies in a Region of Change

Shiraishi Takashi

LYNNE
RIENNER
PUBLISHERS

BOULDER
LONDON

Translated by Paul Warham

Published in the United States of America in 2021 by
Lynne Rienner Publishers, Inc.
1800 30th Street, Suite 314, Boulder, Colorado 80301
www.rienner.com

and in the United Kingdom by
Lynne Rienner Publishers, Inc.
Gray's Inn House, 127 Clerkenwell Road, London EC1 5DB
www.eurospanbookstore.com/rienner

First published in Japanese as *Kaiyō Ajia vs. tairiku Ajia: Nihon no kokka
senryaku o kangaeru* © 2016 by Shiraishi Takashi

Library of Congress Cataloging-in-Publication Data
A Cataloging-in-Publication record for this book
is available from the Library of Congress.

ISBN 978-1-62637-945-9 (hc)

British Cataloguing in Publication Data
A Cataloguing in Publication record for this book
is available from the British Library.

Printed and bound in Japan

 The paper used in this publication meets the requirements
of the American National Standard for Permanence of
Paper for Printed Library Materials Z39.48-1992.

5 4 3 2 1

Contents

Tables and Figures

Tables

Figures

Preface

The chapters of this book represent an extensively edited and rewritten version of four lectures originally given at the head office of Minerva Shobō in Kyoto between May and November 2014 (30 May, 4 July, 25 July, and 7 November). Although I was not so naive as to think that a simple transcript of my lectures could be turned into a book without a fair amount of rewriting, I must admit that the process of correcting and reworking the text ended up taking much longer than I had expected.

Part of the reason was the time it took to check for mistakes and omissions. But I also struggled with a dilemma that is inherent in any attempt to analyze current affairs. Sooner or later, the work of analysis and writing must come to an end, but the global situation continues to evolve on a daily basis. The manuscript inevitably starts to lose its freshness from the moment it is sent to the publisher.

I tried to think of a way to minimize the effects of this problem. My solution was to focus on long-term national strategy alongside the structures and systems of state. Of course, only the reader can decide whether this attempt was successful.

Anything written about current affairs must have an arbitrary cutoff line somewhere, or the book will never be finished. For this project, I defined my "status quo" as the end of August 2015. Of course, several important developments have already happened since, at least one of which has the potential to affect the analysis in this book considerably: the elections that took place in Myanmar on 8 November 2015. The elections brought a victory for Aung San Suu Kyi and the National League for Democracy (NLD) that was much more convincing than I had expected.

As I write this (12 November), the final results have not yet been announced, but it looks certain that the NLD will command a majority in the lower house. It is now likely that representatives from the NLD will be chosen as speaker and president when the Assembly of the Union convenes in 2016, and that "power-sharing" will become the dominant narrative within national politics in Myanmar. This will not be easy, given the gulf between the views on Myanmar's political future held by Aung San Suu Kyi (as well as the NLD and the majority of the population that supports them) and those of the commander-in-chief and the armed forces.

This much is clear from statements made by both sides regarding the present constitution. Will the NLD be able to maintain political stability in partnership with the armed forces? Or, prompted by the overwhelming popular support that exists for democratization and liberalization, will it choose instead to regard the armed forces as an adversary and make changing the constitution the central plank of its policy? It is a delicate situation, one that will need to be watched carefully.

In writing this book, I received extremely valuable comments and feedback from many people. In particular, I would like to thank Professor Miya Kazuho at Kyoto Seika University, Assistant Professor Takagi Yūsuke at the National Graduate Institute for Policy Studies (GRIPS), and Horikawa Kentarō, my editor at Minerva Shobō. As always, I benefited immensely from my discussions with Caroline Hau. I am extremely grateful to all these people and to everyone else who helped put the book together.

Much of the original research that went into the book was carried out under the auspices of a grant-in-aid from the Japan Society for the Promotion of Science for the project Southeast Asia in a Time of East Asian Transformation (principal investigator: Shiraishi Takashi; JSPS KAKENHI Grant Number 23330052) and the Emerging State Project (principal investigator: Sonobe Tetsushi; JSPS KAKENHI Grant Number 15K21728). I would like to take this opportunity to record my appreciation for this valuable support.

—12 November 2015

Introduction

Over the course of the coming four chapters, I discuss a set of questions in connection with history and current affairs in the East Asia/Asia Pacific/Indo-Pacific region and Japan's position within it. Chapter 1 outlines my understanding of the future trends in this region. I want to approach the question in a long-term, say ten- to fifteen-year perspective, up until around 2030. I then examine current events in the chapters that follow and discuss the present situation and future prospects. I look at some of the long-term trends, the current conditions, and the future outlook, while always keeping in mind the history of the region over the past thirty years, from the mid-1980s. I refer to the region with the term *East Asia/Asia Pacific/Indo-Pacific*. I know that this is a convoluted way to talk about the region, but I will explain why I use the term in the course of the pages that follow. For now, suffice it to say that when we try to understand international relations in this vast region from the Pacific to the Indian Ocean, it is important not to be too fixated on any geographical framework. A broader, more flexible perspective makes it easier to understand the dynamics of international relations in the region.

NINETEENTH-CENTURY CIVILIZATION

Let me start with a quote from *The Great Transformation*, a classic in the social sciences, by Hungarian economic historian and political economist Karl Polanyi. He wrote the book during World War II while living in the United States, his place of exile. It opens with the bold declaration that "nineteenth-century civilization has collapsed." The book then continues:

> Nineteenth-century civilization rested on four institutions. The first was the balance-of-power system which for a century prevented the occurrence of any long and devastating war between the Great Powers. The second was the international gold standard which symbolized a unique organization of world economy. The third was the self-regulating market which produced an unheard-of material welfare. The fourth was the liberal state. Classified in one way, two of these institutions were economic, two political. Classified in another way, two of them were national, two international. Between them they determined the characteristic outlines of the history of our civilization. (Polanyi 2001: 3)

Of these four systems, Polanyi himself particularly emphasized the self-regulating market. He believed that two competing principles drove the history of the nineteenth century: the principle of economic liberalism, which aimed at the establishment of a self-regulating market, and the principle of social protection, which aimed at the conservation of humanity, nature, and productive organization. The tensions and clashes between these principles, he argued, were what had caused such phenomena as imperial rivalries, pressure on currencies and exchange rates, unemployment, and class conflict (Polanyi 2001: 138).

But this interpretation is debatable. I believe that the most important reason for the collapse of nineteenth-century civilization was the rise of Germany and the disruption this caused to the European balance of power. This was an outcome of the development driven by German industrialization from the 1870s onward. Rather than looking to the contradictions inherent in the self-regulating market, I believe it makes better sense to explain the collapse of nineteenth-century civilization in terms of the uneven economic development of the European powers, and the failure to maintain and recalibrate the balance of power. I might also add that from our twenty-first-century perspective, the term "nineteenth-century civilization" is an overly Eurocentric way of putting things; probably a term like "nineteenth-century system" would be more neutral and objective.

In quoting Polanyi on nineteenth-century civilization, however, it is not my purpose to offer a competing explanation for why this system collapsed, but rather to draw attention to Polanyi's important insight: that during the "long nineteenth century," from the end of the Napoleonic Wars in the mid-1810s to World War II, what Polanyi referred to as "nineteenth-century civilization" existed in Western Europe, the center of the world system at the time, and that this "civilization" was built on four institutions: the balance of power, the gold standard, self-regulating markets (a market economy), and the liberal state.

THE TWO SUPERPOWERS AND
THE TWENTIETH-CENTURY SYSTEM

What systems provided the foundations for the twentieth-century system that succeeded the nineteenth-century civilization after the latter's collapse? During the Cold War, the bipolar global system was built. The Eastern bloc, centered on the Soviet Union, was built on four systems: imperial control, managed trade, a socialist economy, and the party state. The West, led by the United States, was conventionally known as the "Free World." This too was built on the four systemic pillars: the Pax Americana; a liberal trade system centered on the dollar standard (the dollar-gold standard until the early 1970s) and the General Agreement on Tariffs and Trade (GATT) and eventually, after the end of the Cold War, the World Trade Organization (WTO); the liberal democratic state; and a market economy.[1]

The Eastern bloc dissolved following the collapse of the socialist states in Eastern Europe and the breakup of the Soviet Union. As globalization progressed, the system of the US-led "Free World" appeared to represent the inevitable long-term tendency of world history. Indeed, in the early years of the new millennium, this system seemed set to encompass the entire globe, following US intervention in Afghanistan and Iraq after the terrorist attacks of 11 September 2001. Immediately after the end of the Cold War, Francis Fukuyama spoke of the "end of history," and during the first decade of the new millennium there was much talk of an "American empire." From today's perspective, it is clear that much of this was exaggerated and the product of a passing moment in world history. In fact, as we are well aware now, the twentieth-century system has changed substantially in many ways. The main reasons for this change were the uneven development of the world economy and in particular the economic rise of China and other emerging economies and states. This became clear in the global financial crisis that began with the collapse of Lehman Brothers in 2008. Today, as the global financial crisis recedes into the past, we are aware that global politics and the world economy are undergoing massive changes, even though we do not yet have a good sense of where these changes are taking us. This, I believe, is the "new normal" of the age in which we are living today.

How should we view the changes currently under way in the global system? Or, to put it in more concrete terms, what are the main factors driving these changes, and how are they affecting the global system? These are big questions. On an intuitive level, though, I think there is no question that the main drivers of the changes in the global system, as

Murakami Yasusuke (1992: 351) cogently argued long ago, are industrialization and the technological innovation that underlies it. Industrialization has always taken place unevenly and led to uneven development in the world economy. This means constant changes in the distribution of wealth. Changes in the distribution of wealth lead, sooner or later, to changes to the distribution of power. The balance of power shifts. And this changes the global or regional order. How is this process of change taking place?

Some people hypothesize a "hegemonic shift" and posit that a major war is likely to happen whenever such a shift takes place. But this view perhaps gives excessive importance to the historical fact that US hegemony happened to come about as the result of two world wars. Methodologically, the hypothesis tends to regard states as virtually the sole actors in global politics. This theoretical perspective, which very much simplifies the dynamics of world history, can perhaps be described as "methodological statism." The major paradigms in international political theory include realism, liberalism, and in recent years constructionism, which looks closely at historically and politically constructed identities. In these terms, it is fair to say that the theory of hegemonic shift tilts rather too far toward realism.

We see evidence of a similar point of view in everyday patterns of speech, when people refer to "Japan" doing such-and-such a thing, or "China" doing this or that. This view is built on an assumption that since there is no such thing as a global government, the world exists in a state of anarchy. Within this anarchical world, states act logically as coherent actors in accordance with their own raisons d'état: this leads to an assumption that the best way to analyze international politics is to treat each state as if it had its own individual personality.

GLOBAL GOVERNANCE AND GLOBAL TRENDS

The claim that no world government exists is certainly true. But this is not the same as saying that the world exists in a state of anarchy. Nowadays, we often come across references to "global governance." The phrase should remind us that in fact the world is far from being an anarchy. Although a global government per se may not exist, many international regimes are well established. These include the United Nations, as well as the International Monetary Fund (IMF), the World Bank, and the WTO. On a regional basis, there are organizations such as the North Atlantic Treaty Organization (NATO) and the US-led hub-and-spokes Asian security system. Elsewhere, there are supranational and regional organizations like the European Union (EU) and the Association of

Southeast Asian Nations (ASEAN). Numerous systems, rules, and bodies are in place on a global and regional basis, along with the regulations, conventions, and norms that support them. After World War II, the "Free World" came into being, centered on the United States. This was built on four main supporting systems: the US-guaranteed peace (Pax Americana), the free trade system centered on the dollar standard (until the early 1970s the dollar-gold standard) and GATT/WTO, the liberal democratic state, and the market economy. After the end of the Cold War, with globalization, this became the dominant system, and looked set to spread across the entire globe. I repeat these historical reminders here to underline the fact that the world is far from being a complete anarchy.

It is also a fact that although individual states may behave as coherent actors in international politics, each state nevertheless makes decisions and takes actions based on a given political process. To assume that states can act and think rationally and logically simply does not accord with the reality.

Also, as many commentators have pointed out, nonstate actors have become increasingly important as globalization has progressed. This is another important implication of the term "global governance." For example, financial markets are closely connected across the world, and financial bodies, institutional investors, hedge funds, and rating agencies play important roles alongside central banks and governments. In national security too, nonstate actors such as pirates off the coast of Somalia and the Straits of Malacca, al-Qaeda, and drug cartels are important actors that cannot be ignored. Likewise, in aid to developing countries, institutions like the Ford Foundation and the Bill and Melinda Gates Foundation are performing an important role in setting the global agenda alongside the United Nations, the World Bank, the Organization for Economic Cooperation and Development (OECD) and its Development Assistance Committee (DAC), and government bodies. In an age like the present, when production networks spread over a region across national borders, it is impossible for a country to make plans for its economic development strategy without considering how that country can position itself in the transnational value chains.

THE SOCIAL SCIENCES AS A WAY OF
UNDERSTANDING THE WORLD

As people go international, moving across national borders more frequently and cheaply, concepts of nationality and immigration inevitably change. In this context, what can only be described as global norms are in the process of being made and systems are being built, albeit still in embryonic form for now. This is not to say that differences between civilizations will disappear. Nevertheless, changes are under way that go beyond civilizational differences, although admittedly the extent and nature of these changes vary considerably from one region to another. English is becoming a world language, and global norms are being formed that considerable numbers of people around the world accept as valid and legitimate. Globalization, or the revolution in information and communication technology, has shrunk time and space. People, goods and services, money, as well as information and knowledge now cross national borders, and they circulate on a greater scale and with greater speed than ever before. This has led to the formation of different orders in different regions. The nature of nation-states is changing, and nonstate actors—including foundations, nongovernmental organizations (NGOs), companies, individuals, as well as organized crime syndicates and terrorist groups—are coming to play an important international role, both positively and negatively. Methodological statism is, I believe, inadequate to help us understand this world. This is not to deny the importance of realism. But it does mean that other paradigms, such as liberalism and constructionism, need to be deployed alongside realism to understand contemporary international relations.

There are two more things I would like to say at the outset on this general topic. The first regards trends in the social sciences in the United States. Since the 1980s, political science education at US universities has become very much systematized and professionalized. Signs of this tendency were already there when I was a graduate student in the United States in the 1970s. This has had important bearings on the work produced by US-trained social scientists. In US graduate schools, the mission of political science departments is to educate a new generation of academics who are capable of teaching political science in US universities. Naturally, this means that the priority in terms of quality control is to ensure that the training provided produces scholars capable of teaching political science classes at a certain level as soon as they have graduated with their PhDs and found a teaching position at a university somewhere in the United States. For this, around two years of coursework is normally required, during which students are introduced to realism, liberalism, and constructionism as the chief paradigms of international political science and study the representative texts and key concepts of each.

When these people come to write their dissertations, they tend to produce work based on these paradigms that looks methodologically sophisticated, but is often not very useful for a reader looking to understand a given political phenomenon. In fact, in many cases, after reading books produced by these scholars, I find myself wondering what I have learned from the experience. They seem to spend a lot of time telling you things you already know. After reading books like these for more than forty years, I have become convinced that the world we live in is simply not amenable to being meaningfully analyzed using paradigms like these. In terms of methodology, I use an approach that Peter Katzenstein, a former colleague of mine at Cornell, calls "eclecticism." In other words, I combine a variety of perspectives in different ways depending on the subject, and attempt to make sense of international politics and political economy by giving due importance to history. So that is roughly where I stand, methodologically speaking.

Another trend is the tendency to try to explain social phenomena by analyzing general structures that go beyond individuals: by looking at institutions and structures and, in recent years, at the ideas and patterns of thinking shared by the members of a particular society. This is not something I intend to discuss explicitly here, but it is another tendency that has been quite prominent in the social sciences in recent years—particularly among scholars whose approach is based on the study of institutions. Institutions can be designed, and different institutions produce different outcomes. Take elections, for example. If we imagine replacing a current system with an alternative system, it is possible to analyze with a fair degree of objectivity what kinds of changes might occur in the makeup of the elected body as a result. This is attractive, and I expect this focus on institutions and structures to become even more influential in the future. But there is perhaps a tendency with this approach to pay less attention to the question of *how* a person acts within a given system or structure. This means that questions about what or how people think, particularly people in strategically important positions, and what decisions they make, are perhaps downplayed and understudied. But ultimately it is people who run systems. And this means that the question of how we think about structures and people—or structures and agency—is something to which we need to pay careful attention, particularly when analyzing current affairs, even when we don't discuss it explicitly.

NOTE

1. This describes the system in Western Europe. In East Asia, it was only in Japan that the combination of a liberal democratic system and market

economy was present from the outset. Elsewhere in "Free Asia," democratization came much later: from the mid-1980s in the Philippines, South Korea, and Taiwan and after the fall of the Suharto regime in 1998 in Indonesia. The extent to which Malaysia and Singapore can be considered as democracies is the source of considerable disagreement even today.

1

Long-Term
Trends in Asia

I would like to begin my discussion by looking at long-term trends on a state/national level over the past several decades. Table 1.1 shows the share of the global economy of several important countries and regions of the world. Data are given for four years: 1990, 2000, 2010, and 2018. The figures for 2018 are IMF projections. The table tells us two things right away.

THE RISE OF EMERGING NATIONS
AND CHANGES IN GLOBAL GOVERNANCE

*The Group of Seven's Declining
Share of the Global Economy*

First, let's consider the share of the world economy made up by developed as opposed to developing economies. In 1990 and 2000, the economies of the Group of Seven (G7) countries (United States, Japan, Germany, France, United Kingdom, Italy, and Canada) constituted a total of between 65 percent and 66 percent of the world economy. In other words, during the final quarter of the twentieth century, the G7 made up about two-thirds of the global economy. This was a time when the G7 leaders could take strategic decisions relating to the management of the world economy, as seen classically in the international economic coordination in the years between the Plaza Accord in 1985 and the Louvre Accord in 1987. Since the start of the twenty-first century, however, the share of the world economy represented by the G7 and other developed economies has steadily declined. By 2010, the G7's share had fallen to 50 percent;

Table 1.1   **Share of Global Economy by Country and Region, 1990–2018**

	Monetary Share ($ billions, current prices)				Percentage Share (current prices)			
	1990	2000	2010	2018	1990	2000	2010	2018
World	22,397	32,718	63,990	96,904	100	100	100	100
Advanced economies	17,917	26,132	42,013	56,707	80.0	79.9	65.7	58.5
Major advanced economies (G7)	14,637	21,586	32,304	43,296	65.4	66.0	50.5	44.7
Emerging markets and developing economies	4,479	6,586	21,976	40,196	20.0	20.1	34.3	41.5
North America	6,573	11,028	16,205	23,257	29.4	33.7	25.3	24.0
Canada	594	739	1,247	1,701	2.7	2.3	1.9	1.8
United States	5,979	10,289	14,958	21,556	26.7	31.4	23.4	22.2
European Union	7,047	8,539	16,367	21,454	31.5	26.1	25.6	22.1
Asia Pacific	4,711	7,666	16,984	28,489	21.0	23.4	26.6	29.5
Japan	3,103	4,731	5,495	5,943	13.9	14.5	8.6	6.1
China	390	1,198	5,930	13,760	1.7	3.7	9.3	14.2
South Korea	270	533	1,014	1,702	1.2	1.6	1.6	1.8
ASEAN-5	298	331	1,588	2,902	1.3	1.0	2.5	3.0
Indonesia	113	165	709	1,211	0.5	0.5	1.1	1.2
India	327	474	1,710	2,481	1.5	1.4	2.7	2.6
Australia	323	399	1,247	1,701	1.4	1.2	1.9	1.8

Source: International Monetary Fund, World Economic Outlook Database, October 2013, https://www.imf.org/external/pubs/ft/weo/2013/02/weodata/weoselagr.aspx.

it was expected to drop below 45 percent by 2018. In large part this is due to the rise of the BRICS countries (Brazil, Russia, India, China, and South Africa) and other emerging economies. These developing and emerging economies made up around 20 percent of the world economy in 1990 and 2000, but by 2010 their share had risen to 34 percent. That share was expected to exceed 40 percent by 2018, and by the middle of the 2020s the emerging and developing economies may have a larger share of the global economy than the G7.

Bipolarity, Unipolarity, Multipolarity

The rise of the emerging economies poses a question for global governance: How is the rise of these emerging economies changing the global order? One concept that is widely mentioned in this context is that of "multipolarity." But the term is too imprecise to be particularly useful. During the Cold War, the world was characterized by bipolarity. When the Cold War ended following the collapse of the Soviet Union and the democratization of Eastern European countries, bipolarity was replaced by unipolarity, which lasted for two decades. But with the changing distribution of wealth and power, many people now see the rise of a more multipolar system. To put it differently, multipolarity is a simplistic way of talking about this overarching tendency in the global distribution of wealth and power.

But this tells us very little about how the global system is changing and what kind of world order is now in the making. Under the bipolar system of the Cold War years, the United States and the Soviet Union were rival hegemons engaged in a tense standoff ideologically, militarily, politically, and economically. The two "poles" of the bipolar system were hegemons. With the end of the Cold War, one of the two poles was gone. The remaining single pole was and still is a hegemon, now on the global level. With the rise of a multipolar system, are we then to witness the emergence of many "poles," each hegemonic, with a group of allied and client states/nations, and opposed to or competing with the United States? I don't think this is what most people imagine will happen with the shift from unipolarity to multipolarity, even though it is safe to assume that when China's party state leaders talk about "multipolarity," they mean to make China a hegemonic "pole," as the Soviet Union used to be.

The point I am making is straightforward. We should be careful not to let the similarities in terminology blind us to the differences that exist between unipolarity, bipolarity, and multipolarity. In fact, the meaning of a "pole" in a unipolar or bipolar order is quite different from the significance the term has in a multipolar world. Multipolarity is a simplistic term that tells us little beyond the obvious fact that the distribution of wealth and power is changing unevenly. How should we interpret these changes, then? One approach is to ask how the rise of emerging economies and states might affect the current affairs and the future prospects for global governance.

If we pose the question this way, it should be clear that there are at least two ways of looking at the question. The first is what is generally known as the liberal realist approach, as John Ikenberry presents in his book *Liberal Leviathan: The Origins, Crisis, and Transformation of the American World Order* (2011). Ikenberry argues that despite the rise of the emerging economies, the US-centered world order is strong enough and flexible enough not to collapse easily.

In the years following World War II, Ikenberry notes, the United States established international bodies like the IMF, World Bank, United Nations, OECD, and WTO, as well as global and regional systems including NATO and the United States–Japan Security Treaty.

Looked at purely in terms of the distribution of wealth and power, it is not wrong to say that US wealth and power have declined in relative terms in the decades since. But in the twentieth century, as US power declined, the Western European countries and Japan came back to economic health and supported the US-centered global order as junior partners, and shouldered part of the burden involved in maintaining it. They did this because it was in their interests to do so and because the United States and its allies were bound together by alliances like NATO and the United States–Japan Security Treaty, effectively limiting each signatory party's freedom of action. In this way, they managed the uncertainties that can be brought about by international anarchy.

These reciprocal limitations were also backed up by US systems of constitutional politics. The Western European countries and Japan were engaged in the decentralized and pluralistic policymaking processes of the United States in a variety of ways. As a result, the present US-centered world order mirrors the traditions of constitutionalism that form the basis of the political system in the United States. The world order has therefore emerged as an international extension of the flexible and dynamic framework of system-building at the heart of the US constitutional system. This order guarantees a liberal and open world economy, along with shared norms and the ideals of democracy, human rights, constitutional government, and private property. A comprehensive international network has been built around these shared values. The world order has been adjusted and revised even as US power has declined in relative terms, and these adjustments have enjoyed widespread support. The rise of the emerging economies will do little to change this world order. Indeed, the emerging economies stand to benefit hugely from the maintenance of a stable and predictable order. US power may continue to decline in the future, but the world order the United States has built will endure.

I believe this summary captures what I think are the most important points Ikenberry makes. Even this short summary shows the liberal assumptions inherent in his approach. Ikenberry himself served as a member of the Policy Planning Staff at the US Department of State from 1991 to 1992, and the influence of this kind of liberal realist thinking can often be seen in speeches by US politicians. For example, the speech given by President Barack Obama to the Australian parliament in November 2011, on the subject of US policies in Asia Pacific, was marked by this view of the world. In Japan, I think, experts often find the views of Ikenberry and others who share his perspective too optimistic, and feel that this liberal view of the world underestimates the real difficulties that emerging states, especially China, present. I will come back to this question of how to evaluate his argument later.

From G7 to G-Zero?

The other, contending, view is the idea of a "G-Zero" world presented most prominently by Ian Bremmer (2012). One of the most important points he makes is that there is a crucial difference between emerging and developed countries. In terms of the scale of their economies, the emerging economies and the developed countries are now roughly equal. For example, China's gross domestic product (GDP) in 2013 was $8.9 trillion. This was only half of the equivalent figure for the United States ($16.7 trillion), but bigger than the economies of Japan ($5 trillion) and Germany ($3.6 trillion) combined. Likewise, India's GDP was $1.8 trillion—around the same size as Canada's (also $1.8 trillion) and bigger than Australia's ($1.5 trillion). And although Brazil's GDP of $2.2 trillion was slightly smaller than the United Kingdom's ($2.4 trillion), it was larger than Italy's ($2.1 trillion). In terms of the size of their economies, in other words, these countries have already caught up with the G7 countries.

But per capita income remains much smaller in these countries than in the G7 countries. In 2013, per capita income in Brazil was $10,958, roughly one-third the equivalent figure for the United Kingdom ($39,049) or Italy ($33,909). In the same year, per capita income in China was $6,569: around one-sixth of the figure for Japan ($39,321) or Germany ($43,952). In the case of India, the discrepancy is even starker: India's per capita income of $1,414 was less than 3 percent that of Canada ($53,953). Consequently, and quite naturally, huge numbers of people in these countries long to become more affluent, so that they too can gain access to the same lifestyles many people in developed countries enjoy.

This is natural. But from another perspective, it also means that there is often little political will in the emerging economies and states for measures to address global warming and other global challenges when these measures seem to come at a cost to the interests of their own peoples. This attitude can extend to issues like the protection of intellectual property rights: in the emerging economies, claims that intellectual property rights are a kind of conspiracy cooked up by developed countries to "keep us poor" can be quite persuasive.

One consequence of this (inevitably according to Bremmer) may be that the capacity of global governance to address global challenges will decline as the emerging economies come to have a greater influence and say in international politics. I would enlarge on this somewhat as follows. During the final quarter of the twentieth century, when the G7 countries alone made up two-thirds of the global economy, these countries could take strategic decisions that affected the management of the entire world economy. In the global financial crisis that followed the collapse of Lehman Brothers in 2008, however, the G7 proved incapable of responding to the crisis alone. This led to the replacement of the G7 by the Group of 20 (G20) as the main framework for international coordination. But attempts at international cooperation within the G20 framework collapsed almost immediately, and it is fair to say that the G20 became "G-Zero," as Michael Spence has argued (2011: 320–336).

The Japanese translation of Ian Bremmer's *Every Nation for Itself: Winners and Losers in a G-Zero World* was generally very well received. It is fair to say that in Japan, Bremmer's argument is generally regarded as more persuasive than Ikenberry's, even though I personally find Ikenberry's argument more nuanced. Ultimately, however, I find both arguments too general and vague. The effects of the rise of the emerging economies and consequent changes in global governance differ substantially depending on which area of policy we choose to look at. This should be clear if we review specific examples from a few policy areas. For example, the euro faced a grave crisis between 2011 and 2012, although the situation has improved somewhat since. At the height of the crisis, Japan, China, and other countries in East Asia provided funds for liquidity assistance. Why? Because if the euro collapsed, that disaster would trigger a major crisis across the world's currency and finance systems. In that sense, these countries had no choice: they had to provide funding to protect their own interests, apart from anything else. In early 2011, a forum on global governance was held in Bangkok. The event was organized by Surakiart Sathirathai, former deputy prime minister of Thailand. Recalling that the Asian currency crisis, which started in Bangkok in July 1997, had been labeled in some quarters as the "Tom Yam Kung" crisis, Sathirathai jokingly asked his audience what terms might be used to describe the going crisis affecting the euro: the paella crisis, perhaps, or the spaghetti crisis? Nevertheless, Thailand stumped up the necessary cash. In this sense, it is fair to say that the framework of global governance is still functioning reasonably well—at least in the area of international currency and finance.

International Development and Global Governance

In the field of development, by contrast, the international regime that was dominant in the 1980s and 1990s is clearly undergoing major changes. As early as 2010, the total amount of development funds provided to developing countries by the China Development Bank and the China Export-Import Bank exceeded that of the World Bank.[1] However, China is not a member of the OECD, and naturally is not a member of the OECD's Development Assistance Committee either. This means that China can provide development aid without being bound by DAC regulations, which formed the core of the development aid regime during the second half of the twentieth century. China often refers to development aid as an example of a "win-win" deal. The reality is that when China offers financing for a development project, a Chinese state-run enterprise will place the winning bid, and Chinese engineers and workers will use Chinese-built equipment to construct roads, dams, and port facilities. Under the principle of noninterference in domestic politics, China will happily provide assistance even in countries where there are problems with human rights or governance. This means that the DAC's international aid regime, which was not without significance in previous decades, is already well on the way to collapse.

Today, when Japan offers low-interest concessional loans for infrastructure development in African countries, Japanese companies can no longer compete against Chinese or South Korean companies in untied contract bids for a road construction project. Provided that certain quality controls are in place, a road is a road. From the perspective of the recipient country, the nationality of the construction company is of no real importance. Nevertheless, a Japanese politician might feel justified in asking why Chinese or South Korean companies should benefit from a project carried out with Japanese development aid, especially when Chinese aid projects are inevitably "tied projects" that only Chinese companies can bid for. This is already having an effect on Japanese official development assistance (ODA) policy. As China has become an important player in international development, the rules themselves have started to change. This is apparent in Japan in the field of infrastructure exports.[2]

When it comes to challenges like global warming, emerging economies like India have no intention of taking the initiative in efforts to reduce carbon dioxide emissions. After all, they say, during the nineteenth and twentieth centuries, the industrialized economies of Western Europe, the United States, and Japan used as much energy as they liked, without giving a thought to global warming. Why should we have to scale back our industrialization now, they ask, and sacrifice improvements to our people's standards of living in order to reduce CO_2 emissions? Arguments like this can be quite persuasive domestically and are one reason why international efforts to tackle the problem on a global basis struggle to make progress.

Once we start to look at the current state of global governance in this way, it becomes clear that the capacity of global governance differs substantially from one policy area to another. This is only to be expected, given the fact that each area of policy—currency and finance, commerce, development aid, and so on—has its own distinctive international regime. These regimes differ in the extent to which they are systematized. The extent to which emerging economies see any benefit to themselves in maintaining these regimes also affects their stability. In this sense, the arguments put forward by people like Ikenberry and Bremmer, although they may look straightforward at first glance, in fact offer little substantial guidance in helping us to understand what is actually happening.

I have so far been discussing changes in global governance from the perspective of institutions and structures, but there is another aspect we need to consider, and that is the people responsible for managing these systems. During the presidencies of George W. Bush (2001–2009) and Barack Obama (2009–2017), for example, the international regimes in most policy areas did not undergo radical changes. But concerns have recently been expressed about US leadership in a number of areas. For the most part, people are not worried about the structures of governance themselves. Take what happened in Syria when President Obama threatened a military response in retaliation for any use of chemical weapons, and then failed to follow through on his promise. A situation like this raises questions not so much about governance structures as about the people who occupy the positions of responsibility within them. It is a question of leadership. Within the same system, the performance of global governance will differ greatly depending on whether the sitting US president demonstrates leadership. One problem with Bremmer's argument is that he tends to blend together the distinct problems of leadership, institutions, and structures.

THE RISE OF CHINA AND ITS EFFECT ON REGIONAL ORDER

China as a New Gulliver

The other major trend is the changing distribution of wealth and power across regions and the dramatic rise of China in recent years. As the earlier Table 1.1 shows, North America (the United States and Canada) and Europe (European Union) together made up around 60 percent of the global economy in both 1990 and 2000. From the start of the twenty-first century, however, this percentage started to fall. It was down to 52 percent by 2010, and will almost certainly drop below half by 2018. The main reason for this is the rapidly growing share made up by the Asia Pacific region as the most important center for global economic growth. The increase in China's share has been dramatic. In 1990, China's share of the global economy was just 1.7 percent; this increased to 3.7 percent in 2000. By 2010 it exceeded 9 percent, and it was expected to account for more than 14 percent of the total world economy by 2018. Japan's share was between 14 percent and 15 percent from the Plaza Accord of 1985 until around 2000; this was the peak of Japan's economic strength and influence. China's share was forecast to reach these levels by around 2018, and is likely to rival the United States by the middle of the following decade if its economy continues to grow at rates of 4–5 percent annually. Japan's share, by contrast, will fall to 5 percent or less. How has the distribution of wealth and power in the Asia Pacific region changed over the past two decades? Table 1.2 gives us some idea.

The table compares Japan's economy with those of other countries, with Japan shown as 100. In 1990, the combined total of the economies of China, India, and the ASEAN-7 were equivalent to just one-third the size of the Japanese economy.[3] Even in 2000, the combined economies of China, India, and ASEAN-7 were only half the size of Japan's. During the last quarter of the twentieth century, in other words, Japan was the Gulliver of East Asia. But by 2010, China's economy had overtaken

Table 1.2   GDP in Asia Pacific, 1990–2018

	GDP ($ billions, current prices)				GDP with Japan = 100			
	1990	2000	2010	2018	1990	2000	2010	2018
China	390	1,198	5,930	13,760	12.6	25.3	107.9	231.5
India	327	474	1,710	2,481	10.5	10.0	31.1	41.7
Indonesia	113	165	709	1,211	3.6	3.5	12.9	20.4
Malaysia	43	93	247	443	1.4	2.0	4.5	7.5
Myanmar	n/a	10	49	96	n/a	0.2	0.9	1.6
Philippines	48	81	199	420	1.5	1.7	3.6	7.1
Singapore	38	94	231	348	1.2	2.0	4.2	5.9
Thailand	85	122	318	557	2.7	2.6	5.8	9.4
Vietnam	6	31	112	268	0.2	0.7	2.0	4.5
ASEAN-7	333	596	1,865	3,343	10.7	12.6	33.9	56.3
Australia	323	399	1,247	1,701	10.4	8.4	22.7	28.6
Canada	594	739	1,614	2,273	19.1	15.6	29.4	38.2
United States	5,979	10,289	14,958	21,556	192.7	217.5	272.2	362.7
Japan	3,103	4,731	5,495	5,943	100	100	100	100

Source: International Monetary Fund, World Economic Outlook Database, October 2013, https://www.imf.org/external/pubs/ft/weo/2013/02/weodata/weoselagr.aspx.

Note: n/a = data not available.

Japan's, India's had grown to one-quarter the size, and the ASEAN-7 countries to one-third the size. This trend will continue, so that China's economy will likely be two and a half times as big as Japan's by 2018, with India's half the size and that of the ASEAN-7 countries nearly two-thirds as big.

On a global level, China's economy would still account for only 14 percent of the total by 2018. Even so, China's economy would be larger than Japan's, ASEAN's (counting only the seven countries just mentioned), and India's combined. China will have taken Japan's place and become the new Gulliver of East Asia. As the size of a country's economy grows, government income also increases. The country can invest more in education, science and technology, and military buildup. The effects of this may not be felt immediately, but eventually this spending leads to an increase in national power, to a greater or lesser extent from one country to another depending on how efficiently the funds are used, and other factors. This is not to say that China will necessarily rival the United States in national power if, as expected, its economy grows to roughly the same size as that of the United States by the middle of the 2020s. Nevertheless, as China's economy grows, it is all but certain that its national power will increase too over time. If China's economy continues to grow at a rate of 4–5 percent per year for the next decade or so, it is possible that China will become overwhelmingly the most powerful state in East Asia. People in China are naturally quite aware of this, and people in other countries in the region, including here in Japan, are watching with interest to see what China's economic rise and growing national power will mean for the region in terms of risks, uncertainties, and opportunities. The same thing can be said for the countries of Central Asia, China's hinterland. For most countries in this region, China is already the biggest or second biggest trading partner, so that fluctuations in China's business climate now have a profound impact on the economies of neighboring countries. And there is also no doubt that China represents a major threat to national security for countries that have territorial disputes with China. All these factors mean that the question of how to respond to a rising China is an issue of vital importance not only for Japan and Southeast Asia but for India as well.

How China's Rise Is Seen in Europe

But this is not yet the case in the rest of the world. In Europe, China's rise is welcomed as a major opportunity, and there is as yet little awareness of the risks involved. Evidence of this can be seen in the frequency with which the German chancellor, Angela Merkel, has visited China. From the perspective of Europe, or the Middle East, Africa, South America, and other regions, China is a faraway country on the other side of the globe. The extent to which countries perceive China's rise as a systemic problem varies massively from one region to another. This is an issue of which we will need to be keenly aware for some time.

What are the major points of conflict presented by China's rise? I discuss this question in depth in the next chapter. For now, it is enough to remember that the current period—roughly between 2000 and 2020—represents a vital period of strategic opportunity for China. This is something that all of China's recent leaders—Jiang Zemin, Hu Jintao, and Xi Jinping—have agreed on and mentioned in public statements at various times. From the early 2020s or so, China's economic growth is likely to slow as the working population starts to decline and Chinese society starts aging. This means that the next few years are vital. What is China trying to achieve within this period of strategic opportunity? In the words of a slogan used by the ruling party and government, China's plan is to develop a "rich country, strong army." This phrase, reminiscent of the *fukoku kyōhei* slogan (same translation) that was used with much the same intent in Meiji Japan, basically aims to achieve prosperity through economic growth and to increase military spending and power so that China can exercise its influence as a great power regionally and eventually globally, backed up by its economic and military might. This is what the party says is its basic strategy.

Assuming China's economy continues to grow and China's national power continues to increase under this "rich country, strong army" philosophy, what is likely to happen? As mentioned at the outset, Karl Polanyi argued that what he called "nineteenth-century civilization" was built on four pillars: the balance of power, the gold standard, market economy, and liberal states. This system collapsed during the thirty years between the two world wars and was followed by a bipolar system. The United States built a new twentieth-century system, or the "Free World," based on the Pax Americana, the dollar standard and the GATT/WTO system, liberal democratic states, and the market economy. Pax Americana was supported by the overwhelming military power of the United States and its alliances, particularly NATO in the North Atlantic and the US-led hub-and-spokes system of alliances in Asia Pacific. The dollar standard was originally the gold-dollar standard until President Nixon took the dollar off the gold standard in 1971 and the fixed exchange system was replaced by a floating exchange rate mechanism. Meanwhile, the free trade system that started as the GATT system evolved into the WTO after the end of the Cold War. Domestically, liberal democracy and the market economy became the basic foundations of the political and economic system. In the shift from the nineteenth- to the twentieth-century system, Pax Americana provided the foundation for security, replacing the nineteenth-century balance of power. Economically, a worldwide free trade system was built on a financial system based on the dollar standard and the GATT/WTO.

China as a Free Rider

Since the "reform and opening-up" policy was introduced in 1978, China has experienced dramatic growth within this international system. But although it accepts the Pax Americana, China has continued to bolster its military strength in accordance with its policy of "rich country, strong army." Although China acknowledges the dollar standard, it controls the yuan-dollar exchange rate and does not allow free movement of capital across international borders. Within China itself, the Communist Party maintains what is effectively a single-party state, and despite claims that the economy is based on market principles, state-owned enterprises make up more than one-third of the domestic economy. China also refuses to shoulder any of the costs involved in maintaining the international system. In other words, China is hitching a free ride on the international system led by the United States, while moving forward with its plans for a "rich country, strong army." As China's national power grows, its behavior is increasingly typified by "great power" pretensions and a tendency to push its weight around. If this behavior continues, what effect will it have on international systems? What will happen to those systems if China continues to act in this way when its share of the global economy is more than 20 percent, without shouldering any of the costs of maintaining the international systems? I think there is a serious risk that sooner or later they will become unsustainable and impossible to maintain in the long term.

The question of what is likely to happen to twentieth-century systems following a relative decline in US power has been repeatedly asked over the years. The "hegemonic shift" hypothesis mentioned earlier was originally put forward as an answer to this question. In Japan, Murakami Yasusuke considered the problem from the perspective of systems in his book *Han koten no seiji keizai gaku* [Anticlassical political economy] (1992). Since the 1980s the Japanese government has shouldered its share of the costs of maintaining the international systems, as seen in the international economic coordination following the

Plaza Accord in 1985. There has also been slow but steady progress in the direction of doing more to contribute to maintaining the Pax Americana, mostly in the form of revisions to the so-called Yoshida Doctrine, from initially sending members of the Self-Defense Forces on overseas peacekeeping missions to recent revisions to allow Japan to exercise the right to collective self-defense in certain circumstances without contravening the narrow interpretation of the constitution. At the time of the Asian financial crisis in 1997–1998, Japan proposed an Asian Monetary Fund, and through the Miyazawa Initiative provided considerable funding to support liquidity and public finances in countries that had fallen into crisis. China, by contrast, has hardly done anything in this respect. In fact, China's proposals for an Asia Infrastructure Investment Bank to systematize its ideas of modern-day land-based and maritime "Silk Roads," together with its ideas for a New Development Bank involving the BRICS states, make it unclear whether China wants to maintain the current world systems or break them apart.

As earlier, however, it will still take some time before this becomes a major concern on a global level. More likely, there will remain a continuing difference in the way countries in the Asia Pacific region and the rest of the world perceive China's rise as a risk. And in a decade or a decade and a half, what the party leadership now sees as the window for its strategic opportunity will close. There will be a strong temptation for China to seize as much as it can while the going is good and this period of strategic opportunity lasts. In this sense, I expect the next ten to fifteen years or so to be an extremely difficult period, both within East Asia and for the world as a whole.

Europe and the North Atlantic vs. East Asia and Asia Pacific

What are likely to be the major issues in the East Asia/Asia Pacific region over the next decade? One good way to consider this question is by comparing the region with the Europe/North Atlantic region, where NATO exists as a collective security system. NATO's commander is an American, and in practical terms the United States exerts command over NATO. Since the end of the Cold War, many former Warsaw Pact countries have joined, so that in addition to its members from the Cold War era, NATO now includes the Czech Republic, Hungary, Poland (joined 1999); Estonia, Slovenia, Latvia, Romania, Slovakia, Bulgaria (joined 2004); and Albania and Croatia (joined 2009). European integration has proceeded on the foundations established by this system of collective security, in line with the principles of human dignity, free-dom, democracy, equality, rule of law, and respect for human rights. Consequently, no structural tension exists in terms of alliance relations and the rules and regulations that provide the foundation for system-building between NATO as a body for collective security and the EU as a body for European integration. The recent crisis in Ukraine is a major international problem, caused by Russia's annexation of Crimea and incursions into Ukraine. One of the points of contention is that Ukraine wants to join NATO and move toward closer involvement with the EU for the sake of its national security and economic growth. But from Russia's perspective this would mean NATO and the EU expanding up to its own borders. For President Putin, who bases his popularity on appeals to Russian nationalism, this is totally unacceptable. But it is important to remember that the crisis is not caused by the result of structural tensions between NATO and the EU.

The East Asia/Asia Pacific region, by contrast, does not possess a stable or systemically consistent mechanism for security and political-economic cooperation of this kind. Instead, the region's security is dom-inated by the US-led hub-and-spokes system, built on bilateral security treaties between the United States and Japan, Australia, South Korea, the Philippines, and Thailand and base agreements between the United States and its allies and other countries in the region. Since the normalization of diplomatic relations between the United States and China in 1971, China has accepted US hegemony in the region by acknowledging the United States–Japan Security Treaty and the US-led hub-and-spokes regional security system. Even so, China itself is not a member or part of the system. By contrast, China *is* an important player in the trading sys-tems of the region, and the triangular trade system that existed during the twentieth century, between the United States, Japan, and the rest of Asia, has now been replaced by a different triangular trade network, involving China, the rest of Asia (including Japan), and the United States.

A regional system of trade has therefore come into existence with China as one of its hubs, alongside a regional security system that does not include China. This means that if China chooses to act unilaterally in line with its aspirations and self-image as a great power in relation to territorial disputes in the South China Sea, or takes strong measures against Japan in the dispute over the Senkaku Islands, these actions immediately lead to trade tensions. This is one of the structural charac-teristics of the regional system.

Given these structural characteristics, what are the major challenges this regional system is likely to face within the next decade or so? I can see two major problems on the horizon.

The Next Decade: The Problem of China

The first of these I have already alluded to. It concerns the balance of power. Assuming China continues to rise as a major economic power, it is likely that the balance of power will develop in China's favor unless steps are taken to prevent this. What kind of alliance is possible to maintain the balance of power? When I refer to "maintaining" the balance of power, I suppose what I really mean is: How can we maintain the balance of power in favor of Japan, the United States, and Australia? President Obama's response was the idea of a "pivot" or rebalancing of US strategic priorities to Asia. I will have more to say about this later. The most important aspect involves a redistribution of US military forces, which have previously been deployed evenly between the Atlantic and Pacific, to prioritize the Pacific. In response, Japan is moving to strengthen the systems that support the alliance within Japan and is deepening its cooperation with other US allies and partners across a vast area from the Pacific to the Indian Ocean. Rapid progress is being made to enhance cooperation with Australia in foreign policy and national security, and it is fair to say that the relationship between the two countries can now be called a de facto alliance. There has also been progress on strategic collaboration with the Philippines, Vietnam, Indonesia, India, and other countries. Maintaining the balance of power in the Asia Pacific region so that it works in favor of Japan and its allies is one of the major challenges ahead of us.

Another issue is trade liberalization. Here, progress has been far from impressive. The Doha Round of trade negotiations at the WTO, for example, has been stalled for over a decade. Developing and emerging countries are often reluctant to liberalize trade and commerce, partly under pressure from economic nationalism. Given this, it is inevitable that developed countries will have to take the lead, at least initially, in building systems of trade and commerce better suited to the needs of the twenty-first century, even though they have been becoming protectionist and inward-looking in recent years.

We do not have much time left for this. As we have seen, by the 2020s the developed countries will no longer represent more than half of the world's economy and will be replaced by the developing world and emerging economies as their shares of the global economy flip. In light of this, it should be clear why the Trans-Pacific Partnership (TPP), Trans-Atlantic Trade and Investment Partnership (TTIP), and the Japan–European Union Free Trade Agreement are so important.

The same can be said in other policy areas. But formulating norms and making rules is not at all easy, particularly in areas affecting sovereignty and territorial issues. One can see an example of this in recent attempts to formulate a code of conduct for the South China Sea. As well as the issue of what rules should be made, there is also the question of what method should be used to make those rules. As Ikenberry makes clear in *Liberal Leviathan*, there are essentially two methods for formulating international rules: the imperial method and multilateralism, which involves making rules through negotiations involving multiple countries.

In this context, "imperial" refers to the practice by which a major power makes rules to suit its own interests in a given area of policy and then forces these rules on other countries. This is precisely what China is trying to do in its territorial disputes in the South China Sea. As is well known, China passed the Territorial Waters Act in 1992. Today, based on this piece of domestic legislation, China lays a territorial claim to everything in the South China Sea within its notorious "nine-dash line," or "cow's tongue," and is trying to enforce this by stationing large numbers of law enforcement and navy ships in the area and carrying out surveys on maritime resources, brushing aside the protests of other countries. In the East China Sea, China sends government ships into Japanese waters around the Senkaku Islands on an almost daily basis. In addition to attempting to establish de facto control in this way, China also wants to pursue the imperial approach to making rules within its borders and the wider region. And it is not problematic at all for people in China because they believe, perhaps, that this is what being a hegemon means.

But this is not the only way of making rules. Indeed, the United States is currently promoting the TPP as a step on the way to a Free Trade Area for Asia Pacific (FTAAP), and rule-making within the TPP talks has been based on multilateral negotiations. Of course, national power matters a lot in these negotiations. The United States does get its way quite often, and a lot of the time, the rules that are made suit US interests to a considerable extent. But this does not mean that small countries have no say—we can see this from the interests of "smaller" countries in negotiations over government procurement and intellectual property protection, for example. More influential countries like Japan have even more of a say. And there is another merit to making rules by multilateral negotiations: once rules have been made, a powerful country cannot simply quit if those rules turn out to work to its disadvantage. Once rules have been agreed multilaterally, all countries are bound by those rules.

In the case of imperial rule-making, by contrast, the hegemonic power can abandon the rules as soon as they turn out to be no longer in its interests. This is an important difference. Conflict over these competing methods of making rules is one of the sources of tension in the East Asia/Asia Pacific region today.

It should be clear by now that one political issue in the East Asia/ Asia Pacific region concerns the balance of power and the question of how it should be maintained in one's favor. At the same time, it is useful to remember that a kind of game is under way regarding international cooperation, the questions of what rules should be drawn up in various fields, and how regional cooperation should be carried forward. These state-driven aspects will doubtless continue to be the keynotes of international relations in the region in the years to come. As people in the emerging economies gain more confidence in line with their new prosperity, and start asserting themselves more forcefully, nationalism will become a more important force in the region's politics than it has generally been until now. One likely result of this is that balance-of-power politics will become more important than international cooperation. This will be one of the major trends we will see over the next ten to fifteen years or so.

GLOBALIZATION, URBANIZATION, AND
THE REVOLUTION OF RISING EXPECTATIONS

The other long-term trend I would like to discuss can be summed up in three terms: globalization, urbanization, and the revolution of rising expectations. In this context, globalization can be defined in general terms as a shrinking of distances in time and space. We can understand its effects by looking at the phenomenon and its impact in several different areas. Here I want to discuss the impact of globalization as it relates to the revolution in information and communication technology, global finance and the global value chains, and the movement of people across borders. In terms of urbanization, the simplest way to understand the impact of what is happening may be to note that by 2030, over 60 percent of people in East Asia will live in urban areas. These processes of globalization and urbanization will combine with the growth of the middle classes in the region. Key to assessing the political significance of these developments will be the revolution of rising expectations. I will explain the meaning of this in the course of my discussion.

How Information and Communication
Technology Is Changing Asia

A wide variety of data exist to illustrate the scale and speed with which the revolution in information and communication technology has unfolded.

Let me mention one particularly striking fact. In 2000, just over 700 million people owned a mobile phone worldwide. Of these, 500 million were in high-income countries. By 2010, the number of mobile phone owners exceeded 5.3 billion, including 3.7 billion in middle-income countries and 500 million in low-income countries. The same applies to internet access. In 2000, fewer than 400 million people around the world were online, of whom more than 300 million lived in high-income countries. By 2010, the equivalent figure had risen to more than 2 billion, of whom 1.2 billion lived in middle-income countries.

We can go further. In 2000, most of the world's mobile phones and internet users were to be found in countries with a literacy rate of between 80 percent and 100 percent. By 2010, the technology had become widespread in countries where the literary rate was much lower: from 50 percent to 80 percent. These developments make it almost certain that the vast majority of people in the world will have access to the benefits of information and communication technology within the next decade. In the past, anthropologists carried out fieldwork on "primitive societies" by traveling to study the lives of isolated people living on the islands of the Pacific, the mountains of Southeast Asia, and the savannas of Africa. Today, however, even people in supposedly remote mountainous regions of Southeast Asia can be found shouting "hello" into their mobile phones. In practical terms, the idea of "primitive societies" is losing its meaning. Another factor is that within the next decade, people all around the world will become increasingly connected not only via computers and smart phones, but also through "wearables" and other devices connected to the internet, including automobiles and a growing array of domestic appliances. As the "internet of things" becomes an essential part of our daily lives, it will not just create opportunities for people in developing countries to escape poverty and seize new business opportunities. The new technology will also allow corporations and governments to supervise and monitor huge numbers of people on an individual level at all times. In that sense, it is fair to say that a world of surveillance is coming into existence that would have been all but unimaginable just a few years ago, albeit one different from that forecast by philosopher Michel Foucault.

How is the information and communication revolution changing the world today? We all know what has happened to finance. The significance of financial globalization is well understood, and we see articles about this aspect of change in our newspapers on an almost daily basis. Take, for example, an article that appeared in *Nihon Keizai Shimbun* in 2014 about the growing levels of money leaving emerging economies.[4] A brief summary of the contents follows.

According to EPFR Global, a US research firm, the net outflow of funding from emerging markets worldwide reached approximately $6.4 billion for the week ending 5 February 2014, the highest level since early February 2011. The survey focused on approximately 6,500 emerging-market investment trusts, exchange-traded funds, and hedge funds in emerging markets, amounting to total assets under management of $1 trillion. According to the EPFR's findings, in the latest survey for the week ending 12 February, net outflows amounted to $3 billion in just one week, the sixteenth consecutive weekly period in which there had been a net loss of investment since the week ending 30 October the previous year (2013). The figures were particularly striking for Brazil, Turkey, South Africa, India, and Indonesia. The year 2013 saw double-digit rates of annual decline in the stock markets in Turkey, Indonesia, and Brazil. This flight of funds has also accelerated currency depreciation in these countries. According to the EPFR report, there was a net flow of money away from stock funds in the BRIC countries (Brazil, Russia, India, China) for sixty-eight weeks up to 12 February 2014. Since the beginning of 2013, a cumulative total of $1.5 billion has been lost from Chinese stock funds; similar losses have been seen in Brazilian ($1.1 billion) and Russian ($0.7 billion) stocks.

Little comment is necessary here. The report tells us that the total value of funds in investment trusts, exchange-traded funds, and hedge funds in emerging-economy stock markets is $1 trillion. This is about one-fifth of Japan's GDP, at 100 yen to the dollar. This is the amount that was invested in the emerging economies in February 2014. However, the expectation that the United States Federal Reserve would soon abandon its policy of quantitative easing led to a withdrawal of funds from emerging countries, resulting in a double-digit drop in stock market values in Turkey, Indonesia, Brazil, and other emerging economies in 2013 and a 15 percent to 20 percent fall in currency values in India, Indonesia, and Brazil. The scale of the funds taken out of these markets was not even particularly large: around $1.5 billion from China, $1.1 billion from Brazil, and smaller values from other countries, for a total of only $20 billion or so, equivalent to around 2 percent of the $1 trillion total for emerging countries as a whole. Even so, it was enough to have a substantial impact.

Globalization of Finance and the Crisis That Can Follow

The scale of capital flight from East Asian countries was much greater during the East Asian financial crisis of 1997–1998. In 1996, there was a net inflow of $73 billion (or 7.3 trillion yen) into the five economies of Thailand, Indonesia, Malaysia, the Philippines, and South Korea. In 1997, this became a net outflow of $11 billion (1.1 trillion yen). In other words, a total of $84 billion, or 8.4 trillion yen, of funds left these countries in 1997 alone, leading to a liquidity crisis in these countries. In some countries, partly as a result of an ill-thought-out response by the IMF, the economic crisis led to a serious political and economic crisis.

In economies roughly the size of Indonesia's ($889 billion in 2014) or Thailand's ($374 billion), an outflow of funds equivalent to several billion dollars may have a relatively limited impact: causing a drop in stock market prices or a fall in the value of the currency. But a much larger outflow measured in the tens of billions (equivalent to several trillion yen) may be enough to trigger a liquidity crisis. It is fair to say that, owing to the globalization of finance, the risk of such a crisis grows more severe as the scale of funds managed internationally increases.

Let me touch on one more piece of recent data. This shows the value of currencies being traded on the world's exchange markets on a single day. In 1998, this was equivalent to $1.53 trillion. By 2010 this had risen to $3.97 trillion, and by 2013 to $5.35 trillion. Japan's GDP for 2013 was $5 trillion: in other words, funds slightly larger than Japan's entire GDP are moving across international borders every day. The daily trading value of the world's exchange markets has tripled over the past fifteen years. If this trend continues, the size of funds crossing international borders on a day-to-day basis, already equivalent to Japan's GDP, will increase further in the years to come.

Vast amounts of money are moving across borders every day and are being invested internationally in response to macroeconomic trends. In an age in which such vast amounts move around the world on a daily basis, any country that mismanages its macro economy faces the real risk of a sudden flight of funds that could cause the collapse or bankruptcy of its entire economy. It is important to bear this very real danger in mind.[5]

The Increasingly Steep Slopes of the "Smiling Curve"

The second effect of globalization I would like to discuss concerns global value chains. Table 1.3 shows changes in the intra-regional trade share in recent years. Let me explain what this means. Let us take the example of Japan, China, and South Korea. If we calculate the total value of the exports and imports for these three countries and then work out the total value of the trade carried out between Japan, China, and South Korea as a

Table 1.3   Changes in Intra-Regional Trade Share, 1980–2012

	1980	1990	2000	2005	2010	2012
Asia						
RCEP (ASEAN+6)	33.2	33.0	40.6	43.0	44.1	43.2
ASEAN	15.9	17.0	22.7	24.9	24.6	24.5
ASEAN + China	14.9	15.8	20.1	20.7	20.7	21.2
ASEAN + South Korea	15.1	16.1	22.4	23.2	23.9	24.5
ASEAN + India	15.1	16.5	22.3	23.8	23.4	23.1
ASEAN + Japan	23.4	21.7	26.4	26.0	26.7	27.1
Japan, China, South Korea	10.3	12.3	20.3	23.7	22.1	20.2
North America (NAFTA)	33.2	37.2	46.8	43.0	40.0	40.2
Europe (EU27)	57.5	65.4	65.1	65.0	64.9	63.3
Japan–EU	52.6	61.4	59.8	60.5	59.2	57.4
APEC	57.5	67.5	72.3	69.2	67.0	65.8
TPP	44.0	50.8	53.9	47.0	41.9	42.0
United States–EU	55.0	61.3	57.9	58.7	57.0	55.0

Source: JETRO (Japan External Trade Organization), "Sekai boeki matorikkusu" [World trade matrix], 2015, https://www.jetro.go.jp/ext_images/world/statistics/data/matrix2015.pdf.
Note: Intra-regional trade share is the percentage of intra-regional trade to total trade of the region.

ratio of this sum, the figure we obtain shows trade among the three countries as a ratio of their total trade. In our example, the intra-regional trade share was 20 percent in 2000, and then rose slightly in 2005 and 2010 before returning to the 20 percent level in 2012. The top row of the table shows the figure for the Regional Comprehensive Economic Partnership (RCEP)—that is, the ASEAN countries plus the six countries of Japan, China, South Korea, India, Australia, and New Zealand. Here, the intra-regional trade share was around 33 percent in 1980. This increased to around 40 percent in 2000 and to 43 percent by 2012.

We can compare this with North America, where the NAFTA free trade area involving the United States, Canada, and Mexico shows an intra-regional trade share of 33 percent in 1980, which then rose to 46 percent in 2000 before falling again to around 40 percent in 2012. From this, we can perhaps conclude that the importance of trade with the other two NAFTA countries is falling for the United States. Contrast this with the situation in the European Union, where the intra-regional trade share for the twenty-seven EU member states was already around 57 percent in 1980 and had risen to 63 percent by 2012. In other words, trade among the EU countries is worth two-thirds of the region's total trade.

This raises two questions: Why is this happening? And why is the intra-regional trade share important in considering trade? One reason is that the production process is becoming increasingly fragmented, with every task in the production process now distributed across international borders, according to the principle of comparative advantage.[6] What does this mean in concrete terms?

One frequently cited example is the global value chain of the Apple iPod. The iPod involves several different processes that together produce value: the original idea for an iPod-like device, the process of coming up with a design to give this idea tangible form, the process of sourcing and assembling the necessary components, followed by retail and the provision of services that allow customers to download music in exchange for payment. It is this entire chain that together creates value. This chain of processes can be modeled schematically as the "smile curve," shown in Figure 1.1, to show how value added is distributed across the range of tasks.

There are two main points to note. The first is that the smile curve was historically flatter during the 1970s; the contours of the curve have grown steeper in recent years. The second thing the smile curve shows is that value added is very unevenly distributed along the curve. The tasks involving the greatest added value are what we might call the pre-fabrication processes—in other words, coming up with the original idea and designing the product—as well as selling the finished product and providing associated services. By contrast, sourcing and assembling the necessary components does not involve much added value. We can refine this summary a little by noting that the production of advanced components—rich in ideas, technology, or design—can also bring considerable added value, even if not as great as that involved in pre- and post-fabrication tasks including creating the original idea, planning, design, and services.

This observation not only applies to a single product like the iPod; it also applies to the position a given country's economy occupies in the international division of labor. One example can be seen in a study done by the WTO and the International Input-Output Analysis Group at the Institute of Developing Economies of the Japan External Trade Organization (World Trade Organization and IDE-JETRO 2012). The study notes that in the 1970s, Japanese automakers and other manufacturers tended to concentrate their subcontractors within a single area, where they would then produce their cars or other products. This meant that all the processes, from pre-fabrication to assembly, were performed in the same area and that added value was also quite equally distributed throughout the production process. From the 1990s on, however, and particularly since the turn of the century, the contours of the smile curve

Figure 1.1   The Smile Curve

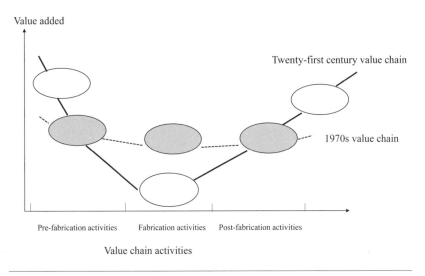

Value added

Twenty-first century value chain

1970s value chain

Pre-fabrication activities   Fabrication activities   Post-fabrication activities

Value chain activities

Source: Baldwin, Tadashi, and Hitoshi 2014: 2.

have gradually become steeper and more pronounced. We can put this another way by saying that increasing fragmentation of the production process has made it easier to see the differences between tasks that bring a lot of added value and those that do not. At the same time, these differences have become distributed along a global value chain that now stretches regionally across national borders.

The reason for this is quite straightforward. The changes have come about because the production process has been fragmented across the region, transcending national borders, with each task now performed wherever it makes most sense in terms of the efficient use of resources. Returning to the iPod, for instance, the idea for the product was born in California, where design was presumably carried out as well. But the products themselves are assembled in factories in China, using components sourced from Murata Manufacturing and other Japanese, Korean, German, and increasingly Chinese component suppliers. To take another example from the field of consumer electronics, in producing its smart phones, Samsung borrowed the original idea from Apple's iPhone, and the design too probably owes a lot to Apple, but the company sources its components from manufacturers in Japan, Korea, and other countries and assembles them in Vietnam.

With the global value chain now stretching across borders, countries that are only just starting out on the path of industrialization have no choice but to rely on cheap labor as their main selling point and can enter the value chain through assembly work, with its small levels of added value. Cambodia has been energetic in following this approach, as has Vietnam, which has provided a package of special incentives to encourage Samsung to locate its smart phone assembly factory in the country. But countries cannot continue to rely on cheap assembly alone. As the economy grows, labor costs rise and people's standards of living improve. Countries need to train and educate more skilled workers and develop supporting industries by promoting small and medium-sized enterprises (SMEs). In this way, they can gradually come to occupy positions higher up the smile curve value chain as their industries develop.

A recent IDE-JETRO preliminary study suggests that with the emergence of technologically sophisticated firms supplying advanced components in China, the smile curve itself is being transformed to China's advantage. Other countries, like Singapore, are strategically developing their human resources and infrastructure and are actively working to attract businesses. As a result, they are rapidly becoming regional hubs in fields such as finance, insurance, and logistics, and are seizing high added value in this way. In short, in an age of globalizing finance, and increasingly liberalized trade, in which companies are operating across international borders, countries now need, as part of their economic development strategies, to consider how to improve their position in global value chains.

The Effect of Low-Cost Carriers

The third effect of globalization is the movement of people. This is something we see reflected in immigration and related issues, which have recently become a subject of debate in Japan, as they have been in other countries for many years, as well as in areas that are already important policy issues, including the "brain drain/brain circulation" problem and tourism. In 2013, for example, the number of foreign tourists who visited Japan exceeded 10 million for the first time. In 2014, this number exceeded 13 million. In part, this increase was due to relatively affordable prices thanks to a depreciating yen, but another major factor was the rise of low-cost carriers. Fares on some of these carriers can be as low as 20,000 yen for a round-trip ticket between Manila and Kansai International Airport. I myself used such a carrier for the return leg of a recent trip, and found the experience quite comfortable, once I'd lowered my expectations for in-flight food and drinks and other services. It's certainly hard to complain when the fare is cheaper than a seat on the *Shinkansen* between Tokyo and Osaka. My Indonesian friends tell me it is now possible to buy a round-trip ticket from Jakarta to Cebu for just $140— cheaper than flying between Jakarta and Bali.

Another recent phenomenon is the growing number of young women taking advantage of cheap direct flights from Kuala Lumpur, the capital of Malaysia, to Bandung in West Java. Bandung's high elevation gives it an enviable temperature of 27 to 28 degrees Celsius even at the hottest time of day, and this, together with a booming fashion industry, draws large numbers of Malaysian women. They travel to Bandung, enjoy a day's shopping, show off their new acquisitions as they stroll around the city, and then have dinner and fly home the next day. Round-trip fares of just $100 or so are making this kind of lifestyle possible for growing numbers of people. This is the world we now live in.

What is the significance of this new pattern of movement of people within the region? I think it could be revolutionary. Think of immigration, for example. One of the objections often heard in the debate about immigration in Japan is that if the country accepts foreign workers, they will bring their families to settle down and live in immigrant enclaves. This might lead to large communities of immigrants who do not assimilate into Japanese society, with all the attendant social costs involved. If we consider Germany's experience with the Turkish community, this is not an entirely unreasonable argument. But in an era where round-trip fares between Osaka and Manila cost only 20,000 yen, and people can fly from Osaka to Bangkok and back for 30,000 yen, is it really likely that people with a certain level of education and decent jobs would want to bring their entire families to settle in a country with a different language, and where their children's future prospects would be limited? I think the possibility is small. From the policy perspective, the important thing is to respect everyone and offer the same pay for the same work. This will allow people to come to Japan as migrant workers, drawn there by the relatively high levels of pay compared to neighboring countries like China, South Korea, Taiwan, the Philippines, Vietnam, and Thailand, using low-cost carriers to return home to visit their families several times a year. I think it is much more likely that we will see this established as a new pattern of migrant labor.

The same thing can be said in relation to the "brain drain/brain circulation" problem. In Japan, support is growing for the view that it must work to attract the highly skilled human resources needed in fields like finance, information and communication technology, science and technology, and academia. This will mean building and maintaining the infrastructure required to attract this kind of talent, in terms of hospitals, schools, housing, and other aspects of daily life. And this is surely a good thing. If Japan builds an attractive environment that makes people from around the world see the country as a place where they want to live, work, and raise children, this will surely benefit Japanese people too. Recent developments make it all but certain that Singapore, China, and South Korea will offer incentives to attract talented workers, and that other countries will soon follow suit. Increasingly, people with the skills to be internationally competitive will move across borders. The numbers of tourists coming to Japan's shores will also continue to increase. The number of foreign tourists visiting Japan is expected to exceed 30 million annually in the next few years. There is plenty of room for the number of skilled foreign workers in Japan to increase further if the country can find a way to replace the current technical internship program with a fairer system of migrant labor. In that sense, the time has come to submit Japan's policies and systems related to the international movement of people to a radical review.

Urbanization and Its Discontents

Another noteworthy long-term trend in East Asia/Asia Pacific is urbanization. The extent of this is clear from Table 1.4. According to the United Nations, in 2000 the urban population of East Asia was around 800 million. But the definition of this population does not include Japan, and when the estimates were published, no census had been carried out in Myanmar since the 1950s, so that country was excluded too. In any case, it is estimated that by 2030, the total population of East Asia will be 2.37 billion, with the urban population having reached around 1.47 billion. This means that around 62 percent of the total population will be living in cities.

The countries of the region can be divided into three quite clear categories. One is made up of countries like China and Indonesia with huge populations, in which around two-thirds of the population will live in cities. Another consists of South Korea, the Philippines, Malaysia, and Singapore. In these countries, an overwhelming proportion of the population will live in cities. In South Korea, it is estimated that the urban population will reach 86 percent. With only a little exaggeration, we can say that South Korea will become something like a larger and

Table 1.4   Urbanization in East Asia, 2000 and 2030

	Urban Population (millions)		Growth Rate (%)	Total Population (millions) 2030	Urban Population by Percentage, 2030
	2000	2030			
China	456.5	877.6	90	1,438.6	61
Indonesia	88.9	188.0	111	276.3	68
Philippines	44.3	86.6	96	113.9	76
Vietnam	19.0	46.0	142	106.9	43
South Korea	37.3	43.1	16	50.2	86
Thailand	18.9	35.4	87	75.4	47
Malaysia	14.2	27.3	92	35.0	78
Cambodia	2.2	8.7	291	23.5	37
Laos	1.0	3.5	248	9.3	38
Far East	803.2	1,468.8	83	2,369.0	62

Source: Calculated from data included in United Nations Department of Economic and Social Affairs, Population Division, *World Urbanization Prospects: 2011 Revision*, https://www.un.org/en/development/desa/population/publications/pdf/urbanization/WUP2011_Report.pdf.

less prosperous version of Singapore in this respect. The third category is made up of the countries of mainland Southeast Asia: Vietnam, Laos, Cambodia, Thailand, and (not included here) Myanmar. In these countries, the urban population is expected to remain below half of the total population. These are the latest predictions for demographic trends over the next decade or so.

Looked at in this way, it is clear that East Asia will become predominantly urban over the next fifteen years or so. The economy will also grow, although of course we cannot tell by how much, so that increasing numbers of people will join the middle classes and become affluent, particularly in the cities. If we define "affluent" as those with an annual household income of $35,000, estimates published by the Japanese Ministry of Economy, Trade and Industry predict that by 2020 the size of the affluent population will be approximately as follows: China, 180 million; India, 67 million; and Indonesia, 12 million (and around 50 million for ASEAN as a whole). Even so, we should remember that "affluent," defined as a household income of $35,000, does not mean "rich" by Japanese standards. In Japan, that would be the equivalent of an annual household of around 3.5 million yen (at 100 yen to the dollar). Incidentally, in Japan around 75 percent of the population have an annual household income of $35,000 or more. This perhaps gives us some sense of understanding what terms like "affluent" really mean in this context. The important thing to remember is that in the years to come, ever larger numbers of people in the region will join the relatively affluent middle classes. In China, this number will be equivalent to 1.5 times the *total population* of Japan; similarly, the equivalent of roughly half of Japan's total population will qualify for this category in India and ASEAN.

As urbanization and economic growth continue in East Asian countries, the numbers of people belonging to the affluent middle class will steadily rise. But not everywhere will develop at the same speed, or to the same extent. Within each country, some areas will develop quickly while others hardly develop at all. It is therefore unrealistic to expect balanced development, and even as economies grow and affluent middle-class populations expand, it is unlikely that we will see in any of these countries anything like the society that exists in Japan, where practically the entire population belongs to the middle class.

The Development Gap

An interesting example of unequal economic growth within a country comes from Indonesia, the important points of a report on which are summarized in Table 1.5. In 2011, Ōizumi Keiichirō published a book called *Consumer Asia* that analyzes the regional characteristics of economic growth in East Asia. Ōizumi observes that in countries like China, Thailand, and Singapore/Malaysia, economic growth has not taken place equally across all parts of those countries. Instead, certain regions—including the Bohai Gulf region around Beijing and Tianjin, the Shanghai region, and the region around Shenzhen and Guangzhou—have developed as "mega-regions," each with an economy roughly equal in size to that of South Korea or Taiwan. This is quite right—and the same applies to other regions, such as Greater Bangkok or the area stretching from Singapore to Johore in Malaysia. Looking to the future, however, it may well be that growth in these areas will slow, and that other regions will emerge as new centers of growth. The predictions shown in Table 1.5 make this point in the case of Indonesia.

There are two interesting aspects of this forecast. One concerns the special capital region of Jakarta. Since the start of the twenty-first century, Jakarta's economy has been growing more slowly than that of the country as a whole, and looking ahead to 2030 the rate of economic growth for the capital region will continue to fall even further. Jakarta is therefore not expected to grow much beyond its present size in economic terms. By contrast, the "suburbs" of Bekasi, Bogor, Tangerang, and Depok are expected to grow at around 7 percent. Another, even

Table 1.5   The Age of Urbanization, Indonesia

	GDP Growth Rate (%), 2002–2010	Share of GDP (%), 2010	Predicted Share of GDP Growth (%), 2010–2030	Predicted Share of GDP (%), 2030
Jakarta	5.8	19	5.1	19
Cities with population 5–10 million[a]	6.7	6	9.1	11
Cities with population 2–5 million[a]	6.4	11	6.9	15
Cities 150,000–2 million[b]	5.9	31	6.3	37
Cities with population under 150,000	5.3	7	1.7	3
Farming villages	5.9	26	2.0	14
Indonesia	5.9	100	5.3	100

Source: McKinsey Global Institute 2012.
Notes: a. In addition to major cities like Bandung (6.7 million), Medan (7.0 million), and Surabaya (7.0 million), also includes parts of the Greater Jakarta conurbation, including Bekasi, Bogor, Tangerang, and Depok.
    b. Pekanbaru (9.8 percent), Pontianak (9.5 percent), Balikpapan (8.6 percent), Makassar (9.0 percent).

more interesting aspect concerns regional cities, particularly those with a population of between 2 million and 10 million. These cities, which include Medan in North Sumatra, Bandung in West Java, and Surabaya in East Java, are expected to grow (like the Jakarta suburbs) at a rate of around 7 percent. Other, somewhat smaller cities with a population of between 150,000 and 2 million are expected to grow by 8 percent to 10 percent; this includes regional hubs like Pekanbaru in Sumatra, Pontianak and Balikpapan in Kalimantan, and Makassar in Sulawesi.

Economic growth will therefore expand away from the mega-region of Greater Jakarta to regional hubs. This itself should be a welcome development, and one that has already taken place in China. But it will not mean that economic development becomes more equal across the country as a whole—something that will lead to serious political problems in the medium to long term. For example, Ōizumi points out that Greater Shanghai has grown massively as a mega-region. However, there is another less positive aspect to this development, which is that huge numbers of educated and ambitious young people from the surrounding areas of Anhui province have been drawn to the city, with the consequence that problems like decreasing birthrates and an aging population appeared much earlier in Anhui and similar places than in Shanghai.

The Revolution of Rising Expectations

For these reasons, I think it is quite unlikely that societies in which everyone belongs to the middle class will be a reality in many of the countries of East Asia even in 2030. Probably somewhere between one-third and two-thirds of the population will still be stuck in poverty, allowing for some differences between countries. But people know quite well from television and social media what an affluent lifestyle looks like, and this will become even more the case as smart phones become more common, movement becomes easier, and urbanization continues.

This leads us to an important political question of how to respond to what has been called the revolution of rising expectations. Over the past thirty years, per capita incomes in these countries have increased dramatically: by thirteen times in China and by two to four times in most of the countries of Southeast Asia. This has led to rising expectations, with more and more people wanting access to the affluence they see around them and demanding to live what they increasingly see as "ordinary" lives.

So, what should be done? Politically, there are only two answers. One is redistribution: taking from the haves and redistributing to the have-nots. The other is economic growth: stimulate the economy, create new employment, and improve living standards. But pork barrel–style distribution of largesse is unsustainable in the long term. And economic growth alone is likely to exacerbate wealth disparities. This means that, politically speaking, the problem ultimately involves finding the right combination of policies so that a country can achieve economic growth while finding ways to redistribute wealth at the same time. Ideally, countries would increase the size of the economic pie and manage dissatisfaction by redistributing it more widely. If governments ignore income redistribution, they risk political instability; but if they allocate too many resources to it, they will be unable to invest in growth for tomorrow. In this sense, we are likely to see everywhere in East Asia the continuation for some time of a politics of economic growth. The purpose of this kind of politics is to achieve economic growth, and there has been a public consensus on this purpose for the past several decades as the quality of people's lives has improved. To maintain this politics, however, governments need not only to continue to grow their economies, but also to invest more in providing a social safety net, correcting income disparities, and redistributing wealth.

What needs to be done to achieve economic growth? What areas do governments need to focus on in particular? Let me summarize the most important points again, including those I have already mentioned. One is macroeconomic stability. As we have seen, huge amounts of money move across international borders every day. Already more than $1 trillion is invested in the emerging economies. In today's world of globalized finance, how a given country maintains its macroeconomic stability can be a question of life or death. One option is to do as China does and impose controls on the movement of capital across borders. But for many countries with far smaller populations and markets, this will have the unintended consequence of discouraging investment from abroad as well. Another solution is to accept the freedom of capital to move across borders and manage the macro economy in such a way as to obtain the trust of institutional investors, hedge fund managers, and the other professionals of the financial world, so that money doesn't suddenly take flight at the first sign of a bump in the road. This is a lesson many countries in Southeast Asia learned from the financial crisis of 1997–1998. It is generally acknowledged that there are basically only two ways of responding to a liquidity crisis. One is foreign currency reserves. A country can stockpile huge reserves of foreign currency. The other is to create a framework whereby countries provide liquidity support for each other, both bilaterally and multilaterally. This second approach aims at making use of the huge foreign exchange reserves Japan and China maintain in the event of a crisis. A framework of this kind came into being through the currency-swap arrangements of the Chiang Mai Initiative in 1999, following the East Asian financial crisis. As a result, it is fair to say that East Asia now has a better safety net to help in the event of a future liquidity crisis.

Avoiding the Middle-Income Trap

Yet another task is to overcome—or avoid falling into—the "middle-income trap," to use a phrase that has come into vogue in recent years. What this means can be shown by the example of Brazil, where per capita national income in 1979 was $4,600. In 2005, this had grown only to around $5,000. In other words, in the space of twenty-six years, per capita income had risen by only $400, at an average growth rate of just 0.6 percent a year. This is called the middle-income trap. What can be done to avoid this trap and ensure that per capita income in middle-income countries (roughly $3,000 to $12,000) rises toward high-income status? This is a question that has been widely debated in recent years. The same prescription has been handed out by the World Bank, the Asian Development Bank, and the OECD: in general terms, human resources training, infrastructure development, and inclusive growth. In other words, the solution is to achieve growth that produces good jobs, and in which the benefits of economic growth are shared widely among the population, and use this to maintain political and social stability.

Of course, the technocrats of East Asia are aware of all this. They know that global value chains stretch across the East Asia region, and that their countries currently occupy a low position on that smile curve, as assemblers of components down in one of the lowest valleys, where only the smallest added value can be obtained. The question for them is this: How can we get out of this valley and climb up the hillside to occupy a position higher up the value chain? This is not an easy question to answer. The fact that a certain task or job within the production process is allocated to a given country means that the country in question has a comparative advantage in that area—this much is easy to understand. But what should governments and their leaders do to attract jobs with a higher added value? We know that technocrats argue that education and infrastructure are important, but what does that mean in concrete terms? This is not a question with easy answers. To understand why, let's look at the example of the Philippines.

Many people in the Philippines speak English. Because of this, in recent years many Wall Street financial institutions and legal offices have moved parts of their back-office support jobs to Manila. This started ten to fifteen years ago, initially with call centers, and spread from there to other types of work with a higher added value. In response, talented university graduates have been drawn to the sector. But why did this happen?

One reason I have already mentioned: widespread proficiency in English. Another factor, which is less commonly mentioned, dates to the Marcos years, and the early years of the 1980s in particular. At that time, the Philippines went through a profound political and economic crisis, during which the Communist Party grew in power and influence. At that time, President Marcos encouraged Filipinos to go overseas as migrant workers, initially to the Middle East during the 1970s. Today, 15 percent of the Filipino work force is employed overseas: as sailors, nurses, engineers, academics, and executives in multinational corporations. This means that today more than 10 percent of the nation's GDP is sent back as remittances from these workers overseas.

What is this money used for? Only around 10 percent of it goes to investment in the general meaning of investment—in bonds or stocks. But quite a lot of the money is used for education. As a result, today even children from supposedly "poor" families (according to conventional Filipino ideas) are able to attend the prestigious private high schools and colleges that were once the preserve of the Manila elite and the middle classes.

As these people have received tertiary-level education at colleges and universities, the Philippines has gradually moved into a position where it now has a comparative advantage in areas like back-office support and in providing human resources to global companies. But what about Laos? Laotians cannot follow the path Filipinos have taken. This has become a major issue looking ahead to the establishment of the ASEAN economic community in 2015.

The Sustainability of the Politics of Economic Growth

Another factor we need to consider is the movement of people. As mentioned earlier, I believe that economic growth will gradually spread from the mega-regions to hub cities in the regions. This will mean that competition between cities becomes important alongside competition between countries. It will no longer simply be a case of Japan competing against China, South Korea, or with the United States, Germany, France, or any number of other countries, but of Tokyo competing against New York, London, Singapore, Hong Kong, and Shanghai, and of Jakarta competing with Bangkok and Manila. And the key to success in this competition will be the extent to which cities can successfully attract talented, ambitious, educated young people from across international borders (see Table 1.6).

At the end of the day, however, what matters most politically is the sustainability of the politics of economic growth. As I have already pointed out, in the foreseeable future, societies in which everyone belongs to the middle classes will not be achieved in most of the East Asian countries. At the same time, the revolution of rising expectations will mean that people will have greater expectations and hopes than ever before of gaining access to what they regard as an ordinary level of prosperity and an acceptable lifestyle. Making economies grow and improving people's standard of living is the only way for governments to respond to these mounting expectations and manage people's dissatisfactions at lingering gaps in wealth. Objectively, therefore, the politics of economic growth will remain a keystone of politics in East Asia for the foreseeable future. There is simply no alternative.

But the fact that this is objectively true does not necessarily mean that this is what will happen in reality. As I have argued, in the case of large discrepancies of wealth and opportunity, there are only two political means

Table 1.6   Numbers of Foreign Students Around the World, 1975–2009

	Number Enrolled Outside Their Own Country (in millions)
1975	0.8
1980	1.1
1990	1.3
2000	2.1
2009	3.7

Study Destination, 2009[a]	Percentage Enrolled
United States	18.0
United Kingdom	9.9
Australia	7.0
Germany	7.0
France	6.8
Canada	5.2
Russia	3.7
Japan	3.6
Spain	2.3
New Zealand	1.9

Source: "Who Studies Abroad and Where," 2011, OECD, https://www.oecd.org/education/skills-beyond-school/48631079.pdf.

Note: a. The English-speaking countries account for a 42.0 percent share.

of response: invest in growth for tomorrow or spend on wealth redistribution to correct the discrepancies today. If, as has happened in Thailand for the past decade, the political system becomes gridlocked and paralyzed, this will only increase the risk of falling into the middle-income trap in the medium to long term. In any country, the available resources are limited, and the question of where to invest those resources is a major question of government strategy or even grand strategy, if we consider national security as one of the areas competing for investment. Normally, a state's grand strategy is shaped when it faces a crisis and a consensus emerges. Various governments implement policies and run their administrations within the parameters allowed by this consensus, but occasionally a revision needs to be carried out. If it is not, it often happens that resource-distribution priorities remain unchanged despite changing circumstances, and eventually the state experiences a crisis.

This happens under both democratic and authoritarian systems of government, but responses to crisis differ dramatically depending on the system of government in place. Under an authoritarian regime, the more serious the crisis becomes, the bigger the danger becomes that a crisis on the grand, strategic level will lead to a crisis in the regime itself. Under a democratic state, the politics of economic growth will gradually grind to a halt, stuck between the competing demands of investment for tomorrow and spending for today, and the country will risk falling into the middle-income (or in Japan's case, high-income) trap. And in today's globalized world, although relatively few citizens may appreciate this as yet, once a free trade agreement was signed between ASEAN and China, for example, industries like shoes in the Philippines and textiles in Indonesia suffered a devastating blow in terms of their competitiveness with Chinese products. Companies went bust and jobs were lost, and there was rising pressure from protectionism in the form of demands for revisions of the free trade agreement.

This can happen in various places. When a crisis hits, implementing protectionist measures is much easier politically than continuing to press on with liberalization. In that sense, the politics of economic growth will continue to be an extremely important subject in the years to come. But how to respond is decided politically, and the responses are outcomes of political processes, not products of economic rationality. Economic growth performance over the next ten to fifteen years will vary from country to country, and these differences will have an impact on the balance of power.

NOTES

1. On the subject of Chinese lending in developing countries, see "China's Lending Hits New Heights," *Financial Times,* 17 January 2011, http://www.ft.com/intl/cms/s/0/488c60f4-2281-11e0-b6a2-00144feab49a.html#axzzleuurZLQp.

2. Lawrence Summers, who together with Treasury secretary Robert Rubin and Federal Reserve chair Alan Greenspan, played a very important role as deputy treasury secretary in steering the Clinton administration's response to the Asian financial crisis of 1997–1998, published the article "A Global Wake-Up Call for the U.S.?" *Washington Post*, 5 April 2015. In "Time US Leadership Woke Up to New Economic Era," *Financial Times*, 6 April 2015, he argued that the fact that the United States did not succeed in persuading the United Kingdom and its other European allies to stay out of the Asian Infrastructure Investment Bank project was a sign that the United States was losing its role as the underwriter of the global economic system. With China's economic size rivaling that of the United States, and emerging markets making up half the world's output, the global economic architecture needed substantial adjustment. Although he does not put the case in quite the same startling terms that Ian Bremmer uses, it is fair to say that the thrust of this argument is of essentially the same type: radical changes to the distribution of the world's wealth and power will ultimately bring about wide-ranging changes in global governance.

3. I use the term *ASEAN-7* for the sake of convenience to refer to seven of the ten countries of Southeast Asia, excluding Brunei, Cambodia, and Laos, even though at this time Vietnam, Laos, Cambodia, and Myanmar were not yet members of ASEAN.

4. "Shinkōkoku no manē ryūshutsu ga kōsuijun, saidai de shū 6500-oku en ni" [High levels of capital flight from emerging economies, up to ¥650 billion a week], *Nihon Keizai Shimbun*, 25 February 2014.

5. One example of a macroeconomic crisis that led to a geopolitical crisis comes not from East Asia but from Ukraine. The ongoing crisis in Ukraine is normally viewed in terms of the Russian annexation of Crimea and the question of whether Ukraine is even sustainable as a nation-state. This observation is not wrong, but if we ask how the current crisis began, the answer is quite simple: it began from a macroeconomic crisis. In spring 2013, the US Federal Reserve Bank announced that it might end its policy of quantitative easing. This prompted much of the funding that had been pouring into newly emerging economies to flee back to the safety of the United States. As a result, the interest rate on Ukraine's dollar-denominated government bonds shot up from around 7.8 percent in April 2013 to 11.6 percent in July. This triggered a macroeconomic crisis in Ukraine, and since institutional investors in the United States, Europe, and Japan do not buy Ukrainian government bonds, Russia stepped in with a rescue package, with the condition that Ukraine stay out of the EU. Immediately after this, however, a mass movement opposed to the government of President Viktor Yanukovych started, and once the government fell the political crisis soon led to a geopolitical one. In the case of World War I, war broke out when the balance of power collapsed. But in the twenty-first century, it may be the case that a macroeconomic crisis can lead to a geopolitical crisis. This is one of the lessons of the current situation in Ukraine.

6. On this subject, Richard Baldwin's "Misthinking Globalization," delivered as the keynote speech at the International Symposium on Global Value Chains: Quo Vadis?, held at the National Graduate Institute for Policy Studies in Tokyo on 5 July 2013, is very insightful and worth studying.

2
The Geopolitical Framework

There are two main questions I would like to address in this chapter. As discussed in the introductory chapter, regional security in East Asia/Asia Pacific is built on the US-led hub-and-spokes security system. Economically, a triangular trade system has evolved over the years and now links the United States, China, and the rest of Asia, including Japan. Within this trading framework, transnational production networks have evolved across national boundaries. Since the beginning of the twenty-first century, states have signed a series of bilateral and multilateral free trade and economic partnership agreements to encourage firms to invest in their countries and to improve the functioning of their production networks. International aid, investment, and trade have all developed under the name of economic cooperation. But the security and trading systems have started to experience structural tensions. The rise of China has changed the balance of power in the East Asia/Asia Pacific region and made the future prospects of the regional systems uncertain. The United States is promoting the TPP, encouraging further development of the trading system under US leadership, while at the same time "pivoting" to maintain the balance of power in its favor. China's own strategy has at times attempted to change the status quo unilaterally by force, while at other times China has been actively looking to extend its influence by providing economic cooperation and investment to neighboring countries. These developments have accelerated geopolitical and geoeconomic changes in the region. What was the United States trying to achieve under the Obama administration, and what is the strategic thinking that informs US policy in the region? We can ask the same question about China: As an increasingly important regional and global power, what is China trying to achieve under the leadership of Xi Jinping? And how are international relations in the region changing as a result of the growing rivalry between the two major powers?

US POLICY IN ASIA PACIFIC

The Pivot to Asia

Let's start by looking at the thinking that informs US policy in Asia Pacific. The thinking is nicely expressed in a speech President Barack Obama (2011) gave in the Australian parliament in November 2011. The speech contains the clearest and most systematic account of his Asia Pacific policy as it has been in place as of this writing.

The speech contains four main points. First, Obama stated that the United States is a "Pacific nation." What does this mean? From the perspective of East Asia, the United States is a country located on the other side of the Pacific Ocean. Therefore, people in Japan, China, and other East Asian countries have a fear or hope that as China rises in wealth and power, the United States may eventually withdraw from the region. By declaring that the United States is a Pacific nation, Obama responded to these hopes and fears by stating that the United States remained an indelible presence in the region by dint of its geography. Obama emphasized the same point in a speech he gave in Japan in 2009. This is the essential point for President Obama's Asia Pacific policy, as it has been for the policy of every US president since the end of World War II.

What is it that the United States aims to achieve by insisting that the nation is an integral part of the region? What are the purposes of US foreign and national security policy? President Obama put the second point this way: the United States "seek[s] security, which is the foundation of peace and prosperity. We stand for an international order in which the rights and responsibilities of all nations and all people are upheld. Where international laws and norms are enforced. Where commerce and freedom of navigation are not impeded. Where emerging powers contribute to regional security, and where disagreements are resolved peacefully. That's the future that we seek."

He referred to "emerging powers." There are several ways of interpreting this phrase, perhaps. But the fact is that the phrase is often used along with references to "freedom of navigation." This suggests that Obama had China primarily in mind rather than any other country. He talked about resolving disagreements peacefully and made clear his opposition to any attempt to "change the status quo by force," to use an expression that has become common recently.

What is the United States doing toward these ends? This is the third point. President Obama put forward a policy of "rebalancing" or a "pivot." He put it this way (Obama 2011): as a Pacific nation, the United States will uphold its "core principles" in the region, and "will play a large and long-term role" in "close partnership with our allies and friends." The United States is working to "put our fiscal house in order" and "reducing our spending." As the wars in Iraq and Afghanistan come to an end, "we will make some reductions in defense spending." Nevertheless, "our presence and mission in the Asia Pacific" remain "a top priority." Further:

> We will allocate the resources necessary to maintain our strong military presence in this region. . . . We will keep our commitments, including our treaty obligations to allies. . . . And we will constantly strengthen our capabilities to meet the needs of the twenty-first century. Our enduring interests in the region demand our enduring presence in the region. The United States is a Pacific power, and we are here to stay. America's defense posture across the Asia Pacific . . . will be more broadly distributed . . . more flexible . . . and more sustainable.

As well as "maintaining our strong presence in Japan and the Korean Peninsula," the United States will enhance its presence in Southeast Asia. The United States will collaborate with allies and partners "from the Pacific to the Indian Ocean." In Japan, "our alliance remains a cornerstone of regional security." The United States is also working with Thailand and the Philippines. "Our commitment to the security of the Republic of Korea will never waver. We also reiterate our resolve to act firmly against any proliferation activities by North Korea."

The US presence will be "enhanced across Southeast Asia." The United States has a partnership with Indonesia, is working with Malaysia, and is deploying ships to Singapore. It will have "closer cooperation with Vietnam and Cambodia." It welcomes India "as it looks east and plays a larger role as an Asian power."

The United States will "reengage with our regional organizations." Obama noted that he would be "the first American president to attend the East Asia Summit." The United States will "address shared challenges, such as proliferation and maritime security, including cooperation in the South China Sea."

The United States will "continue our effort to build a cooperative relationship with China. All of our nations have a profound interest in the rise of a peaceful and prosperous China. China can be a partner, from reducing tensions on the Korean Peninsula to preventing proliferation. We'll seek more opportunities for cooperation with Beijing . . . to promote understanding and avoid miscalculation." At the same time, the United States will "continue to speak candidly . . . about the importance of upholding international norms and respecting the universal human rights of the Chinese people."

The United States seeks free markets, "economies that are open and transparent, trade that is free and fair," and will cooperate economically to build "an open international economic system where rules are clear." The Trans-Pacific Partnership is a "potential model for the entire region." The United States will maintain support for the G20 as "the center of global economic decision-making."

This is what President Obama said in the Australian parliament. Following the speech, in January 2012 the Department of Defense issued a document with the title "Sustaining US Global Leadership: Priorities for Twenty-First-Century Defense," which envisioned the Asia Pacific region as the focus of US security strategy (US Department of Defense 2012: 2).

Following this, US secretary of defense Leon Panetta, in his speech given at the Shangri-La Dialogue in Singapore, explained the significance of this US repositioning by stating four main principles.[1] First was the principle of abiding by international rules and order. Second was the expansion of partnerships with countries in the Asia Pacific region. Third was the maintenance and strengthening of the US military presence: Panetta underlined several areas in Southeast Asia and the Indian Ocean in which the US military presence would be strengthened by stationing marines in Darwin, organizing joint military exercises with Thailand (Cobra Gold), enhancing the US military commitment in the Philippines, deploying littoral combat ships to Singapore, and increasing bilateral defense cooperation with Vietnam. Fourth was force projection—the deployment of US naval power around the world. In the past, the United States deployed its naval assets half in the Pacific and half in the Atlantic. But by 2020 this was to be adjusted, with 60 percent placed in the Pacific and 40 percent in the Atlantic. The United States would also keep six aircraft carriers stationed in the Pacific, and would also deploy littoral combat ships in the region.

This account helps us to understand President Obama's Asia Pacific policy and why it has been referred to as "rebalancing" or "pivoting" to the region. Obama's speech in the Australian parliament was structured around four main points: (1) the United States is a Pacific nation; (2) the United States would maintain its military presence in the Asia Pacific region; (3) the United States would strengthen its collaboration with allies such as Japan, Australia, South Korea, and the Philippines, as well as strengthen its partnerships with countries such as Indonesia, Singapore, and India, and also contribute to regional cooperation and strengthening political collaborations; and (4) for the latter purpose, the United States would build a free, fair, open, and transparent international political system, for which TPP provides a model. The most important point is to stress that the United States would maintain its military presence in Asia Pacific and that there would be no cuts to the budget for maintaining US presence in the region, even though the wars in Afghanistan and Iraq would be over and the United States would reduce its military spending in the future. For this purpose, the United States would adjust the balance of its military forces, rebalancing the deployment of its forces between the Pacific and the Atlantic and pivoting to the Pacific.

From Foreign and Security Policy to the Economy

This rebalancing represented an important strategic decision for the Obama administration, but critics have raised several concerns regarding the long-term sustainability of the policy. The most important is the argument that US national strategy has undergone a major shift since the end of the Cold War. During the Cold War era, the Soviet Union was a clear and present threat. This meant that US strategy was built on simple foundations: how to control this threat and defend the peace and prosperity of the United States together with the "Free World." Since the end of the Cold War, however, the world situation has changed. In some ways, it has become more complicated. As James Woolsey, who headed the Central Intelligence Agency (CIA) under the Clinton administration, once said: "We have slain a large dragon, but we live now in a jungle filled with a bewildering variety of poisonous snakes" (Brands 2014: 246).

In this changed world, what the most important priorities should be for US policy has become a highly contentious political issue. The American public gave priorities to rebalancing the government budget, reinvigorating the US economy, creating jobs, and promoting globalization over foreign and international security policy issues. This new set of priorities was neatly encapsulated in President Clinton's famous declaration, "It's the economy, stupid!" This of course did not mean that the United States ceased to be the global hegemon. But Clinton was keen to minimize the cost of playing that role—in particular the human cost. A good illustration was his response to the crisis in Somalia, as depicted in the film *Black Hawk Down*. His successor, George W. Bush, placed the war on terror at the foundation of national strategy after the terrorist attacks of 11 September 2001. But the wars in Afghanistan and Iraq did not go as smoothly as the United States hoped, and with the global financial crisis in 2008 and the election of Barack Obama as president, the war on terror is no longer seen as the single most important issue in national strategy. As is well known, President Obama was extremely cautious about military interventions, as we can see in his response to the crises in Ukraine and the Middle East. Like Clinton, he was keen to minimize the cost to the United States.[2]

Seen in this way, it is clear that US strategy in the post–Cold War era has been more inward-looking and less consistent than during the Cold War era. Yet the United States is still the global hegemon, and international crises will come to the United States, however much successive presidents want to focus on domestic issues. As a result, Clinton's foreign policy and national security policy were often ad hoc and based on impromptu responses to events as they occurred, particularly in his first term. During the Cold War, it was said that a president would typically spend around 60 percent of his time on foreign policy issues. President George H. W. Bush, it is said, devoted more than 75 percent of his time to international affairs. He was a president with a personal interest in foreign policy, and I must say we were fortunate to have him as US president at a major turning point in international relations marked by the end of the Cold War and the Gulf War. In contrast, President Clinton had almost no interest in foreign policy and during the early years of his presidency he apparently spent only around 25 percent of his time on foreign policy (Halberstam 2001: 435).

I also have the impression that George W. Bush's war on terror suffered from a lack of attention to detail. In going to war in Afghanistan and Iraq and ousting the Taliban and Saddam Hussein, his administration apparently gave little thought to such questions as postwar pacification, reconstruction, and nation building. As a result, the Taliban is once again extending its power and influence in regions along Pakistan's border with Afghanistan. The Islamic State of Iraq and Syria (ISIS) has expanded its control over the border regions between the two nations. All these developments are sad evidence of US strategic inconsistency since the end of the Cold War.

Obama's China Policy: Engagement and Hedging

Another problem often raised in connection with President Obama's Asia Pacific policy is its China policy. Critics say that although the government's basic stance can be named "engagement and hedging," there are too many fluctuations and inconsistencies in the way it is put into practice.

Historically speaking, US policy toward China underwent a major transformation in the wake of the Tiananmen Square massacre in 1989 and the end of the Cold War. During the Cold War era, strategic collaboration with China was useful in helping the United States to counterbalance the Soviet Union and stabilize the regional order in East Asia. But diplomatic relations between the two countries were gradually normalized, as symbolized by the visit of Mikhail Gorbachev to China in May 1989. It was shortly after this visit that troops of the People's Liberation Army (PLA) forcefully suppressed the protesters in Tiananmen Square. The number of people killed is unclear—some estimates say 700 people, others say 2,000—but images of the protest and its violent suppression were broadcast live on televisions around the world. This event destroyed the image of China that the American public had cherished since President Nixon's visit in 1972, as a country that was steadily deepening its friendship with the United States. President Reagan once described the country as "so-called Communist China," implying that China was not really the communist dictatorship many people thought it to be. But the Tiananmen massacre made it clear that China was not merely a so-called communist state but rather a true Marxist-Leninist party state just like the Soviet Union and its Eastern European satellite states (which were soon to collapse in 1989) and North Korea (Mann 1999).

In the years that followed, after numerous twists and turns, US policy on China shifted to one of engagement and hedging. The basic principle of the strategy was to engage with China and provide incentives to encourage China to accept the status quo and the regional order in Asia and to play the role, as Robert Zoellick put it, of a "responsible stakeholder." But at the same time the United States would "hedge" in various ways to ensure China would not threaten the US-led regional order. The balance between the two strands of this strategy has shifted from time to time, at times emphasizing more engagement and at other times more hedging.

We saw the shifting balance of engagement and hedging under President Obama. In his first year in office, Obama, and also Hillary Clinton as secretary of state, inclined toward an engagement policy. In July 2010, however, Clinton strongly criticized China's conduct in the

South China Sea at the ASEAN Regional Forum held in Hanoi. In December 2010, just before Hu Jintao's visit to Washington, D.C., Clinton declared that there was no such a thing as a United States–China "Group of Two" and that the idea of these two managing world affairs was out of the question. By then, the balance of US policy toward China was clearly turning in the hedging direction. The same can be said of Obama. Although he stressed the importance of engaging China in his speech in the Australian parliament, his main focus was the promise that the United States would maintain its military presence in the Asia Pacific region and would strengthen political cooperation with its allies and partners in the region. In this sense, it is fair to say that the speech was more inclined to hedging than engagement.

What kind of developments did we see during Obama's second term? National Security Adviser Susan Rice made statements that seemed to accept China's ideas for "a new model of major power relations." Likewise, John Kerry was not especially critical of China as secretary of state. Not a few now wonder whether the US government is once again inclined in the direction of engagement.

The Inconsistency of US Policy on China

This view is probably accurate enough as an observation of the current state of affairs. The question is *why* US policy on China has been so inconsistent. One helpful source for understanding this question is the book *The Rise of China vs. the Logic of Strategy*, by Edward Luttwak (2012).

Luttwak points out that the United States has three China policies. One is the policy of the Treasury. Numerous US companies have invested in China or have been engaged in economic activities there. Cheap manufactured goods imported from China benefit American consumers. Furthermore, China buys the US Treasury bonds for its foreign currency reserves, and thus ensures that funds flow back into the United States. Chinese economic growth therefore benefits the United States. This, says Luttwak, is the Treasury's China policy in a nutshell (Luttwak 2012).

Another is the China policy of the Department of Defense. The Pentagon has always inclined in the direction of hedging. Historically speaking, I think—and this is my own understanding, not something that Luttwak argues in his book—it is fair to say that from the 1970s until the middle of the first decade of the twenty-first century, regional order in Asia was maintained by a deal between China and the United

States: China agreed to accept the United States as hegemon in Asia, while in return the United States agreed to guarantee China's security. In other words, we can say that for many years China has contained its own ambitions to be a regional hegemon. This was a major compromise for the ruling elite and the public in China who believed in their own country's right to be a major power. In return, however, China obtained a stable strategic environment and access to cutting-edge technology, including military technology. As a result, China successfully rose to economic prominence with the assistance of the United States (in the form of the World Bank) and Japan. In this sense, it was not a bad deal for China. And for the United States, its China policy was strategically significant during the Cold War with the Soviet Union. But all this changed in the twenty-first century. Particularly after the global financial crisis of 2008, as the Chinese ruling elite and people gained confidence, and as a new generation took its place among the country's elite, restoring China's rightful place as the Asian hegemon has become a foremost foreign policy priority (White 2013). It is within this context that China has worked to strengthen its military and has taken unilateral actions in the South China Sea. In response to these developments, the policies of the US Department of Defense have tilted even more to hedging in recent years.

In addition to the policies of the Treasury and the Department of Defense, two other branches of government, the State Department and the National Security Council (NSC), play an important role in the decision-making on the China policy. Depending on the thinking and policy positions of the secretary of state and the national security adviser, as well as their high-level policy advisers, the two agencies may tilt the policy either to hedging or to engagement. Americans, particularly many of the professionals responsible for formulating foreign and national security policy, are pragmatic people. They tend to believe that shared interests should lead to a mutually beneficial relationship. Their first instinct, therefore, is to start with engagement. Only after developments prove them wrong do they shift to hedging.

Keeping these dynamics of policymaking in mind can help us to understand better the pendulum-like swings of US policy on China. As discussed, the administration usually starts with an emphasis on engagement and gradually shifts toward hedging over time. Secretary of State Hillary Clinton emphasized engagement during her first year, and then switched to hedging from her second year. I think we will see something similar happen with Secretary of State John Kerry and National Security Adviser Susan Rice in due course, even if they are slower to learn than Clinton. I believe there are signs they are moving more in the direction of hedging recently.

Furthermore, in order to see trends in US foreign and security policy clearly, it is important to pay attention not only to the executive branch but also to Congress and more broadly to conversations in the foreign and security policy community. From this perspective, we can see that US policy on China is likely to shift even more in the direction of hedging in the years to come. In March 2015, for example, John McCain (Republican, chairman of the Senate Armed Services Committee), Jack Reed (Democrat, ranking member, Senate Armed Services Committee), Bob Corker (Republican, chairman, Senate Foreign Relations Committee), and Bob Menendez (Democrat, ranking member, Senate Foreign Relations Committee) sent a letter to Secretary of State John Kerry and Secretary of Defense Ash Carter, and argued that the United States needed to come up with a comprehensive strategy for addressing China's activities to expand its effective control in the East China Sea and South China Sea. In particular, the letter drew attention to China's land-reclamation activities on many reefs and atolls in the Spratly Islands in the South China Sea for the purpose of building runways and other structures. Once these are complete, the letter noted, these facilities will serve as the bases for China's State Oceanic Administration ships, People's Liberation Army navy ships, PLA air force fighters and patrol planes, and other logistics and defense materials. This will improve the quality of command and control, surveillance, and the overall military capability of China. The letter said these developments are "a direct challenge not only to the interests of the United States and the region, but to the entire international community," and argued that the US government needed to respond strategically to address the challenge.

The Military and Political Dilemma

Another important consideration we need to bear in mind is that the US "rebalancing" strategy faces a complicated dilemma between military rationality and political rationality. In 2014, China's national defense budget was around 808 billion yuan ($132 billion). This was 12.2 percent up from the previous year (an increase of approximately 88 billion yuan or $14 billion). On a nominal scale, China's national defense budget has increased forty times in twenty-five years, and quadrupled over the past decade. As many people have pointed out, these figures do not include everything that China invests in national defense. For example, equipment procurement costs and research and development investments are not included. It is generally estimated that the size of China's defense budget is roughly double the declared amount. By making such a huge investment in the military, China is fast advancing with the mechanization and informatization of the People's Liberation Army, improving its capacity to win in "informatized local wars" and carry out its "historical missions in a new stage of the new century." More concretely, this means expanding the military capability to prevent Taiwan from going independent. Part of this mission involves being able to block the United States from military access and engagement in the area, and the military capacity to interfere with US military activities in the region, or what is known as antiaccess/area denial (A2/AD) capability (Japan Ministry of Defense 2014: 33–35). How has the United States responded to these developments? The phrase often used is "air-sea battle." According to the concept developed by the Department of Defense in its *Quadrennial Defense Review* report in February 2010, the United States would use missiles to neutralize China's A2/AD capacity in an emergency such as a Chinese invasion of Taiwan or similar full-scale military operations by the PLA. What kind of roles would the carrier strike group based in Yokosuka play in such a situation? What about the marines in Okinawa? As China's A2/AD capability is enhanced, it will be a major military risk if the US continues to deploy the important military personnel and assets in Yokosuka and Okinawa. And given the current progress of communications and aerospace technology, robotics, automation, and miniaturization, it is certainly feasible that rapid progress will be made toward developing a fully automated cyber-defense system that can be operated remotely. Once this revolution in military technology becomes a reality, we can ask whether it makes sense to maintain the carrier strike force at Yokosuka and the marines in Okinawa. Military experts are already asking these kinds of questions. At the same time, however, it is important to consider the political impact of any measure the United States takes in the region. If the United States were to relocate its carrier strike force from Yokosuka to Hawaii or to move the marines from Okinawa to Guam, this would have a huge political impact on the stability of the region. Simply put, once discussion starts based on a widespread perception that the United States has started to review its forward deployment strategy, this would instantly change Chinese expectations and actions, and could easily destabilize the region. In that sense, it would not be a rational political decision. This is the dilemma the United States and its allies face, the dilemma inherent in the emerging reality being created by China's strengthening of its military and the ongoing revolution in military technology. It will only grow more serious in the years to come.

Just to avoid any misunderstanding, I should emphasize that at this point, the US Department of Defense remains committed to a strategy of forward defense. The regional security system centered on the United States and backed up by bilateral security treaties and base agreements between the United States and Japan, the Republic of Korea, and Australia remains effective. US military personnel and assets are stationed throughout the region, and the system continues to be vigorously maintained. As long as this system remains in place, the progress of military technology—automation, cyber weapons, informatization, and miniaturization—presents no problems.[3] But we have to be alert and cautious about the idea of "offshore balancing." In a nutshell, this is the idea that it would be better for the United States to withdraw from the region militarily, and maintain equilibrium in the region by balancing China, Japan, and Russia against each other. Only if this balance of power is about to collapse would the United States intervene, and play the role of balancer. But I have very serious doubts whether the security order in the Asia Pacific region can be maintained in this way.

Two Types of "Gardening" in Diplomacy

A metaphor I find useful for understanding US foreign policy and national security is to compare diplomacy to gardening, as George Shultz did (1993: 128). There are two types of gardening: the process of designing and creating the garden in the first place, and the process of upkeep and maintenance. Looking back on US policy in East Asia and the Western Pacific since World War II, it is fair to say that the work of creating the garden took place in two main stages: from the late 1940s to the beginning of the 1950s, and during the 1970s. What does the garden look like today? The Korean Peninsula is divided in two, with the Republic of Korea, a US ally, occupying the southern half of the peninsula, and US troops stationed there. Japan is also a US ally and home for US bases, with the US-Japanese alliance, redefined in the 1990s, remaining crucial for regional security in the Western Pacific. China agreed to acquiesce to the US-led regional order in the 1970s. Formerly there were also important naval and air force bases in the Philippines, but these had to close down in the wake of the People Power revolution of 1986. Since the 1990s, the Philippines has been replaced in part by Singapore as an important base for the US military presence in Southeast Asia. Indochina turned to socialism in the 1970s, and the US bases that had been established in Thailand during the 1950s and 1960s closed in the 1970s. Since the 1990s, Australia has played an increasingly important role as a US ally in the Western Pacific.

This summarizes the design and creation stage of the gardening process. In short, the design of the garden has not changed substantially from the 1980s to the present. In Europe, the situation has been quite different, and the layout of the garden has had to change considerably to accommodate geopolitical changes, including the collapse of socialist states in Eastern Europe, German unification, the collapse of the Soviet Union, and the eastward expansion of NATO and the EU. Compared with Europe, the major changes in the geopolitical structure of East Asia have been less dramatic and more incremental: the "reform and opening" policy in China, the Tiananmen massacre, the Doi Moi (Renovation) policy in Vietnam, the end of the Cold War and the arrival of peace in Indochina, and the rise of the region as a major center of global economic growth and the development of a regional manufacturing network—all these developments led to the regionalization of East Asia with an inherent tension between its security and trade systems. In recent years, China has spent heavily on its military, and with Xi Jinping espousing what he calls the "China Dream," many people now wonder whether China has embarked on an attempt to change the entire design of the garden under its own hegemony.

The United States is not really interested in altering the design of the garden. Yet there is a growing concern that the layout of the garden may change despite US preferences if China is allowed to seek its own interests. What should be done? President Obama's speeches on Asia Pacific outlined the US strategy clearly. The basic idea is to encourage the gradual evolution of the regional security system centered on the United States. Key to this, I believe, will be making the US-Japanese and US-Australian alliances closer and deeper, transforming the regional hub-and-spokes security system into a network of alliances and partnerships with trilateral security relations at its core.

CHINA'S RISE AND ITS STRATEGY

Maintaining the Status Quo

What is China trying to achieve? We have seen that US foreign and national security policy is essentially one of "gardening," or working to maintain the status quo. For the United States, the basic aim of foreign policy is to prune and weed and generally maintain a garden that is already in place, or (to put it in other words) to maintain and support a regional political order organized in accordance with a set of norms and rules. From China's perspective, however, China played little part in constructing the regional order and has little incentive to maintain it now. Nevertheless, from the 1970s until the middle of the first decade of this century, China agreed to accept US predominance and chose to prioritize economic development within the US-led regional order. China did not have the capacity to challenge the United States, and by becoming a "junior partner" was able to obtain major military and economic advantages. This continued without any disruption until the breakup of the Soviet Union and the end of the Cold War. When the Soviet Union collapsed, there were debates within the Chinese leadership, with some arguing that China should assume the now vacant position as leader of the socialist world. Deng Xiaoping thought differently. He made a strategic decision that China was not yet strong enough for this ambition, and believed that China should first concentrate on building up its strength. This is the policy of *taoguang yaohui* ("bide our time while building up our strength"). But this decision did not mean that China's leaders had abandoned the idea of their country as a major power and the rightful hegemon in Asia. They merely decided to put these ambitions aside for strategic reasons. The ultimate aim is to restore China to its rightful position as the most powerful state in Asia. This has continued as what Xi Jinping describes as the "China Dream." What we face today is a situation in which China's ruling elite have become more confident in their power. Spurred on by the growing chauvinism of the Chinese people, they are now taking steps to make their "China Dream" a reality.

One of the crucial events that directly sparked this change was the global financial crisis in 2008. This was preceded by remarkable economic growth in China, which lasted more than thirty-five years from the end of the 1970s. A look at the size of China's economy, measured in GDP (in current prices), underlines the scale of this growth. In 1980 China's GDP was $202 billion, equivalent to 19 percent of the Japanese economy and just 7.3 percent that of the United States. By 2010, this had grown to some $5.879 trillion, outstripping the scale of the Japanese economy. This was equivalent to thirtyfold growth over the past thirty years. If the Chinese economy continues to grow at an average of between 5 percent and 6 percent over the next decade, it will rival the economy of the United States in scale by the mid-2020s. In 2009, China overtook Germany to become the world's largest exporter, and since 2008 has held the world's largest stockpile of foreign currency reserves with holdings of over $1.809 trillion.

People tend to think that China will continue to develop as it has over the past thirty years and expect that China will in due course become the regional hegemon in Asia and a global superpower alongside the United States. But there are problems with this kind of linear thinking. The United States is engaged in "gardening," and its policy is geared to maintaining the status quo. China is looking to change the design of the garden itself.

The fact that China wants to change the regional order does not mean it can make it happen. As I have said, once its share of the global economy exceeds 20 percent, China will find it increasingly difficult to concentrate solely on pursuing its own interests. At the moment, China is free-riding on the global free trade system built on the dollar standard and the WTO. Meanwhile, China's party state leadership is investing 2 percent of GDP (to cite only the official figures) into military spending every year under the slogan of "rich country, strong army." China is using this power to unilaterally "settle" territorial and sovereignty disputes under the name of "core interests." China likewise acts with scant regard for other countries in areas where no global governance systems are yet in place, despite their decisive significance for national security, such as cyberspace and outer space. If this behavior continues, instability is inevitable in both the global and the regional order, and this will lead to greater pushback against China from other countries. As Edward Luttwak (2012) says, if China remains in a state of "great state autism," the counter-effects will only grow more serious in the years to come. Will China's ruling elite sooner or later break out of its "great state autism"? We cannot know whether this will happen, but even if it does, it will most likely happen a decade or two from now. China will have to decide what position it wants to occupy in the world. The country's leaders cannot expect other countries to follow China simply because China is larger than any other country. The Chinese say they want to be respected, but they cannot buy respect with money. As long as they remain in a condition of "great state autism" and continue to make self-centered decisions with scant regard for other states' interests, it is quite possible that China will find itself mistrusted and hemmed in on all sides by hostile powers.

Xi Jinping's Grand Strategy

As China's supreme leader, Xi Jinping occupies three important positions: general secretary of the Communist Party, president of the People's Republic, and chairman of the Central Military Commission. What thinking informs the strategic decisions Xi Jinping and his fellow leaders are taking? Although we can attempt to read the various signs, we cannot really tell for sure. We should also be aware that state strategy often becomes clear only with the benefit of hindsight. We can look back on a series of decisions and discern a thread of thinking running through those decisions. In many cases, however, the reality is that the decisionmakers are forced to take decisions under the pressure of time, without fully weighing up pros and cons. In that sense, a state's "grand strategy" is often more like a kind of "grand narrative." Decisionmakers are not necessarily conscious of themselves as drawing up a long-term strategy. My impression is that the people in central decisionmaking positions in China are essentially maintaining the basic state strategy that has been in place since the 1980s, albeit with some gradual modifications in politics, the economy, and foreign and security policy. Needless to say, it is quite possible for major strategic decisions to result from this kind of gradual fine-tuning and adjustment.

What are the notable features of the government under Xi Jinping? What do his government's statements tell us and what has his government been doing since he came to power? Xi Jinping was chosen as successor to Hu Jintao as general secretary of the Communist Party and chairman of the Central Military Commission in 2012. He officially became president of the People's Republic of China the following year.

When he was chosen as general secretary of the party in 2012, various groups with divergent interests existed within the party. He was chosen as a leader who would be acceptable to a majority of these differing stakeholders. As a result, it was widely expected that he would not antagonize these groups by taking unnecessary risks and would prioritize government stability—at least in the first few years. It was thought that he would wait to address serious long-term problems.

In fact, he embarked on a major anticorruption campaign in January 2013. Since then, he has purged and punished numerous senior officials, including several deputy ministers and senior Communist Party figures, including former Politburo Standing Committee member Zhou Yongkang, former vice chairmen of the Central Military Commission Xu Caihou and Guo Boxiong, and former director of the General Office of the Communist Party Ling Jihua (Kamo 2015: 64–66).

There were probably several aims behind this, but analysts generally agree that Xi Jinping was looking for ways to strengthen his own power base, as well as breaking up the vested interests of the state-owned enterprises, pushing ahead with reforms of the People's Liberation Army, and bolstering his support among the people. It should also be noted that Xi Jinping is not alone among China's leaders in having a sense of crisis regarding the long-term viability of the party state system in China. Indeed, shared awareness of this concern is probably another factor that has made possible an anticorruption campaign on this scale (National Institute for Defense Studies 2015: 93).

With these moves, Xi Jinping has succeeded in consolidating his power within the central decisionmaking cadres, far beyond what Hu Jintao achieved. This is obvious if we look at the various commissions and "leading groups" that decide and coordinate policy within the Communist Party. Xi Jinping is the chairman of all important committees, including the Central National Security Commission, responsible for coordinating internal law and order and foreign and security policy; the Central Comprehensively Deepening Reforms Commission, which leads the reform programs of the party state; and the Central Leading Group for Military Reform, in charge of reforming national defense and the armed services under the Central Commission. He is also head of the Central Leading Group for Financial and Economic Affairs, which in the past was always placed under the premier of the State Council (Kamo 2015: 68).

The Difficult Reality of the Chinese Economy

What developments can we see taking place under Xi's leadership? As far as the economy is concerned, the issues are quite clear. Since the global economic crisis in 2008, China has implemented a massive economic stimulus package worth some 4 trillion yuan. Around a third of that has been invested in manufacturing, and around a quarter in property development and infrastructure, triggering a remarkable investment boom. This has resulted in massive spending on capital investment, and an accumulation in many companies of assets with low profitability. Take the materials industry, for example, where excessive capital investment has led to excessive production capacity, market collapse, and declining production. The situation is becoming worse, and it is now proving difficult to gain returns on investment. Asset prices rose wildly and then slumped, and this has had a major impact on many industries, from materials to furniture and domestic appliances. Low-profit investment was carried out on a massive scale in the regions. Regional governments calculated that if the economy grew, their revenue would increase and they would be able to pay off their debts. But excessive investment and unsustainable debt burdens have brought local-government and private-sector joint property investment to crisis point in many places.

Even with a buildup of bad debt, if some aspects of a company's business are making a profit, it can use that profit to repay its loans or arrange refinancing with a bank, and thus avoid defaulting. But the efficiency of investment will certainly be adversely affected. In the past few years, around 50 percent of GDP has been invested, for an economic growth rate remaining around 7 percent. Many people claim that even this figure cannot be trusted. Leaving that question aside for now, there can be little doubt that investment is less efficient and effective than it was in the years when the growth rate was over 10 percent. The only way to increase productivity is to promote innovation and invest strategically in new industrial areas. But this has not happened. In fact, since the 2008 economic crisis, the state-owned enterprises have come to occupy an even larger share of the Chinese economy, and since they generally enjoy a monopoly or something close to one, these companies have very little interest in innovation. We cannot expect much from this quarter. In 2012, a senior figure in a Chinese think tank said that if China's economic growth rate dropped below 7 percent, around a third of the state-owned enterprises might find it difficult to remain profitable.[4] Clearly, the time has come for a major rethink of the way China's economy is managed.

What is to be done? One useful pointer is the concept of the "financial seizure" put forward by Tsugami Toshiya (2015b) in his book *The Struggles of the Giant Dragon*. Tsugami uses the GDP deflator (the difference between nominal and real GDP rate) as a proxy variable for inflation, and uses this to calculate real interest rates. Until recently, he says, the interest rate for savings was negative in real terms with interest rates regularly running at negative 5–8 percent for savings and negative 1–3 percent for loans. This meant that China was essentially taking wealth from depositors and using it to subsidize borrowers (companies, particularly state-owned enterprises). The contribution made by consumers to China's economic growth has therefore been much smaller than in other countries, and this was a major reason why consumption accounted for just half of GDP. Investment, by contrast, using nominal GDP growth rate as a proxy variable for return on investment, has consistently shown a high rate of 18–21 percent over the past decade. And since the nominal rate of interest on loans remains around 7 percent, this has led to major profits.

If companies can expect to earn an operating revenue that is much higher than the cost of funding, even businesses that would otherwise be unprofitable can make money. This inevitably leads to excessive investment. This is what has happened in China. Over the past year or two, however, the situation has changed dramatically. The nominal growth rate has fallen to around 8–9 percent, while nominal interest rates are around 7.5 percent. This means that companies can no longer expect to earn the same revenue that they previously enjoyed. The "financial seizure" has vanished, and borrowers must now look to invest in businesses that will make a profit. It seems almost certain that in the long term, this will transform the Chinese economy from one led by investment to one driven by consumption. But even if this transformation does take place as expected, the process will naturally involve some difficult adjustments. In fact, they have already started, and this is the situation we are seeing today (Tsugami 2015b: 111–112).

Building a "Moderately Prosperous Society"

What are the prospects for the Chinese economy in the longer term? One thing that will surely have an important impact is the country's aging society. By the beginning of the 2020s, the ratio of people aged over sixty-five to the working-age population (aged fifteen to sixty-four) is expected to exceed 20 percent. Total labor input has already peaked, and will soon start declining. In the long term, this means that even in the best-case scenario, the labor force is likely to show negative growth of around 0.2 percent from 2016 to 2025 and negative growth of around 0.4 percent for 2026 to 2030. GDP growth is also expected to fall from 7 percent to around 5 percent, although this will depend on productivity growth to some extent.

When Xi Jinping refers to the "new normal," he is in effect saying that this process has already started to affect the Chinese economy. He is trying to manage the expectations of the Chinese people by warning them not to expect the same high rates of economic growth they enjoyed in the past, and at the same time instructing the party cadres both in the center and in the regions that public investment no longer be the driving force of economic growth.

A policy response to this situation is already under way. For example, until recently, local governments relied on subsidiary companies known as local government financing vehicles (*rongzi pingtai*) for much of their funding. These companies borrowed large amounts of funds from the banks, issued bonds, and raised funds, and invested these funds in real estate development. They provided crucial funding support to local governments. However, this system came to an end in 2015;

since 2016, local government financing has been limited to municipal bonds (Tsugami 2015b: 88). If the Chinese economy maintains a growth rate of around 7 percent while shifting from an investment model to a consumption-led economy, the reforms will be successful. But if the growth rate plummets to as low as 2 percent to 3 percent, the economy will be in for a hard landing (Tsugami 2015b: 2–5).

In the context of foreign and security policy, we also need to pay attention to the activities of state-owned enterprises in China's economic cooperation. Several important things are happening in this area. One is that Xi Jinping and the other leaders have shifted from the previous policy that prioritized competition within the domestic market, to a policy of encouraging monopolies or oligopolies by the state-owned enterprises. Many areas of industry, including railways, power, and communication, are now dominated by a single state-owned enterprise holding a share of more than 80 percent. Negotiations are currently under way, for example, under the auspices of the State Council, for a merger of the country's two major producers of trains and rolling stock, the China Southern Locomotive and Rolling Stock Corporation and the China Northern Locomotive and Rolling Stock Corporation. If the merger goes through, this will lead to the birth of a giant company with close to a 100 percent share of the domestic market for trains and subway cars and sales of nearly 4 trillion yuan. The aim of the merger is to concentrate economic resources and give an impetus to orders of high-speed rail and other projects from overseas.

In power, the State Grid Corporation, which operates 80 percent of the domestic national electricity grid, merged the fifteen substation companies under its control into one. In the nuclear power sector, which is trying to strengthen exports of nuclear power plants and technology, negotiations are ongoing for a merger between the State Nuclear Power Technology Corporation and the State Power Investment Corporation.[5]

The macroeconomic conditions for economic cooperation centered on infrastructure exports are also coming into place. *Nihon Keizai Shimbun* has predicted that by 2015 China's foreign direct investment will exceed inward foreign direct investment and that China will become a net exporter of capital.[6] Indeed, statistics from China's Ministry of Commerce suggest that direct investment into China from January to November 2014 was worth $106 billion, while outward foreign direct investment from China for the same period was up by 12 percent from the previous year to $90 billion. The government of Xi Jinping is actively supporting overseas expansion of Chinese companies under the slogan of its "Going Out" (*Zou chuqu*) policy. In December 2014, the

State Council reduced or scrapped regulations limiting fundraising by foreign currency for companies wanting to invest overseas.

This is the current situation and outlook for the economy. What about China's foreign and security policy? One thing we should keep in mind is that the Chinese economy is unlikely to keep enjoying rapid growth. At the same time, since the global financial crisis, China's leaders have come to believe that the United States is destined to decline. They believe that this is "our time," and that "our economy" is better managed than that of the United States. They have said things they should probably have left unsaid, and they have done things they ought not to have done. It will take some time to exorcize their hubris and for things to return to normal (Tsugami 2015b: 11).[7] This is significant in the context of China's foreign and national security policy.

Many commentators have drawn attention to the remarks made by Hu Jintao to diplomats at the eleventh Conference of Chinese Diplomatic Envoys Stationed Abroad in 2009. In the midst of the international financial crisis, he said that this was a time when China had to maintain stable and relatively fast economic development, but that the country was facing important new opportunities and difficult challenges and that China's diplomatic activities should contribute to protecting its interests of sovereignty, safety, and development. In saying so, Hu Jintao amended Deng Xiaoping's famous "Eight-Character Dictum" of "hide one's capacities, bide one's time, and seek achievements." Under Hu, this was revised to "bide one's time, and actively seek to do as much as one can." In November 2012, he said that considering the overall situations, both domestic and international, the country faced an important strategic opportunity to develop and grow, and called on the Chinese people to "rise to the challenge to seize this strategic opportunity calmly but aggressively and achieve the great objective of realizing a moderately prosperous (*xiaokang*) society by 2020."[8]

Under Xi Jinping, this position of proactively seizing opportunities and achieving objectives has grown steadily more pronounced, as has been widely noted as regards his rhetoric. At the third group study session of the CCP Politburo, held in January 2013, for example, Xi Jinping said that China would walk the path of peaceful development, but added that "we will neither relinquish any legitimate interests nor can we sacrifice the core interests of the nation."

How is Xi Jinping's government managing foreign relations? First, let's look at China's relationship with the United States. In June 2013, Xi Jinping visited the United States for the first time since he was appointed general secretary of the Communist Party and head of the military council, for a summit meeting with Barack Obama at Sunny-lands, California. According to media reports, the chief items on the agenda were formulating a code of conduct in cyberspace and North Korea's nuclear program. But according to informed sources with access to the Chinese Ministry of Foreign Affairs, Xi Jinping himself wanted to gain concessions from the United States on cyber terrorism and territorial issues in the East and South China Seas by using bargaining chips such as the resumption of six-party talks on North Korea. However, President Obama did not consent to China's proposal for a "new model" of major power relations, which China defined as: avoiding clashes and conflicts, developing a win-win relationship, and mutual respect for core interests. Obama's refusal was certainly based on the fact that many people in the United States regard China as a threat. In recent years China has increased tensions through its unilateral actions on territorial disputes with its neighbors, and the country has also caused endless frictions with the United States and other powers through its suspected cyber espionage and some unusually close encounters between Chinese military planes and US aircraft.

China's "Counter-Rebalancing" Strategy

Another important speech by Xi Jinping on diplomacy and relations with neighboring countries and the wider region came at a Peripheral Diplomacy Work Conference held in October 2013. The Japan-based *Chūgoku Tsūshin* [China News] newspaper reported on this forum in detail. Xi Jinping said that the important tasks for the conference were to consolidate experience, evaluate the current climate, and ensure that everyone was facing in the same direction. The conference would help to open the way toward the future and settle on a strategic target for diplomatic activities in the region for the next five to ten years. It would decide the basic direction and overall allocation of priorities and clarify a roadmap and implementation plan for actions to find solutions for the serious problems China faced in regional diplomacy. He made the following observations:

> The strategic aims of our country's regional diplomacy are to achieve the objective of our "Two Centuries" struggle, to bring about the great rejuvenation of the Chinese nation, to comprehensively develop our relations with neighboring countries, to solidify friendships with our neighbors, to deepen mutually beneficial cooperation, to maintain and

make full use of this period of important strategic opportunity for China's development, to defend the national interests of sovereignty, safety, and development, to promote friendly political relationships between China and the countries of the region, to solidify economic bonds, to deepen security cooperation, and to intensify exchanges between peoples and cultures. Our basic guidelines on regional diplomacy are good will and partnership with our neighbors, developing friendly relations that will reassure and enrich our neighbors and ensuring that our dealings with neighboring countries are marked by the principles of closeness, sincerity, consideration, and tolerance. Developing friendly relationships with neighbors is a consistent part of China's regional diplomacy.

We must push ahead with a comprehensive approach to regional diplomacy, devoting our energy and strength into maintaining the peace and stability of the region. Walking the path of peaceful development is a strategic choice made by the Party based on the tide of the times and China's fundamental interests. Maintaining peace and stability in the region is an important objective of China's regional diplomacy. We must work to deepen mutually beneficial, win-win relationships in the region. We must make an integrated plan for resources in areas including economy, trade, science and technology, and finance. This plan must make full use of our comparative advantage and find points of strategic agreement with other countries in the region to deepen mutually beneficial cooperation. We will actively participate in regional economic cooperation, joining hands with suitable countries to accelerate infrastructure interconnectivity and communication and completing the construction of the "Silk Road" Economic Belt and the "Twenty-First Century Maritime Silk Road." We will speed up the implementation of a regional free trade area and widen the scope of trade and investment cooperation, and construct a new framework for regional economic integration. We must deepen regional financial cooperation, actively promote preparations for the Asian Infrastructure Investment Bank, and perfect the regional financial security network.

We will promote regional security cooperation. Security cooperation with the other countries of the region is a shared need. We will build a new view of security based on mutual trust and benefit, equality, and cooperation, and support the concept of comprehensive, shared, and cooperative security as we push ahead with security cooperation with other countries of the region. We will actively participate in regional and sub-regional security cooperation, deepen cooperation mechanisms, and increase mutual strategic trust.[9]

This speech reflects the fundamental ideas behind Xi Jinping's approach to regional diplomacy. Essentially, his strategy is to emphasize that China pursues "peaceful development" and is eager to develop friendly relationships with its neighbors through economic cooperation. By doing so, he tries to reassure neighboring countries in the region that they have no reason to worry about China's rise. In this sense, the strategy can be called "counter-rebalancing" in response to the strategy put forward by President Obama. China will not give up its "legitimate interests" or sacrifice its "core interests," but it wants to reassure neighboring countries that they do not need to worry and to "stabilize, control, and shape" the region by developing close relationships with its neighbors, treating them as partners, and working to develop friendly neighborly relations.[10] China's aim is to "construct a stable and advantageous external environment."

An important part of this strategic framework is the Belt and Road Initiative (originally translated more literally from the Chinese as "One Belt, One Road"), which unites the concept of a Silk Road Economic Belt and a Twenty-First Century Maritime Silk Road. The purpose is clear. Economic cooperation, including trade and infrastructure investment, is an important instrument of China's foreign policy. The aim is to strengthen diplomatic relations with neighboring countries through economic cooperation, with a special emphasis on infrastructure development.

At a conference on interaction and confidence-building measures in Asia held in May 2014, also attended by Russian president Vladimir Putin and leaders of several Central Asian countries, Xi Jinping spelled out a "New Asian Security Concept," and expressed China's ambition to establish a new regional order that excludes the United States. In addition to the six countries (China, Russia, Kazakhstan, Kyrgyzstan, Tajikistan, and Uzbekistan) participating in the Shanghai Cooperation Organization (SCO), the other countries represented at the conference included Bahrain, Bangladesh, Cambodia, Egypt, India, Iran, Iraq, Israel, Jordan, Pakistan, Palestine, Qatar, South Korea, Thailand, Turkey, the United Arab Emirates, and Vietnam.

In late November 2014, Xi Jinping gave a speech on foreign policy at the Central Conference on Work Relating to Foreign Affairs. In this speech, he said, "We will place cooperation and win-win relationships at the center of China's new international relations," giving instructions that China's diplomats should avoid friction with Japan and other neighboring countries. This was the first time the conference had been held for eight years, since August 2006. According to a report in *Nihon Keizai Shimbun* in 2014, he stressed that China would seek to maintain a stance of cooperation in its diplomacy with neighboring countries, and would seek to "make progress in relationships with regional major powers and build sound and stable major power relations."

With the Senkaku Islands and other sovereignty disputes in the South China Sea in mind, Xi Jinping said, "We will staunchly defend our territorial rights and maritime interests, and will deal with disputes over territories and islands in an appropriate manner," but at the same time he stressed that "differences and disputes among nations must be resolved peacefully through dialogue and consultation. We are opposed to any appeals to force or threats. China must adapt itself to the trends of development in the world," adding that China must avoid frictions with surrounding countries in order to avoid isolation from the international community, and must create an international environment favorable to China's development.[11]

CHINA'S RISE AND ITS BEHAVIOR IN THE REGION

Territorial Issues in the South China Sea

So far, we have looked at China's foreign policy—or more accurately, we have reviewed some of the statements Xi Jinping has made about China's basic stance and its foreign policy direction. But what has the Chinese government actually been doing? We can summarize China's actions on the ground over the past few years as follows.

China regards territorial disputes in the South China Sea as a sovereignty issue and part of its "core interests." Accordingly, it has shown no sign that it is prepared to make any compromise. Quite the opposite: since 2007–2008, China has become increasingly assertive and acted unilaterally, by using force to impose its own position on other countries (see Figure 2.1). Let me give some recent examples: between May and July 2014, the China National Petroleum Corporation set up an oil-drilling rig in disputed waters around the Paracel Islands, which both China and Vietnam claim. Vietnam protested, and there were clashes between Chinese government ships and Vietnamese coast guard and fisheries' monitoring vessels. In the Spratly Islands in the South China Sea, China has built a 3,300-meter runway on Fiery Cross Reef for military purposes. China has already constructed a 3,000-meter runway on Woody Island, one of the Paracel Islands. If China builds another runway on Scarborough Shoal, over which it now exercises de facto control following a trial of nerves with Philippine government vessels in 2012, China will place itself in a good position from which to exercise de facto control over the South China Sea.[12]

China has also let its official ships enter the waters around the Senkaku Islands in the East China Sea. In November 2013, China declared the establishment of an air defense identification zone in the

Figure 2.1   The South China Sea

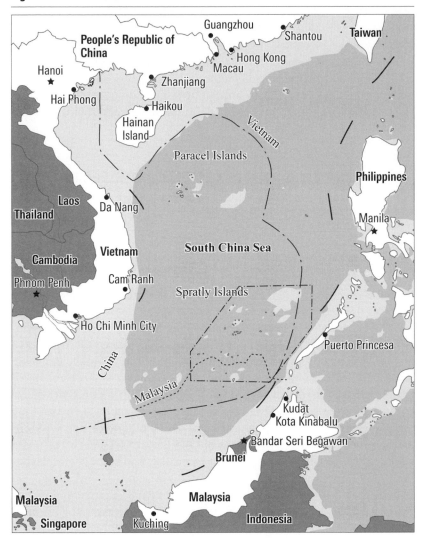

East China Sea, which includes the Senkaku Islands. Between May and June 2014, Chinese air force fighters repeatedly "buzzed" aircraft from Japan's air self-defense force, raising concerns about the risk of an accidental collision.

Chinese provocations have repeatedly been directed against US armed forces in the South China Sea. In December 2013, for example,

Chinese ships obstructed the activities of the USS *Cowpens*, which had as its mission to monitor the Chinese aircraft carrier. In August 2014, planes from the Chinese navy obstructed the missions of P-8 Poseidon surveillance aircraft. Following these events, at a meeting during the Asia Pacific Economic Cooperation (APEC) summit meeting in Beijing in November 2014, Abe Shinzō and Xi Jinping agreed to work toward a maritime communication mechanism to prevent unintended clashes. Barack Obama and Xi Jinping also agreed to build a similar communication mechanism to prevent accidental clashes between US and Chinese naval ships or air force planes. Despite the apparently mutual and conciliatory nature of these agreements, they can be seen as indications of how unilateral and aggressive China's actions in the region have been.[13]

The Belt and Road Initiative

What about the Belt and Road Initiative? Xi Jinping first spoke of the idea of a Silk Road Economic Belt in September 2013, and this was followed by the idea of a Twenty-First Century Maritime Silk Road and a new Asian Infrastructure Investment Bank (AIIB) in October 2013. As we have seen, he referred to both initiatives again at a regional diplomacy roundtable forum the same month.

In October 2014, twenty-one nations from Asia and the Middle East, including China, signed a memorandum in Beijing to move toward establishing the AIIB. In December 2014, the Silk Road Fund was founded with an investment of $40 billion from several Chinese government banks.

The Silk Road Economic Belt, which is the "belt" part of the initiative, is envisaged as two routes: one from Beijing to Europe through Central Asia and Russia and another from the Xinjiang Uyghur Autonomous Region through Pakistan to the Gulf. The Shanghai Cooperation Organization and the Conference on Interaction and Confidence-Building Measures in Asia already exist for political cooperation in this vast continental region. Economic cooperation through and along this "belt" will be built on these frameworks of political cooperation and will presumably strengthen political cooperation at the same time. The question is: What strategic significance does this initiative have for China?

It is significant as its energy lifeline. China currently uses more than 10 million barrels of oil a day, and its dependence on imports is already over 60 percent. In other words, China currently imports between 6.5 and 7 million barrels of crude oil every day. This is expected to increase further in the future. Ten years from now, China's oil consumption is expected to rise to 19 million barrels, roughly equivalent to the current levels of consumption in the United States. By that time, its import dependence is expected to increase to 70–75 percent. At the same time, China's consumption of natural gas is growing, and its imports will expand considerably over the next decade. Given this prospect, securing a stable supply of energy resources is clearly a vital part of Chinese strategy.

From this perspective, Russia and the former Soviet states of Central Asia occupy a vital strategic position. Turkmenistan has the world's fourth largest reserves of underground natural gas, and China currently imports huge amounts of natural gas from this country.

In 2014, Russian president Vladimir Putin and Xi Jinping signed a long-term contract to supply natural gas via a pipeline from Lake Baikal in Siberia through Heilongjiang province to Beijing and Tientsin. Another pipeline runs from Central Asia, via the Xinjiang Uyghur Autonomous Region to Shanghai, Guangdong province, and Fujian province.

Some people also locate the strategic significance of the "belt" in the importance of Central Asia as a market and distribution routes to Europe. Evidence for this can be found in proposals for a series of new high-speed railways, including routes through Eurasia and Central Asia, and a new trans-Asian route.[14]

However, given the population and economic scale of the countries of Central Asia, it is hard to see that the region would have much value as a market. There are five countries in Central Asia: Kazakhstan, Kyrgyzstan, Tajikistan, Turkmenistan, and Uzbekistan. In 2013, their populations and GDP numbers were as follows: Kazakhstan, 17.6 million, $252 billion; Kyrgyzstan, 5.7 million, $7.9 billion; Tajikistan, 8.3 million, $9.2 billion; Turkmenistan, 5.8 million, $47.2 billion; Uzbekistan, 30.2 million, $59.1 billion. Altogether, the five countries have a population of 68 million people and their combined economies are worth around $375 billion—both about the same as Thailand (68 million people, $401 billion).

Logistics by Rail and by Sea

What about the significance of the Belt and Road Initiative for distribution and transportation? It takes around fifteen days to transport goods overland from the coastal area of Jiangsu province to Dusseldorf. To build a good transportation and distribution network in a single country may bring significant benefits. But moving goods overland from the Xinjiang Uyghur Autonomous Region in the interior of China to Europe via Central Asia would mean passing through the customs inspections of many states. Given the time and costs involved in passing through customs, it is hard to see how a "Eurasian land bridge" of this kind would bring significant benefits in logistical terms. By contrast, container ships can carry large volumes of freight from Guangdong to the port of Piraeus in Greece in around fifteen to twenty days. Once the goods are unloaded, Greece allows direct access to the EU, which should surely give this route a comparative advantage from the logistical perspective.

I am not saying that a high-speed rail link would be of no value. It is important to note that the Eurasian land bridge is at least in part an attempt to address some of the problems that China currently faces at home. As part of its war on terror in the wake of the terrorist attacks of 11 September 2001, the United States effectively placed Afghanistan under de facto occupation and steadily expanded its influence in Central Asia. But the United States started to withdraw its troops from Afghanistan in 2011. It was in parallel with this development that China, Russia, and the countries of Central Asia started joint military training exercises within the Shanghai Cooperation Organization framework, and started meetings of their defense ministers. China's northern border was a strategic front in the 1960s to 1980s during the period of uneasy relations with the Soviet Union. Today, however, relations between China and Russia are relatively stable, even though this stability is not built on deep mutual trust. China's influence is steadily increasing in the former Soviet countries of Central Asia as China's economy continues to grow.

Meanwhile, the Xinjiang Uyghur Autonomous Region has been rocked by Uyghur separatism, terrorism, and the threat of Islamic fundamentalism. Given the need to maintain internal security and order and to develop its interior economically, it is important for the Chinese government to support economic development in Central Asia, make these countries more dependent on China, isolate the Uyghur separatist movement and related terrorist activities, and insulate Xinjiang from the rising influence of Islamism in Central Asia and the Middle East. Infrastructure building is also important as part of international public works projects that create an outlet for China's surplus production capacity of steel, cement, and other products, and to earn time for reforming state-owned enterprises.

As we have seen, the Chinese government is integrating and amalgamating state-owned enterprises and encouraging them to seek markets overseas. As China's economic growth gradually slows, there is a good chance that increasing numbers of state-owned enterprises will not remain

profitable if they are active in China alone. China's economic cooperation, with its focus on infrastructure development, is at least partly driven
by internal policy purposes.

China obtains its oil supplies by tanker—from the Middle East, particularly from Saudi Arabia and Iran, and from Nigeria and Angola, via
the Cape of Good Hope. At present, China imports around 6.5 to 7 million barrels of crude oil per day, as already mentioned. If we assume
that a 200,000-ton tanker can carry around 2.5 million barrels of oil,
this means that China needs about three tankers' worth of crude oil
every day. If the journey from the Gulf to the East China Sea and South
China Sea via the Indian Ocean and the Straits of Malacca takes eight
days, there are normally around twenty-four massive Chinese tankers on
the seas transporting oil supplies. If China's crude oil imports increase
to around 10 million barrels a day, this would mean that forty large
tankers would be on the move at all times. There can be no doubt that
one of the aims of the Maritime Silk Road—the "road" component of
the Belt and Road Initiative—is to secure the sea lanes from the Middle East to the South China Sea and East China Sea via the Indian
Ocean and the Straits of Malacca. Also, given the risk that the Straits
of Malacca could be a choke point in a time of crisis, building a pipeline
to supply oil to the Chinese interior from the coastal regions along the
Indian Ocean makes geopolitical and geoeconomic sense. China already
has an oil and gas pipeline in operation from Kyaukpyu in Myanmar to
Kunming in Yunnan province. The China-Pakistan Corridor, which runs
from Kashgar in Xinjiang through Islamabad and Karachi to Gwadar,
is also said to have the same aim.[15]

THE SOUTH CHINA SEA AND
MAINLAND SOUTHEAST ASIA

A Never-Ending Game of Go

I mentioned earlier that George Shultz's "gardening" analogy offers a
useful way of thinking about US foreign policy. Is there a similar
metaphor that might help us to understand China's foreign policy strategy? One possibility is an idea given by Henry Kissinger, who has compared China's strategy to the game of *Weiqi*, better known in the West
by its Japanese name of Go (Kissinger 2011).[16]

I think this is quite perceptive. If I were to add anything, I would say
that this is a game of Go that is never-ending. I would also say that the

strategy is not always determined by a single player or a single deci-sionmaking group and that the strategy often emerges out of moves that multiple players make, such as central party state leaders, provin-cial party state officials, and state-owned enterprises. If we set aside the question of how and to what extent the central party state elite decide the strategy and impose their will on local party bosses and state-owned enterprises, however, the Go metaphor is useful to under-stand how China plays the game of international politics, what aims and beliefs are shared broadly by the party elite, and how strategy emerges in China.

What kind of game is China playing and what pattern is it trying to create on the board? I believe the following is not too off-the-mark as a summary of the basic strategy. First, China is trying to promote the idea of a "new model" of major power relations with the United States and seeking to manage this relationship on the basis of mutual respect for core interests and the avoidance of conflict. At the same time, it is look-ing to meet the US "pivot" toward Asia Pacific with its own counter-rebalancing strategy.

China wants to make South Korea economically dependent on China and turn it into a buffer state. China wants to steer it as much as possible in a more neutral direction. Japan is to be isolated. In the South China Sea, China will use force to gain de facto control over an increas-ingly wide area, and in the long term it aims to turn this entire maritime area into a Chinese lake. It is building up defensive capabilities in the sea lanes from the East China Sea and South China Sea via the Straits of Malacca to the Indian Ocean and the Middle East.

In Southeast Asia, and particularly in the countries of mainland Southeast Asia, China wants to provide large-scale infrastructure proj-ects and other types of economic cooperation to make these countries dependent on China and create a buffer zone between China and its rivals. It is constructing energy lifelines across the region stretching from Central Asia to the Middle East and Europe, and is carefully man-aging its relationship with Russia and promoting political and economic cooperation in this region.

In sum, China's basic strategy is to oppose the US-led alliances in the Atlantic (NATO) and Asia Pacific (the hub-and-spokes regional security alliance) that have until now served as the two major pillars of the global order, by constructing a Eurasian economic union. As part of this strategy, in East Asia, China is looking to turn the Korean Peninsula and mainland Southeast Asia into buffer zones, and to incorporate them into its own sphere of influence if it can.

Sovereignty Disputes in the South China Sea

The question is how to assess this strategy and its implementation. What China has been doing in recent years in the South China Sea and East China Sea is well known. China claims sovereignty over almost the entire South China Sea within its "nine-dash line," and is engaged in a series of standoffs with other countries in the region that claim sovereignty over various small islands and shoals within this maritime area, namely Vietnam, the Philippines, Malaysia, and Brunei. China is also in conflict with Indonesia over the exclusive economic zone around the Natuna Islands.

China's position on the territorial issues in the South China Sea has changed over the years. In the 1990s, after China passed the Territorial Waters Act in 1992, sovereignty disputes over territories in the South China Sea emerged as a major point of contention between China and ASEAN countries until around 1998 or 1999. There was then a period of relative calm that lasted until around 2007.

In 2002, China and ASEAN signed a joint declaration on a code of conduct in the South China Sea. In 2003, China and the Philippines agreed on a joint oil and gas exploration deal, while China and ASEAN signed a joint declaration on a strategic partnership for peace and prosperity. Such agreements played a key role in calming the animosity between China and some of the ASEAN states over sovereignty issues in the South China Sea.

Beginning in 2007, however, tensions began to rise again, particularly between China and Vietnam. One reason was the decision of China's Hainan province to establish a new administrative region named Sansha, a prefectural-level "city" incorporating the Paracel and Spratly Islands and the Macclesfield Bank shoal.

Another reason was that Chinese fishery patrol boats began repeatedly to capture Vietnamese boats fishing in the waters around the Paracels, an area claimed by both Vietnam and China, but under de facto Chinese control. This made the issue of territoriality in the South China Sea a major point of contention at the ASEAN Regional Forum (ARF) held in Hanoi in 2010. China and ASEAN reached a basic agreement on implementing the code of conduct on the South China Sea at the ASEAN Regional Forum in Bali in 2011, even if it is fair to ask how seriously China is prepared to honor the agreement.

At the East Asia Summit also held in Hanoi in 2010, ASEAN decided to invite the United States and Russia to join the ASEAN+6 forum (Japan, China, South Korea, India, Australia, New Zealand), beginning the following year, to form an ASEAN+8 forum. It also launched a new meeting of defense ministers based on the ASEAN+8 framework.

But China started becoming even more assertive in 2012. The ASEAN foreign ministers' meeting in 2012 was held in July in Phnom Penh, Cambodia. The meeting became embroiled in disputes over its statement on the issue of sovereignty in the South China Sea, where Vietnam and the Philippines were engaged in increasingly testy disputes with China, and for the first time since the foundation of ASEAN in 1967 the meeting failed to agree on a joint statement. Chinese interference was to blame.

In the lead-up to the conference, China had lobbied Cambodia as host nation, in an attempt to make sure that discussions at the forum did not work out to China's disadvantage. Hu Jintao visited Cambodia in April 2012 and announced that China would give Cambodia a total of 450 million yuan in grant aid and low-interest finance. Defense Minister Liang Guanglie visited Cambodia for the ASEAN defense ministers' meeting in May and signed off on 120 million yuan of grant aid assistance.

In June, He Guoqiang, eighth in the Communist Party hierarchy and secretary of the Central Committee for Discipline Inspection, met Prime Minister Hun Sen and signed off on a deal for a grant of $420 million of financing and a gift of two aircraft. These promises of assistance reaped their intended rewards, to the extent that China's foreign minister, Yang Jiechi, expressed his thanks to Hun Sen immediately after the ASEAN foreign ministers' meeting for having respected China's "core interests."

In retrospect, it is clear that the ASEAN response to the sovereignty issues in the South China Sea underwent a major change in 2012. From 2010 onward, as seen at the ARF, the ASEAN+8 defense ministers' meetings, and similar forums, ASEAN was a convenient lever for countries like Vietnam and the Philippines that had territorial disputes with China in the South China Sea.

This is why in the run-up to the ASEAN foreign ministers' meeting in 2012, China went on the offensive with a package of generous grants for Cambodia, and ensured that the foreign ministers' meeting would not succeed in releasing a joint statement on the South China Sea issue. China worked to ensure that Vietnam and the Philippines could no longer use ASEAN as a lever.

But this did not mean that Vietnam and the Philippines would give up all their attempts to deal with the South China Sea issue internationally. Nor did it mean that they would simply be subdued by China's exercise of power into quietly accepting China's position on the South China Sea, the exclusive economic zone, or the coastal shelf.

If they could no longer use ASEAN as a lever, they would simply look for other approaches instead. This is a role that the United States is ideally suited to play. Hillary Clinton attended the ARF in 2010 as secretary of state and emphasized the strong interest of the United States in freedom of navigation in the South China Sea. In 2011, the United States attended the East Asia Summit as part of the ASEAN+8 framework.

The speech we looked at earlier by Barack Obama to the Australian parliament was delivered just before he attended the East Asia Forum. In this sense, the speech served to give an outline of his policy position at that forum. And from 2012 on, the United States has regarded strengthening its military presence in the Asia Pacific region as a fundamental part of its new national defense strategy.

Japan has also decided to help the Philippines, Malaysia, and Vietnam strengthen their coast guard capabilities, including by providing patrol vessels. Military cooperation has also started among ASEAN countries. The navies of the Philippines and Vietnam have agreed to enhance cooperation, including by carrying out joint naval exercises. And the navies of Indonesia, the Philippines, Vietnam, and Brunei are planning joint patrols designed to prevent illegal fishing in the waters around the Natuna Islands.

China's Shortsightedness

In sum, it is fair to say that since 2012 China has driven the countries of ASEAN, particularly the Philippines, Vietnam, and Indonesia, which have territorial disputes with China in the South China Sea, closer to the United States, Japan, Australia, and India. And clearly, the more China is perceived to be a threat, the more useful a framework of the Indo-Pacific, rather than that of East Asia or Asia Pacific, will be for regional cooperation. In this sense, China's machinations in the lead-up to the 2012 ASEAN foreign ministers' meeting can be described as shortsighted. Since 1999, in the name of building an East Asian community, China had treated the ASEAN+3 (Japan, China, South Korea) as the main framework for regional cooperation, excluding the United States, and gradually expanded its influence within this framework. From 2007, however, China has made itself into the biggest single risk factor for countries like Vietnam, the Philippines, and Indonesia.

The situation has remained unchanged in the years since. China continues to try to change the status quo by resorting to force in its sovereignty disputes in the South China Sea. This is quite clear from China's decision to drill for natural resources using a state-owned enterprise near the Paracels, and to construct a runway and port facilities on the Fiery Cross Shoal. What we should pay attention to is how other countries have responded.

The United States has made its stance clearer than ever: it will not accept unilateral attempts to change the status quo by force. In remarks at the Shangri-La Dialogue in Singapore in May 2014, Defense Secretary Chuck Hagel highlighted four security priorities for the United States: encouraging the peaceful resolution of disputes, upholding the freedom of navigation, and standing firm against coercion, intimidation, and aggression; building a cooperative regional architecture based on international rules and norms; enhancing the capabilities of allies and partners; and strengthening the regional defense capabilities of the United States. On the question of territorial disputes, he said that while the United States would "take no position on competing territorial claims . . . we firmly oppose any nation's use of intimidation, coercion, or the threat of force to assert those claims." China, he said, had "restricted access to Scarborough Reef, put pressure on the long-standing Philippine presence at the Second Thomas Shoal . . . and moved an oil rig into disputed waters near the Paracel Islands." Hagel criticized these "destabilizing, unilateral actions" (National Institute for Defense Studies 2015: 236–237).

In addition to enhancing the capabilities of Japan, Australia, and other allies, and promoting coordination, the United States is also working to secure access to the Asia Pacific region and maintain the US military presence in the region. Since 2011, the US secretary of defense has held meetings with ASEAN countries simultaneously with the ASEAN defense ministers' meeting forum. In 2014, Secretary Chuck Hagel invited defense ministers from the ten ASEAN countries to Hawaii for an unofficial summit. In April 2014, the Philippines signed an agreement on enhanced defense cooperation with the United States, creating the legal framework for the United States to rotate troops into the Philippines for extended stays. Similar agreements have been reached with other countries in the region. In April 2014, President Obama visited Malaysia, releasing a joint statement on a comprehensive partnership including maritime security. The United States also signed a comprehensive partnership with Vietnam in July 2013, and a nuclear cooperation agreement in May 2014. Also, during a visit to Vietnam of the chairman of the Joint Chiefs of Staff in 2014, an agreement was reached to promote cooperation in the fields of maritime security, search and rescue, and education and training. In addition, during the visit of Pham Binh Minh to the United States, the US government announced a partial lifting of export restrictions to Vietnam on equipment useful for maritime security. The United States and Indonesia also signed a comprehensive partnership agreement in 2010 (National Institute for Defense Studies 2015: 9, 17, 27, 236–237, 241–242).

How ASEAN Countries Have Responded

None of this means that ASEAN has altogether lost its significance as a "lever." In 2014, the ASEAN foreign ministers' meeting expressed deep concern about tensions between China and Vietnam (albeit without mentioning China explicitly) caused by China's exploratory offshore drilling for resources, and called for prompt ratification of a code of conduct for the South China Sea. At the ASEAN foreign ministers' meeting, the ASEAN+3 foreign ministers' meeting, and the ARF, all held in August, an agreement was reached to start practical negotiations on drawing up a code of conduct as a matter of priority—though doubts remain about the seriousness of China's commitment on this issue (National Institute for Defense Studies 2015: 9, 135).

ASEAN countries have also been taking steps to help themselves. Vietnam decided to acquire six submarines from Russia, three of which were in operation by 2014. During Prime Minister Nguyen Tan Dung's visit to India, an agreement was reached for the early implementation of a loan of up to $100 million to allow Vietnam to purchase naval vessels from India. Vietnam was also considering asking the Permanent Court of Arbitration to intervene in the sovereignty disputes in the South China Sea in accordance with the United Nations Convention on the Law of the Sea (National Institute for Defense Studies 2015: 31, 131, 144).

In the Philippines, the Armed Forces of the Philippines Modernization Act was amended in 2012 to provide approximately $1.8 billion for modernization of the armed forces over five years, in addition to the regular budget. In 2012, the Philippines began a process of arbitration based on the UN Convention on the Law of the Sea as regards its sovereignty disputes in the South China Sea. The Philippines also deliberately ran a ship aground on the Second Thomas Shoal close to the Mischief Reef under de facto Chinese control in the Spratly Islands, and now stations a small garrison of soldiers there. In March 2014, Chinese government ships attempted to blockade the shoal, preventing the Philippines from bringing in a merchant marine vessel to send in new garrison staff and new supplies, and forced the vessel to leave the area (National Institute for Defense Studies 2015: 11, 25–26, 132).

In Indonesia, in 2010 the government announced that it would build a "minimum essential force," and has since been steadily increasing its defense budget and procuring significant amounts of major equipment. The navy has released blueprint plans to develop green-water capabilities by 2024. In 2014, General Moeldoko, then commander of the armed forces, announced an enlargement of the garrison stationed in the Natuna Islands. President Joko "Jokowi" Widodo announced in a speech shortly after taking office in October 2014 that making Indonesia a "global maritime fulcrum" would be one of the important policy priorities of his government. In addition to building new port facilities, stimulating the fisheries industry, and strengthening the navy, the plan also aims to improve the country's ability to respond to territorial issues, by boosting its capabilities to exert effective control over territory, particularly its territorial waters, and improving the country's maritime defense capabilities. As part of this plan, the new government toughened up its efforts to patrol illegal fishing by foreign vessels, and since December 2014 has destroyed or sunk fishing boats from Vietnam, Thailand, and China caught fishing illegally in Indonesian waters (National Institute for Defense Studies 2015: 30, 143, 149).

It is clear that China's actions in the South China Sea since 2007 have more or less canceled out any efforts it had made through its ASEAN diplomacy in the years from 2000 to 2007. Yet it must be said that the chances of any change in China's hardline stance in the South China Sea seem remote indeed, given Xi Jinping's remarks that China will never compromise on issues of sovereignty or territory. This is clear from China's thinking on regional diplomacy. As we have seen, Xi Jinping and his foreign policy advisers insist that China has no intention of giving up what it sees as its legitimate rights or sacrificing its core interests, but within those limits will "develop close relationships with its neighbors, treating them as partners and working to develop friendly neighborly relations, seeking to reassure neighboring countries" and to "stabilize, control, and shape" the region and "construct a stable and advantageous diplomatic environment." In the South China Sea, China has problems with Vietnam, the Philippines, Malaysia, and Indonesia (Brunei also has a dispute with China in the South China Sea, but from China's point of view Brunei hardly counts as worthy of notice), while in the East China Sea, China is in conflict only with Japan over the territorial issue. China most likely sees a burden on this scale as an inevitable and acceptable cost of defending its core interests.

China's Economic Cooperation: Development in the Greater Mekong Subregion

What is China doing, then, to "develop friendly neighborly relations . . . reassure neighboring countries and . . . stabilize, unite, and shape" the region? As we have seen, it is pushing ahead with economic cooperation under the framework of what has come to be known as the Belt and Road Initiative.

China is making huge investments in economic cooperation in mainland Southeast Asia. This is taking the form of development of the Greater Mekong Subregion. This program began as an initiative of the Asian Development Bank in 1992, involving Thailand, Cambodia, Laos, Myanmar, Vietnam, and China (Yunnan province and the Guangxi Zhuang Autonomous Region).

Approximately $10 billion was invested between 1992 and 2007, and another $22 billion from 2008 to 2012. These investments went heavily to building infrastructure in the areas of transportation and power generation and distribution, including seventy projects in the sphere of transportation ($15 billion) and thirty-two in energy ($5 billion), with the aim of building a regionwide transportation network including the North-South Economic Corridor, the East-West Economic Corridor, and the Southern Economic Corridor (see Figure 2.2).

For China, this important program is intimately tied to development of the domestic economy, particularly of Yunnan province and the Guangxi Zhuang Autonomous Region. For this reason, development of the Mekong region was designated as one of five priority areas for cooperation and strengthening economic and trade relations between China and ASEAN as early as the ASEAN-China Summit in 2001. In 2003, the action plan to implement the joint declaration on the ASEAN-China strategic partnership for peace and prosperity contained an agreement to build transportation infrastructure (building a Kunming-Singapore railway, railways and roads from Kunming to Yangon and Myitkyina, and improving rail links from Yunnan province to Vietnam), and to implement a Greater Mekong Subregion intergovernmental agreement on regional power trade as part of the Mekong River Basin Development Cooperation project.

Ōizumi Keiichirō says that China's aim in developing the Mekong River region is to make use of the framework of wider projects like the Asian Development Bank's Greater Mekong Subregion program, the ASEAN Mekong Basin Development Cooperation project, and Thailand's Mekong Economic Cooperation strategy (Ayeyawady-Chao Phraya-

Figure 2.2   Economic Corridors in the Greater Mekong Subregion

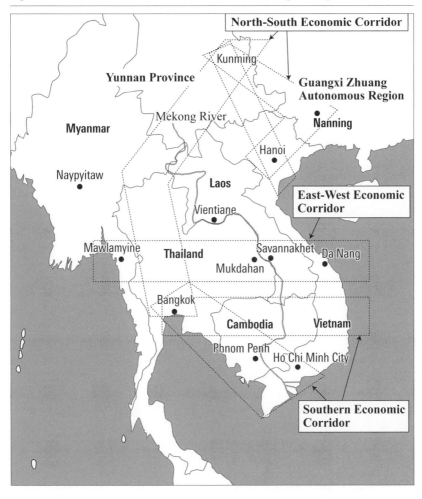

Mekong Economic Cooperation Strategy), while ensuring that these contribute to the economic development of the southern regions of China.[17]

What have been the main effects of China's economic cooperation
in mainland Southeast Asia? In simple terms, in constructing wide-ranging
infrastructure such as highways, high-speed railways, and electricity
grids, China is constructing a hub-and-spokes-style regionwide system
of infrastructure that will stretch from its hub in Kunming, the provincial capital of Yunnan, down south through mainland Southeast Asia via
Nanning in the Guangxi Zhuang Autonomous Region to Hanoi, via Laos

and Thailand to Bangkok, and across Myanmar to Yangon, eventually reaching the South China Sea and Indian Ocean.

The question is how significant this will be. A road is a road, whoever builds it. But once highways are built and high-speed railway links are in place, then people, goods, and money follow—and, in wartime, tanks too. To what extent this will change the geopolitical and geoeconomic makeup of the region in the long term is an important question.

East-West Links from Vietnam to Myanmar

What response are we witnessing to these moves? If China is establishing a hub-and-spokes system of regional infrastructure reaching south from a hub in Kunming, and trying to incorporate mainland Southeast Asia into its sphere, it is sufficient to respond by building east-west connections linking Da Nang and Ho Chi Minh City in Vietnam via Laos and Cambodia to Bangkok and Yangon and Dawei in Myanmar. In fact, such projects are already under way.

In 2007, Japan designated the Mekong region a priority area for economic cooperation and in 2008 hosted a Mekong-Japan foreign ministers' meeting attended by Vietnam, Laos, Cambodia, Thailand, and Myanmar. At the Mekong-Japan summit meeting in 2012, an agreement was reached on the Tokyo Strategy 2012, with Japan promising 600 billion yen in official development assistance. This has since been implemented.

In July 2015, at the seventh Mekong-Japan summit meeting in Tokyo, Japan announced that it would provide around 750 billion yen in aid to the Mekong region over a three-year period from 2016 to 2018. The aim, clearly, was to connect the countries of mainland Southeast Asia, east to west, from Vietnam to Myanmar.

THE BELT AND ROAD INITIATIVE
AND THE *TIANXIA* ORDER

Prospects for the Belt and Road Initiative:
Myanmar and Sri Lanka

What are the prospects for the Belt and Road Initiative from a wider perspective? Of course, we cannot tell what the future holds, but despite China's bold moves, I am not convinced that China's strategy will gain the "territory" it is hoping for on the Go board. Two countries where

China previously invested considerably in economic cooperation provide useful pointers in this regard: Myanmar and Sri Lanka.

Let's look at the case of Myanmar first. In 2010, elections were held under the new constitution, and in 2011 the country underwent a transition to civilian rule under a new government headed by President Thein Sein. In August of that year, Thein Sein gave a speech to the National Assembly in which he vowed to improve the lives of the people through national reconciliation and economic growth. Government policy underwent a dramatic change, as Thein Sein steered his administration in the direction of openness and liberalization.

In September, he met with Aung San Suu Kyi and opened a dialogue with the National League for Democracy, released political prisoners, recognized the right to form labor unions and strike, and revised the political party registration law. In the meantime, a ceasefire was agreed and negotiations on a peace treaty started with the ethnic minority armed groups that had been fighting against the government. In economic policy, the foreign investment law was amended for the first time in twenty-four years to make the country more attractive to foreign investment, and in April 2012 a managed floating exchange rate system was introduced.

In tandem with these reforms toward political and economic liberalization, foreign policy also underwent a shift. The biggest change was the decision to cancel construction of the Myitsone Dam hydroelectric project that was being built with Chinese aid at a total cost of some $3.6 billion. Thein Sein met US president Barack Obama at the East Asia Summit in November 2011; this was followed by a visit to Myanmar by Secretary of State Hillary Clinton in December.

In October 2011, the Japanese government also announced the resumption of previously suspended official development aid to repair hydroelectric facilities, and in April 2012, President Thein Sein visited Japan, reaching an agreement at a meeting with Prime Minister Noda Yoshihiko to restart yen loans that had been frozen since 1987. In October 2011, Thein Sein visited India, where he reached an agreement with Prime Minister Manmohan Singh to speed up progress on the Kaladan Multi-Modal Transit Transport project, which is to provide a major new trade route with India by building port facilities and transportation infrastructure along the Kaladan River, which vertically transects Myanmar. These moves should not be taken to mean that Myanmar has suddenly lurched in the direction of the United States, Japan, and India. Nevertheless, taken together they clearly suggest that the new government is looking to build a new, more evenly balanced foreign policy, moving away from the previous almost total dependence on China that marked the country's foreign policy during the Than Shwe era.

In Sri Lanka, there was a change of government in January 2015, when Maithripala Sirisena took over as president from Mahinda Rajapaksa. In March, the new government announced it was canceling a major project in which a Chinese company was to have invested a total of around $1.5 billion. The reason given was a lack of clarity in the contract. Rajapaksa had promoted Chinese-funded infrastructure projects during his time as president, but Sirisena had been critical of this policy during the election campaign and moved swiftly to change direction following his victory. The new government also announced that it no longer intended to allow the use of Sri Lankan ports by submarines of the Chinese navy, another policy approved by the previous government under President Rajapaksa.

China has been building ports and distribution bases in countries including Myanmar, Bangladesh, Sri Lanka, and Pakistan, in what is called its "String of Pearls" strategy. The change of government in Sri Lanka, at the very center of the string, raises the possibility that the strategy may not work out as planned.[18] What these examples in Myanmar and Sri Lanka demonstrate is clear. Chinese offers of economic assistance are welcome in many countries at the time they are made. But there is no guarantee that their effects will survive a change of government. What guarantee is there that the same thing will not happen in other countries where China is currently pushing the Belt and Road Initiative hard, such as Russia, Central Asian countries, and Pakistan? Take China's relationship with Russia, for example.

Sino-Russian relations grew much closer in the 1990s, when the two countries signed a number of agreements and treaties: military cooperation agreement in 1993, a constructive partnership agreement, a mutual nonaggression pact, and an agreement to establish a tripartite stability zone in Central Asia in 1994. These culminated in the signing of a Sino-Russian friendship treaty in 2001. China and Russia then signed two protocols in 2005 and 2008 officially demarcating the 4,300-kilometer borderline between them. Trade also expanded, from around $5 billion in the 1990s to $84 billion in 2009. In that year, China overtook Germany to become Russia's biggest trading partner. In the field of energy, a 1,000-kilometer oil pipeline linking China and Russia was completed in 2009. This is one part of a deal in which Russia will provide 300 million tons of oil to China from 2011 to 2030, in return for $25 billion in Chinese financing (Shambaugh 2013: 113–114).

Yet this is likely to be a rather limited partnership built on a shared recognition of mutual benefits, as political scientist David Shambaugh has argued. This can be understood easily in view of the current situation. Russia has annexed Crimea and is using force to turn the eastern part of Ukraine, with which it shares a border, into a buffer zone. The United States and Europe have imposed sanctions as a result. Russia's biggest export is energy resources. China has a major strategic interest in securing a stable supply of energy in the medium to long term. A major incentive currently exists for the two countries to cooperate for their mutual benefit. President Putin has visited China to meet Xi Jinping, and promised that Russia will provide a stable supply of energy to China, in return for an agreement by China to increase its trade with Russia and promises of financing and economic cooperation. These agreements have strengthened the Sino-Russian relationship to something approaching a de facto alliance.

However, this relationship is built on the mutually beneficial relationship that happens to exist at present. I do not see any evidence of systemic foundations or the kind of mutual trust that would be necessary to maintain an alliance-like relationship into the post-Putin era. Something similar can be said of other countries that are currently China's partners: North Korea, Cambodia, Pakistan, Iran, and others.

A Twenty-First-Century Revival of the Sino-Centric Tributary System?

There is also the question of what principles China would uphold to put together a Sino-centric order if it did manage to bring large parts of the geopolitical Go board under its influence. The current US-centered global order is based on the sovereign-state system. This means that the sovereign state is the basic unit of the international community, that treaties are based on agreements between sovereign states, that norms and practices come into being in the course of long-term relationships, and that ultimately international order is built on the foundation of these treaties, norms, and practices.

What principles does China propose to use as the foundations for a new Sino-centric order? Some Chinese commentators and public intellectuals refer to the coming new order as a *tianxia* order, using a Chinese term literally meaning "all under heaven." What would a *tianxia* order mean? Are they suggesting a revival of the Sino-centric tributary system that some China historians argue previously existed during the Southern Song, Yuan, Ming, and Qing Dynasties? Will a twenty-first-century version of this tributary system really form the foundation for a new *tianxia* order?

I have already addressed this question elsewhere (Shiraishi and Hau 2012: chap. 4), so for now I will merely make the following observations. In today's international order, the formal equality of sovereign states and, more generally, the principles of freedom, fairness, and transparency are widely accepted. These norms and the system built on them have spread around the world and have come to be shared by increasing numbers of people as a result of globalization and what we might call "Anglo-Americanization" over the past two centuries under the influence of first the British Empire and then the United States as hegemonic powers and the rise of English as an international lingua franca. It is hard to imagine a radical restructuring of this order in the coming years—even in East Asia, let alone the wider world—simply because of China's economic rise. The prospect of any revival of a kind of twenty-first-century tributary system based on the principle of formal inequality and hierarchy is, I think, very remote.

In the field of world systems theory, some scholars have tried to expand the concept of the tributary system in recent years. But one of the unspoken assumptions of their argument is transparency of language and the overwhelming importance of economic interests. Or, to put it in slightly simpler terms, according to this theory, no matter how arrogant the Chinese government may be, the countries and peoples of the region will ultimately put their own economic interests first, giving rise to a de facto order centered on China.

But in historical terms, it is also true that the limits of the Sino-centric order were truly exposed when the language of order collapsed. For example, an imperial letter brought by a Ming emissary from the Hongwu emperor to the "king of Japan" contained the following passage: "When this letter shall reach you, if you submit as a vassal, then offer tribute to my court. If you do not, you should immediately raise an army and prepare your defenses" (Tanaka 2012: 67, 259). To deny or refuse to take part in this language was tantamount to denying the entire Sino-centric tributary system itself. In 1273, the king of Pagan in Upper Burma received a similar letter from the Chinese emperor and had the emissary from the Yuan court put to death. In Japan, the Kamakura shogunate also beheaded emissaries from Yuan China, in 1275 and 1279. Later, Toyotomi Hideyoshi received a vassalage letter from the Ming court investing him as the "king of Japan" and bearing a gold seal, which he sent back to China. At the very foundation of the *tianxia* order was the practice of accepting an unequal, hierarchical relationship on the level of language—but it is hard to imagine any such order being accepted internationally in the twenty-first century.

Can China Build a New Order with Power and Money?

So what is likely to happen? If China continues to behave in accordance with its own self-image as a great power, but other countries respond by saying, "So what?," it is likely that the *tianxia* order will become nothing more than bullying and money diplomacy. We have seen several instances of this already. In 2010, when China's foreign minister, Yang Jiechi, was criticized at the ARF meeting in Hanoi for China's actions in the South China Sea, he is said to have responded angrily by dismissing the complaints and noting that China was far bigger (and more important) than any of the other countries at the forum. And when Premier Li Keqiang visited the United Kingdom in 2014, the Chinese government was adamant that he should meet the queen. To make this happen, China put together a deal with British companies worth some 2.4 trillion yen. These examples demonstrate an attitude that says, "We are a major power; smaller countries should be quiet and not complain. If you keep quiet and do what we want, we will take care of you." But China cannot build a Sino-centric global order simply by pushing its weight around and dispensing money. Other states will go along with China while China dispenses money, only to desert it when the tap runs dry. In that sense, although China's foreign and national security policy looks as if it is aiming boldly to capture large parts of the strategic board, it is fair to say that its behavior is rooted in a narrowly defined, not to say narrow-minded, concept of national interest, and is opportunistic. The problem is that such self-centered and opportunistic behavior is having an impact on global systems in a variety of ways and that this impact is growing more serious as time passes.

Another important question is how we should understand China's foreign and national security policy in relation to the dynamics of Chinese internal politics. Most commentators agree that Chinese politics has developed in the context of a contest between a "left-wing" conservative and a "right-wing" reformist faction. In his book *The Struggles of the Giant Dragon*, Tsugami Toshiya (2015b) characterizes the two groups as follows. Conservatives, he says, are made up of people who set a high value on the traditional theory of Marxism-Leninism, and the control of power by the Communist Party; have a strong sense of resentment/victimhood regarding China's history of invasion and quasi-colonialization; and tend for these reasons to be extremely nationalistic, and strongly suspicious of the "West" and its universal values (freedom, democracy, human rights, and so on). The reformists, by contrast, are made up of people who prioritize the market economy; are reformist-minded; and are open to collaboration and cooperation with the "West" and its universal values (Tsugami 2015b: 32). As we have already seen, following the global financial crisis of 2008 the Chinese government introduced economic stimulus measures worth 4 trillion yuan and its economy recovered dramatically. But now the party is over and the Chinese economy is facing the end of its bubble. The recent arrest of Zhou Yongkang, a former member of the Politburo Standing Committee and secretary of the Central Political and Legal Affairs Commission, on charges of major corruption, exposed the collapse of China's system of governance and laid open before the public his personal interference in the judiciary and long history of illegal acts.

It is therefore easy to understand why the Chinese ruling elite under Xi Jinping feel a sense of crisis about the sustainability of the party state system, and why to ensure the long-term survival of this system they have started to manage people's expectations by speaking of a "new normal," as well as embarking on market-driven structural reforms of the economy, local government finances, and the judicial system. Based on this analysis, Tsugami Toshiya (2015b: 157–158) suggests that Xi Jinping himself probably belongs to reformists. He notes that although the Chinese phrase *yi fa zhi guo* is generally interpreted to mean "rule by law" rather than "rule of law," Xi Jinping emphasizes the importance of modernizing the state's governance systems and capabilities, and suggests that a shift from a "rule by law" to "rule of law" may be under way.

The only realistic way to transform the Chinese economy from an investment-led growth model to a consumer-driven economy is to implement an economic policy driven by market-economy reforms. Whether left- or right-wing, this is the only way to go. Similarly, in light of the crisis of legitimacy affecting the entire party state system following the arrest of Zhou Yongkang, any governance reform to address this question head-on will require the introduction of the rule of law. But carrying out reforms of this kind will inevitably raise an awkward question: When will the Chinese Communist Party itself be placed under the law? Related to this is the question of what the leadership of the Communist Party actually means in concrete terms.

If the leadership of the Communist Party is equated with the leadership of Xi Jinping as general secretary, introducing the rule of law would mean that all the machinery of state and the entire nation—party,

PLA, government, National Congress, judiciary, and the Chinese people themselves—would be placed under the law, except Xi Jinping.

I also find Tsugami's argument that Xi Jinping belongs to reformists unconvincing. If we are to use the left-wing/right-wing framework, I believe that Xi Jinping is closer to the left, as David Shambaugh, Michael Pillsbury, and others have argued.[19] Far more important than any of this, however, is the fact that questions are now being asked about the party and the People's Republic of China: Who do China and the Chinese Communist Party really belong to?

Who Does China Belong To? The Purpose of Politics

During the process of transition from Hu Jintao to the current Xi Jinping government, Bo Xilai (member of the seventeenth Politburo and Communist Party secretary for Chongqing) was removed from office and several of his political allies, including Zhou Yongkang (member of the Politburo Standing Committee) and Ling Jihua (chief of the General Office of the Communist Party), were also purged.

One of the contentious points at that time was the political risk posed to China's party state by people who had "lost out" in the society's rush to prosperity. As we have seen, the Chinese economy has grown massively since the 1980s. In the thirty years from 1980 to 2010, per capita income grew nineteenfold. There was a huge expansion in the numbers of the middle-income (household income $5,000 to $35,000) and affluent classes (household income over $35,000), and is predicted that by 2020, 390 million people will belong to the upper-middle income bracket (household income $15,000 to $35,000) and 180 million to the "affluent" class. Even so, more than half of the Chinese population remains stuck in the lower-middle income bracket (household income $5,000 to $15,000) or in actual poverty (household income under $5,000). Making matters worse is the fact that today the poor understand quite well what a prosperous life looks like. And as the fight against corruption demonstrates how rotten the "tigers" have become, the truth about party corruption is now clearly exposed. Because of this, considerable numbers among those who have "lost out" in the market economy are nostalgic for the days of Mao, when "everyone was equal and we were all poor together." This idealization of the revolutionary past has been described as "Red nostalgia" (Endō 2012). When Bo Xilai became party secretary for Chongqing at the end of 2007, he appealed to this nostalgia and turned it to his own ends by starting the Sing Red movement that encouraged people to sing revolutionary songs in a manner reminiscent of the

Cultural Revolution. He also launched the Striking Black (*Dahei*) movement to get rid of gangsters and eradicate corruption. As part of this campaign, he arrested the directors of private-sector companies on false charges and confiscated their personal assets, which he invested in the Sing Red movement and cheap housing. He also arrested and punished a succession of senior political figures in the Chongqing government who disagreed with him, and attempted to build his own "independent" kingdom in the southwest. In reviewing the excesses of the Cultural Revolution, the Communist Party banned the personality cult and demagogic political movements, but it did not—could not—get rid of Mao Zedong. As a result, there are still large numbers of people in China today who respect and admire Mao, and such people are particularly numerous among those who have lost out in China's recent economic growth. Bo Xilai attempted to mobilize these people. The fear that if left unchecked this movement might easily lead to a second Cultural Revolution seems to have prompted the party's central leadership to come together and deprive Bo Xilai of his position and power.

What is at issue here is the purpose of politics. What purpose is the party state there to serve? Who does China belong to? To put it differently, when Xi Jinping speaks of the "China Dream," what does the word "China" mean? And when he refers to the ideal of building a "rich country, strong army," what is the "country" he is talking about? Does China belong to the Second Generation Reds (*Hong erdai*), the quasi-aristocratic class of the children of the founders and senior cadres of the People's Republic? Does it belong to the elite princes of the party, to the Communist Party, or to the people as a whole? These are the questions that are being asked. Although the Second Generation Reds retain a powerful position close to the center of the party state, Xi Jinping and other elite leaders are responding to these questions by appealing to the idea of a "China Dream," the slogan of "rich country, strong army," and nationalism. In this way, they hope to overcome the current crisis of legitimacy of the party state. But the real question is how the leaders will convince the people to buy into their narrative.

CHANGING INTERNATIONAL RELATIONS IN EAST ASIA

The Indo-Pacific Framework

As we have seen, recent years have been marked by US rebalancing, the rise of China, and China's increasing adoption of a "major power" stance in its foreign policy. What changes have these developments brought to international relations in the East Asia/Asia Pacific/Indo-Pacific region? As I have mentioned, a structural tension exists in East Asia between the regional security system and its system of trade and investment. The security system consists of a US-led hub-and-spokes system, with the United States–Japan alliance as its cornerstone. In recent years, this security system has become more networked, as a result of bilateral and multilateral cooperation between Japan and Australia, Japan and India, and Australia and India, and trilateral cooperation between the United States, Japan, and Australia, and between the United States, Japan, and India. There has also been increasingly close security cooperation between Japan and Australia and the countries of ASEAN.

The trade and investment system is different. This system is built on trilateral trade involving China, the rest of Asia including Japan, and the United States. Some progress has been made in recent years with the signing of the ASEAN-plus free trade agreement and more recently with steps toward concluding the TPP negotiations. To put it another way, whereas the trading system cannot exist without Chinese participation, China is not a participant in the region's security systems. And whereas China is the largest trading partner for almost all the countries in East Asia, in the field of national security it is the United States that is the most important ally or security partner for most of the countries in the region. This means that the rise of China and its tendency to adopt a great power stance in its relations with other countries has increased tension in the regional systems. The countries in China's neighborhood all hope to derive economic benefits from China's rise. But if China continues to push its weight around as a "major power" and insists on pressing its own rules on other countries, its neighbors will resist. Immediately after the East Asian financial crisis of 1997–1998, many countries in the region perceived US intervention in the countries in crisis as a threat and created a new cooperation mechanism that excluded the United States. This new mechanism took East Asia as its regional framework and aimed to create an East Asian community. China's recent actions in the South China Sea and East China Sea, however, mean that today it is China that is perceived as the major risk in the region. In 2011, the East Asia Summit was enlarged from an ASEAN+6 to ASEAN+8 format, and the TPP idea emerged as a steppingstone toward the creation of an Asia Pacific free trade area. And now the framework for regional cooperation is expanding from the Asia Pacific region to the Indo-Pacific, with the United States as a crucial player.

This is not simply about "containing" China. But neither is it merely a question of encouraging China to act as a "responsible stakeholder," making its own contribution to maintaining and developing the global and regional order, as Robert Zoellick, deputy secretary of state under George W. Bush, put it. As the word "rebalancing" clearly suggests, the United States is looking to deal with China through a combination of engagement and hedging, while acting at the same time to maintain the balance of power in Asia Pacific and in a wider area reaching from the Pacific to the Indian Ocean.

Since the global financial crisis of 2008, realist power politics, or "rebalancing," has become most important in the international relations of the region, rather than the politics of regional cooperation prevalent in the years from 1997–1998, when the crisis hit the region, until 2007. Many countries in the region are trying to derive benefits from the economic rise of China, while looking to achieve balance in security and keeping a close eye on the movements of Japan, the United States, and Australia. The two examples of South Korea and Southeast Asia show two different approaches to this balancing act.

US-Korean Relations as the "Linchpin" of the Pacific

First, let's look at South Korea. In July 2014, Xi Jinping visited South Korea and reached an agreement with South Korean president Park Geun-hye on a free trade agreement between China and South Korea. China had already signed free trade agreements with Hong Kong, Macau, Taiwan, and ASEAN, and the free trade agreement with South Korea represented a kind of wrapping-up of its efforts in this area. Meanwhile, President Obama referred to the US alliance with South Korea as the "linchpin" of Asia Pacific. In South Korea, this has led to a tendency to agree with the view of Yun Duk-min, chancellor of the Korea National Diplomatic Academy, who says that "Korea is increasingly valuable to both the United States and China." This, I think, represents the majority view of South Korean strategic thinking.

At their meeting in July 2014, the leaders of China and South Korea agreed to conclude a free trade agreement by the end of the year, and to carry out a joint research project on the comfort women issue. In addition, the two leaders confirmed that they would coordinate their stance on North Korea, that they were irrevocably opposed to North Korea's development of nuclear weapons, and that they would cooperate to make the Korean Peninsula nuclear-free. On national security, they reached an agreement for regular strategic dialogue between the Chinese state councilor responsible for foreign policy (vice premier–level official) and South Korea's director of the National Security Office. At a joint press conference, the two leaders emphasized the significance of their meeting, saying that it represented an important turning point for the future development of relations between China and South Korea.

South Korea is an ally of the United States, and its leaders, from President Park down, must surely understand that South Korea is expected to coordinate with the United States and its other allies—Japan, the Philippines, Australia, and others—to help maintain a balance against China. But the reality is different, as this example shows. What is happening is that South Korea is not responding to the US "rebalancing" and not working closely with Japan either—because of the comfort women issue, as President Park puts it—while aligning itself with China to seek its own interests, in both national security and economic cooperation.[20]

As Edward Luttwak has argued, in preparing for a possible attack by North Korea, South Korea relies on the United States as a deterrent against full-scale warfare, and on China as a deterrent against a more limited, short-term attack (2012: 229). In economic terms, China is already South Korea's biggest trading partner. As Table 2.1 shows, in 2000, 22 percent of South Korea's exports went to the United States (the biggest single market for its exports) and 12 percent went to Japan, which was also a bigger export market than China, with 11 percent. By 2012, however, China accounted for 24 percent of South Korea's total exports. Meanwhile, the US share of South Korea's total exports declined to 11 percent and Japan's share to 7 percent by 2012. The United States occupies a position of decisive importance in science and technology, and as is well known the number of people from South Korea who study in the United States is much higher than the number from Japan. Japan remains important as a source of parts and components, but this is little understood by the general public, although it is well known to executives at big companies like Samsung. I believe this has led to a de facto strategic decision among the South Korean public that if the country skillfully manages its relations with China and the United States, this will be enough to ensure success both in terms of economic growth and in containing and deterring the North.

The "G2 strategy" of depending on the United States and China both for deterrence of North Korea and for South Korea's economic growth is becoming a national consensus in South Korea. The China–South Korea joint statement of July 2014 shows this clearly. The summit meeting was marked by three main agreements. The first is related to economic cooperation: not a trilateral agreement involving Korea, Japan, and China, but a bilateral free trade agreement between South

Table 2.1   South Korean Trade, 1995–2012 ($ millions)

	1995	2000	Percentage (2000)	2005	2010	2012	Percentage (2012)
Total exports	131,360	172,692		285,484	471,071	551,806	
1. China	9,144	18,455	11	61,915	116,838	134,323	24
2. United States	24,344	37,806	22	41,500	49,992	58,807	11
3. Japan	17,048	20,466	12	21,027	28,176	38,796	7
4. Hong Kong	10,682	10,708	6	15,531	25,294	32,606	6
5. Singapore	6,689	5,648	3	7,407	15,244	22,888	4
6. India	1,126	1,326	1	4,598	11,435	11,922	2
7. Germany	5,965	5,154	3	10,304	10,702	7,510	1
8. Vietnam	1,351	1,686	1	3,432	9,652	15,946	3
9. Indonesia	2,958	3,505	2	5,046	8,897	13,955	3
10. Mexico	941	2,391	1	3,789	8,846	9,042	2
Total imports	135,110	160,482		261,238	425,265	519,711	
1. China	7,402	12,799	8	38,648	71,574	80,785	16
2. Japan	32,606	31,828	20	48,403	64,296	64,363	12
3. United States	30,420	29,286	18	30,788	40,589	43,654	8
4. Saudi Arabia	5,432	9,641	6	16,106	26,820	39,707	8
5. Australia	4,897	5,959	4	9,860	20,456	22,988	4
6. Germany	6,584	4,625	3	9,774	14,305	17,645	3
7. United Arab Emirates	1,558	4,703	3	10,018	12,170	15,115	3
8. Qatar	232	2,292	1	5,599	11,916	25,505	5
9. Indonesia	3,325	5,287	3	8,184	13,986	15,676	3
10. Kuwait	1,068	2,716	2	5,977	10,850	18,297	4

Source: Asian Development Bank, "Key Indicators for Asia and the Pacific," various years, http://www.adb.org/statistics.

Korea and China. The second is an agreement regarding joint historical research. This amounted to an agreement that Japan was the cause of the region's problems and that it was Japan's failure to respond to "reasonable" concerns about interpretations of history that was making improved relations between Japan and South Korea impossible. The third regarded the denuclearization of the Korean Peninsula. This agreement is quite significant, particularly in terms of thinking about what might happen on the Korean Peninsula if North Korea collapsed and was united into a single state with South Korea. What would happen? Denuclearization, I think, and probably a Greater Korea as a neutral state. Of course, one major hurdle stands in the way before this can happen: the US troops stationed in South Korea. In previous years, President Roh Moo-hyun demanded that the United States should obtain permission from the South Korean government when wanting to deploy troops stationed in South Korea outside the country. It is possible that such a request might be made—if not under the present government, then under the next, or at some time in the near future. We do not know what would happen next, but we need to be aware that this is the direction in which South Korea is moving.

Mainland and Maritime Southeast Asia

What about countries in Southeast Asia? Partly because the ten countries located in this region are all members of ASEAN, there is a tendency to discuss them together, but the countries of mainland and maritime Southeast Asia differ considerably in the issues they face in both national security and economic development. I will discuss the national strategies of some of the most important countries of the region in the next chapter. For now, I want to make some general observations about the region and underline some of the overall trends.

One is the basic difference between mainland and maritime Southeast Asia. Mainland Southeast Asia consists of the five nations of Vietnam, Laos, Cambodia, Thailand, and Myanmar. In this region, located between China on the one side and Bangladesh and India on the other, Chinese influence has increased substantially in recent years, and in this sense the tendency to view these countries through the lens of their proximity to China makes some sense. In terms of their political systems, too, these countries have something in common both with one another and with China: Vietnam and Laos are communist party dictatorships, Cambodia is under the dictatorship of Hun Sen, and Myanmar, despite recent reforms and moves toward openness and liberalization, remains halfway to democratization, whatever media reports may suggest to the contrary. Thailand is ruled by a military junta, and although Prime Minister Prayut Chan-o-cha has said that the country will transition to civilian rule in 2016, we do not know whether this will in fact happen or even what "civilian rule" would mean. I tend to see political instability and uncertainty continuing there. In sum, the countries of mainland Southeast Asia are all ruled by authoritarian governments, politically comfortable for China.

Maritime Southeast Asia consists of Indonesia, Singapore, Malaysia, Brunei, and the Philippines. These countries are located across a vast region stretching from the Pacific to the Indian Ocean, horizontally in a line from Japan and Taiwan to India and Sri Lanka and vertically in a line from Malaysia to Australia via Indonesia. Its location right in the center of the Indo-Pacific makes maritime Southeast Asia highly strategic.

Prime Minister Abe has visited all these countries to promote security cooperation. This region occupies a pivotal position geopolitically in the security of the Indo-Pacific. Therefore, it makes sense to see maritime Southeast Asia as a part, in fact the backbone, of the Indo-Pacific in terms of security. In terms of their political systems, the Philippines and Indonesia are democracies, and although many people would no doubt object to any description of Singapore and Malaysia as "liberal" democracies, there can be no doubt that they are democracies.

These differences between mainland and maritime Southeast Asia are likely to become more pronounced in the years to come, along with the rise of China. There is a straightforward reason for this. There are three major factors that need to be noted in terms of understanding the foreign and security policy of the countries of Southeast Asia. One is the US-led hub-and-spokes regional security system with the US alliances with Japan and Australia as its backbone. Some Southeast Asian states can build their national security policies with this system as a given. Other states perceive this US-led regional security system as a threat. Which category a country belongs to in this sense leads to significant differences in that country's foreign policy and national security strategy. Another factor is whether a country has a territorial dispute with China in the South China Sea. For obvious reasons, countries that do not have sovereignty disputes with China in the South China Sea—such as Thailand and Cambodia—are less likely to perceive China as a sovereign threat. Yet another factor is the extent to which these countries are integrated into the global economy. Together, these three factors create major differences in the foreign policies and national security strategies of the countries of Southeast Asia.

Let me give one example of what I mean: the differences between the foreign policy and national security strategies of Vietnam and Thailand. Vietnam is a country that has a territorial dispute with China. In terms of national power, there is a massive difference between Vietnam and China, in population, in the size of their economies, in military power, and in other metrics. For Vietnam, the question of how to manage this asymmetry vis-à-vis China is a major challenge for its foreign and national security policy. And what is the answer? Vietnam is a one-party state, and although it is not averse to the idea of pursuing cooperation with the United States in foreign and national security policy, so long as the United States continues to regard Vietnamese human rights violations as a problem, and continues to call for democratization of Vietnam's political system, Vietnam needs to beware of the risk of "peaceful transformation." This means that Vietnam cannot build its own national security policy entirely around the US-led hub-and-spokes regional security system. Also, over the past fifteen years, Vietnam has become integrated into the global economy, and Vietnam's trade dependency ratio had reached 175 percent by 2013. Even so, as Vietnam's geographical location makes evident, there is a risk that the region around Hanoi and Hai Phong might be sucked into the Guangzhou economic zone if present trends continue unchecked. Seen in this light, it makes perfect sense that the Vietnamese government is paying careful attention to its foreign and security relations with China, while moving forward with security cooperation with Russia, Japan, India, and the United States, using ASEAN as a lever in its negotiations with China and taking part in negotiations on the TPP. Thailand, by contrast, has no border with China and of course no sovereignty issues with it either. It is a US ally, even though US bases in the country closed in the 1970s. It is also deeply integrated into the global economy (with a trade-dependency ratio of 118 percent by 2013). There are major concentrations of manufacturing industries in the region around Bangkok, and Thailand is the major hub in the Southeast Asian production network, particularly in the automobile industry. As a result, Thailand does not regard China as a threat. State strategies differ substantially from one country to another. Geopolitical and political economic factors are extremely important in deciding state strategy. They differ significantly between mainland and maritime Southeast Asia (with Vietnam as a kind of halfway house or intermediate case).

ASEAN as a Lever

The second factor is the importance of ASEAN as a lever. With Indonesia as a partial exception, the countries of Southeast Asia are small and middle powers with relatively little influence on international politics. All of them therefore use ASEAN as a kind of lever to boost their influence and impact. Lee Kwan Yew, the former prime minister of Singapore, once said at a private dinner that ultimately Singapore's diplomacy was all about leveraging.

Singapore is a city-state with a population of 5.5 million people, and although its per capita income is the highest in Asia, its economy is quite small. It has neither political nor military power. But when Singapore speaks as a member of ASEAN—if Singapore's position becomes the consensus position within ASEAN—then larger powers like Japan, China, and Australia will listen to what it says. And if Singapore can succeed in making its position the consensus of the ASEAN+3 (Japan, China, South Korea) then its opinion will also attract the attention of the United States and the European Union. Likewise, if influential figures in the US government listen to advice from Singaporean government leaders when considering Asia policy, Singapore can use the United States as a lever to have an impact on neighboring ASEAN countries.

This was the thrust of Lee Kwan Yew's remarks. I believe this thinking is shared by many leaders of ASEAN countries, consciously or otherwise. If there is one country where this tendency is less pronounced in the region, that is Indonesia, which sees itself as the major power in ASEAN. But the idea of using ASEAN as a lever is widely shared throughout the other countries of the region. This idea of how countries can use ASEAN to their advantage is one we should keep in mind when thinking about the future of ASEAN.

Changes in Regional Cooperation Frameworks and ASEAN

What is happening in ASEAN? I have already mentioned the changes that have taken place in the framework of regional cooperation as it has played out over the past several decades, from the "Asia Pacific" framework in the 1990s, through the "East Asia" framework in the years after the East Asian financial crisis, when the United States was perceived as a threat, to the "Asia Pacific" framework in the period since 2007–2008, when China has come to be perceived as a threat, and into the current age, when the still unfamiliar phrase "Indo-Pacific" is being used as the latest framework for regional cooperation. It is important to note in this context that in regional cooperation—whether free trade agreements or financial cooperation like the Chiang Mai Initiative built on the ASEAN+3 framework—cooperation normally has some kind of "plus sum" as its objective, and that the question of how to hedge what risk is crucial in determining what framework of cooperation ASEAN countries choose. An ASEAN economic community will be in place by the end of 2015. With this in mind, negotiations are under way for the Regional Comprehensive Economic Partnership, a free trade agreement involving ASEAN plus the six nations of Japan, China, South Korea, India, Australia, and New Zealand. The prospects for these negotiations, however, are not as bright as those for the TPP; some ASEAN nations, including host country Malaysia, are lukewarm about the idea of the RCEP, in part because of serious reservations about China. In geopolitics, in addition to the

ARF, since 2010 the ASEAN Defense Ministers Meeting–Plus (ADMM+) has provided a forum for meetings of defense ministers from ASEAN+10, and this is becoming an important setting for discussions on regional security issues.

What are the prospects for an ASEAN economic community, then? The ASEAN project differs substantially from the European Community project. The European Community (or European Union) is a political project that aims to create a polity that transcends sovereign states, based on the Europeanist ideology of "we Europeans." This project is built on the lessons learned from the two catastrophic wars of the twentieth century. The ASEAN Community project is based on no such political will and no such Asianist ideology.

With the exception of Thailand, all the countries of ASEAN gained their independence from colonial rule in the years after World War II, and nationalism has remained a major force until today. Consequently, the most important role most countries look to ASEAN to perform is to act as a lever, helping them to achieve objectives that would be hard for small and middle powers to achieve on their own. In other words, in joining an ASEAN economic community and an ASEAN security community, the primary consideration for all the countries in the region is the question of how it will benefit them as a country: there is in principle no question of any country sacrificing its own interests for the sake of ASEAN.

Seen from this perspective, it should be clear why an ASEAN economic community is important. Multinational corporations, Japanese companies among them, have built transnational production networks across the region. For all the countries in the region, investment by multinational corporations, along with an expansion and deepening of these production networks, will bring major benefits in terms of economic growth, job creation, and improved standards of living. A crucial part of making this a reality will be to make ASEAN into a single investment region, by eradicating tariffs on components. This would make the region a single integrated production area and allow the production network to be managed more efficiently. This is the purpose of an ASEAN economic community.

The idea is premised on multinational production networks transcending national borders and on putting together a framework, both tangible and intangible, that will contribute to managing those networks. In this sense, an ASEAN economic community represents an attempt to create a high-quality free trade agreement for developing economies. Yet many problems remain. While trade in goods is being liberalized, there has been little progress on the liberalization of services, and even less progress on nontariff barriers and the harmonization of regulations.

Another important point to note about an ASEAN economic community is the creation of a political coordination mechanism for large-scale infrastructure projects across national borders. This is particularly noticeable in mainland Southeast Asia (in the Greater Mekong Subregion), where a look at the map is enough to show how the construction of highways, soon to be joined by high-speed rail links, crisscrossing a wide region from north to south and east to west, is turning Kunming, the capital city of Yunnan in China, and Bangkok, into two major hubs. The Bangkok metropolitan region is also home to a heavy concentration of automobile plants and other industries, many of them belonging to Japanese corporations. In recent years the production network has started to expand from the Bangkok region to surrounding countries, under the framework of Thailand+1. This too is premised on the provision of the large-scale infrastructure across a wide region. In the medium to long term, this is something that will have major significance for the development strategies of the countries of mainland Southeast Asia.

US Military Strategy and ASEAN

Geopolitically, mainland and maritime Southeast Asia occupy different positions in US strategy. From the 1960s into the 1970s, the United States became mired in Vietnam during the Johnson and Nixon presidencies. By 1970, as part of a search for a path to withdrawal and "peace with honor," the United States announced what has become known as the Nixon Doctrine, a set of principles for its military engagements overseas. Essentially, the doctrine stated that while the United States would honor its treaty obligations and help to maintain the nuclear deterrence system, in other conflicts it would restrict itself to providing military aid and naval and air support. The countries involved would be expected to assume responsibility for providing manpower on the ground. In Vietnam, this meant that the responsibility for defending South Vietnam lay with South Vietnam itself, and in line with this doctrine the United States was able to withdraw its ground troops from Vietnam (Wakatsuki 2006: 15).

Forty-five years later, this doctrine still remains important in US thinking about mainland Southeast Asia. The situation in maritime Southeast Asia, however, is quite different. Freedom of navigation in this region, particularly from the East China Sea to the South China

Sea, and through the Straits of Malacca, Sunda, and Lombok to the Indian Ocean, is of primary importance to US naval strategy. In maritime Southeast Asia, the US military commitment has remained unshaken. This makes a vital difference in terms of the US military commitment in mainland and maritime Southeast Asia.

The two subregions, with Vietnam as a partial exception, differ in their perception of China as a threat. They also differ in their development strategies, mainly because of the progress in the construction of cross-border regional infrastructure in mainland Southeast Asia. I would not argue that ASEAN will be less important in the future due to these factors. An ASEAN economic community will remain and may find ways to develop beyond 2015. But I would be surprised if the ASEAN security community creates a robust role for itself in the East Asia/Asia Pacific/Indo-Pacific region in the near future.

There is one more thing I should say about mainland Southeast Asia. As we have seen, Japan and China are competing for infrastructure development projects in the region. Generally speaking, China is building infrastructure from north to south, while Japan has been active in infrastructure development along the east-west lines. This competition has increasingly opened the region to the outside world, and Bangkok is developing rapidly as a regional hub. What should we expect to happen next?

If you travel west from Bangkok, you will eventually hit the Andaman Sea close to the small town of Dawei in Myanmar, where conditions happen to be ideal for a deep-water port. If a highway were constructed from Bangkok and an industrial zone built in Dawei, the town would make an ideal location for Thailand+1 development. The Japanese government is getting involved in the development of Dawei, following requests from the governments of Thailand and Myanmar. In July 2015, during the Mekong-Japan summit meeting, Prime Minister Abe signed an agreement with Myanmar's president Thein Sein and Thailand's prime minister Prayut Chan-o-cha on joint development of a special economic zone in Dawei. According to the Japanese Ministry of Economy, Trade and Industry, developing the special economic zone will require total investment of more than 800 billion yen. But there are some 1,600 Japanese companies in Thailand (figures for April 2015), and for these companies, direct access to the Indian Ocean from Bangkok would be a major boost, opening new sales routes to India, the Middle East, and Africa, and helping to reduce logistics costs.[21] Developing Dawei is likely to take fifteen to twenty years. But as the project progresses, it is almost certain to bring even bigger differences between the economic development strategies of mainland and maritime Southeast Asia.

NOTES

1. On the new national defense strategy, see US Department of Defense 2012.

2. Hal Brands's *What Good Is Grand Strategy?* (2014) provides a good historical analysis of US national strategy. On US strategy since the end of the Cold War, see Zbigniew Brzezinski's *Second Chance* (2007).

3. On recent trends in US defense strategy, see the Reagan National Defense Forum keynote speech delivered by Secretary of Defense Chuck Hagel at the Ronald Reagan Presidential Library in Simi Valley, California, 15 November 2014, https://www.defense.gov/Newsroom/Speeches/Speech/Article/606635, in which Hagel discusses the importance of cutting-edge manufacturing technology in terms of national defense, including robotics, autonomous systems, miniaturization, big data, and advanced manufacturing, including 3D printing.

4. Tsugami Toshiya, "2015-nen no Chūgoku: Shū Kinpei seiken no yukue" [China in 2015: The future direction of Xi Jinping's government], Japan Science and Technology Agency, China Research and Communication Center, seventy-ninth study session, 15 January 2015. For the enormous position state-owned enterprises occupy in the Chinese economy, it is useful to note that in 2010 the market share of major state-owned enterprises in various industries was as follows: communications, three companies, 96.2 percent; air transportation, five companies, 76.2 percent; automotive, six companies, 74.0 percent; electricity, eight companies, 70.6 percent; shipping, three companies, 60.7 percent; banking, four companies, 48.5 percent (72.7 percent if all state-owned banks are included); petrochemicals, four companies, 45.3 percent (76.6 percent if all state-owned companies are included).

5. "Chūgoku dokusen kigyō, kokunai kyōsō jūshi yame, sekai shinshutsu" [China's monopolistic companies shift from focus on domestic competition and start to look overseas], *Nihon Keizai Shimbun*, 9 December 2014. Recent reports suggest that the Chinese government has plans to merge the 110 central state-owned enterprises and reduce their number to around 40 by 2020. The aim is to reduce excessive facilities and redundant investment, and to create huge mega-companies capable of competing on a worldwide basis. During an earlier phase of reforms of the state-owned enterprises during the 1990s, the focus was on increasing the private sector's share of the economy by breaking up and privatizing state-owned enterprises. This time, however, the purpose of the reforms is specifically stated to be to strengthen the control of the party and national government, and it is likely that the state-owned enterprises' share of the Chinese economy will increase even further; "Chūgoku, kokuyū kigyō o kyodaika, kokka shudō de tōgō kasoku, shijō o senyū, hizumi mo" [China's mammoth national enterprises: Mergers increasing under state leadership, leading to market monopolization and some distortions], *Nihon Keizai Shimbun*, 15 September 2015.

6. "Shihon jun'yushutsu-koku ni tenjiru Chūgoku" [China becomes a net capital exporter], *Nihon Keizai Shimbun*, 4 January 2015.

7. In his book *The Party: The Secret World of China's Communist Rulers*, Richard McGregor (2010) introduces the following incident, which took place when a senior manager of a financial institution visited Beijing in 2008 for a meeting with Wang Qishan, vice premier of the state council in charge of

finance and commerce. During the meeting, Wang apparently made it clear that China had little to learn from his visitors, apparently saying: "You have your way. We have our way. And our way is right!" (p. xvii). Wang Qishan is a straight-speaker, but this kind of arrogance is quite common, particularly in recent years. In 2012, Wang Qishan was appointed to the Politburo Standing Committee of the Communist Party of China, where he currently directs the government's anticorruption campaign as secretary of the Central Commission for Discipline Inspection.

8. "Saikin no Chūgoku jōsei to wagakuni no taiō" [The recent situation in China and Japan's response], *Kokusai Jōsei Kenkyūjo*, 3 December 2013.

9. See Swaine 2015 and "Chūgoku: Kyōryoku o gaikō no kaku ni" [China: Placing cooperation at the heart of diplomatic policy], *Nihon Keizai Shimbun*, 29 November 2014.

10. Wang Jiarui, director of the International Liaison Department of the Communist Party of China (2015).

11. See Swaine 2015.

12. Based on National Institute for Defense Studies 2015: 7–8 and information provided by Abe Jun'ichirō, 22 May 2015.

13. National Institute for Defense Studies 2015: 16. China is also adopting a tougher stance on its border with India. From 2004 to 2009, during Manmohan Singh's first period as prime minister, Sino-Indian relations improved and strengthened, particularly in terms of the economic relationship. However, from around 2008, China started to criticize Indian de facto control in Arunachal Pradesh, and India started to accuse China of a retrograde stance on the border dispute. Since taking office in 2014, Narendra Modi has sought to keep economic cooperation separate from territorial and security issues. When Xi Jinping visited India in September 2014, the two leaders agreed to establish an industrial park in Modi's home state of Gujarat, and released a joint statement promising some $20 billion of Chinese investment. At the same time, India has been increasing the number of police posts along its border with Tibet, and is taking part in national security cooperation with Japan and the United States, as well as United States–Japan–India and Japan-Australia-India security dialogues.

14. One recent essay analyzing the geopolitical implications of China's regional infrastructure building across Eurasia is Alfred W. McCoy's "The Geopolitics of American Global Decline: Washington Versus China in the Twenty-First Century" (2015). However, this essay completely ignores the difficulty of building alliances on the Eurasian continent, as well as the challenges posed by Islamism, and can therefore only be described as a weak analysis of the emerging new "great game" in Eurasia.

15. Based on information from Gotō Yasuhiro of *Nihon Keizai Shimbun*, 9 June 2015.

16. Kissinger compares US diplomacy to chess, in which the game finishes when one player checkmates the opponent's king. Similarly, in US diplomacy, as soon as one issue is resolved, diplomats move on to the next problem. But Chinese diplomacy, Kissinger says, is like a game of Go, in which each foreign policy initiative is connected to all the others. I think this is an acceptable analogy, though I rely more on George Shultz's gardening metaphor because the upkeep of an existing garden is the basic objective of US diplomacy.

17. Ōizumi Keiichirō, "Dai Mekon ken (GMS) kaihatsu puroguramu to CLMV no hatten," 2018, https://www.jri.co.jp/MediaLibrary/file/report/rim/pdf /2716.pdf. For a systematic analysis of China's regional diplomacy, economic cooperation, and security policy, I recommend Aoyama Rumi, *China's Foreign Policy in Asia* (2013). Aoyama's analysis is full of insights into the role of the Yunnan government and state-owned enterprises in development of the Greater Mekong Subregion, a subject I do not have space to discuss at any length here.

18. Akita Hiroyuki, "Chūgoku ga ki o momu shimaguni no hanran," *Nihon Keizai Shimbun*, 27 March 2015.

19. Shambaugh, *China Goes Global* (2013); Pillsbury, *The Hundred-Year Marathon* (2015).

20. "Chū-Kan FTA, nennai daketsu mezasu, ianfu mondai de kyōdō kenkyū," *Nihon Keizai Shimbun*, 3 July 2014; "Chū-Kan mitsugetsu, ayausa haramu," *Nihon Keizai Shimbun*, 4 July 2014.

21. "Nihon, Myanmā tokku sanka," *Nihon Keizai Shimbun*, 21 June 2015.

3
Strategic Trends in Southeast Asia

In this chapter, I discuss recent trends in some of the countries of Southeast Asia. In Japan, there is a tendency to treat "Southeast Asia" and "ASEAN" as more or less synonymous terms. It is true that the ten countries of Southeast Asia are all members of ASEAN, but as I pointed out in Chapter 2, it would be wrong to assume that they share the same foreign and national security policies or that they are all alike in their economic development strategies. Strategic thinking differs considerably from country to country. My purpose here is to look at their domestic structures, international environments, and strategic thinking, and then ask how and why they differ.

RELIGIOUS AND ETHNIC DIVERSITY

Buddhist, Muslim, and Christian

Let me begin by looking at some of the main characteristics of Southeast Asia as a region—or more accurately "subregion," since the whole of East Asia is increasingly regarded as a discrete region in recent years—from a comparative perspective. One striking characteristic of Southeast Asia is its ethnic and religious diversity. For example, Myanmar and Thailand are both Theravada Buddhist countries, but the region close to the border between Myanmar and Bangladesh is home to the Rohingya Muslims, and in recent years there have been frequent violent conflicts between the Rohingya and the Buddhist Burmese. Meanwhile, numerous minority groups have been engaged in armed resistance against the Burman-led central government since Burma became independent after the war. Peace talks have been under way between the central government of Myanmar and armed groups belonging to the Karen, Kachin, and other ethnic minority groups since the transition to a new government in 2011.

From the southern part of Thailand to Malaysia and Indonesia and as far north as the island of Mindanao in the Philippines, the majority of Malay people are Muslims. In the southern regions of Thailand, ethnic Malays have been engaged in an insurgency against the Thai government for many years. The overwhelming majority of Filipinos are Christians, most of them Catholics, but in Mindanao and Sulu, the Moro Islamic Liberation Front fought a separatist war for independence for many years, until a peace agreement was reached in 2014. At present, attempts are under way to establish a Bangsamoro autonomous government for the region within the framework of the Republic of the Philippines. Likewise in Indonesia, an independence movement in Aceh in North Sumatra lasted until the middle of the first decade of the twenty-first century. There were also bloody sectarian conflicts between Muslims and Christians in Poso, in central Sulawesi, and across the Moluccas (Maluku), historically known as the "Spice Islands." Another separatist movement continues in Papua (Indonesian New Guinea) to this day, albeit on a relatively small scale.

The ethnic and religious diversity of Southeast Asia means that national unity continues to be a major challenge. At the same time, more than half a century since most of the countries of the region gained independence from colonial rule, "identity politics" is coming to the surface not only as separatist movements and sectarian conflicts but also in a variety of unpredictable forms. How to manage and control these challenges is a vital issue for the governments in the region.

Social Changes in Southeast Asia

One useful resource for seeing what is happening in Southeast Asia is "Understanding the Major Social Changes in East Asia Based on Population Censuses" (2015). According to the 2010 census, the population of Thailand was 66 million people, the overwhelming majority of whom are Buddhist Thai. However, there are also around 1.5 million Malays, the majority of whom reside in the four southern provinces of Songkhla, Pattani, Yala, and Narathiwat. Their language, religion, and customs are different from those of the Thai majority. This is the social setting in which political unrest remains in southern Thailand. In addition, there were a total of nearly 2 million foreign workers in Thailand—counting only those residing in the country legally. According to the 2010 census, these consisted of workers from Myanmar (1.3 million), Cambodia (280,000), Laos (220,000), and China (140,000); if we take into consideration people working in Thailand illegally, we can estimate that there are more than 2.5 million people in Thailand from Myanmar, Cambodia, and Laos. Human trafficking in Thailand has come to international attention as a serious problem in recent years, in part because of foreign workers residing there illegally.[1]

Malaysia, with a population of 28 million, takes pride in its identity as a multiethnic state with a mixed population of Malays, Chinese, and Indians. For many years, however, the Muslim population has been increasing relative to the other groups, and in the 2015 census Muslims made up 61 percent of the population. The Chinese population, by contrast, dipped below 30 percent for the first time in the 1991 census, and in the 2015 census had fallen to just 25 percent of the population. At the same time, education levels are steadily improving, and 68 percent of the total population now have at least a secondary education, an increase of 8 percentage points compared to 2005. The figure for the Bumiputera ("Sons of the Soil," mainly Malays) rose from 61 percent to 71 percent, so that it is fair to say that the Bumiputera policy of positive discrimination for Malays is achieving results, at least in the field of education. Malaysia has the third highest national income per capita in ASEAN, after Singapore and Brunei, at over $10,000 in 2014. This explains why a large number of foreign workers are drawn to Malaysia from neighboring countries, both legally and illegally. According to the 2010 census, there were 2.3 million workers from Indonesia, Bangladesh, Myanmar, and other countries, and counting only those living in Malaysia legally, foreign workers had already exceeded the population of Indian descent with Malaysian nationality (1.9 million) (see Torii 2015: 30).

In the Philippines, the population was 92 million in 2010, and passed 100 million in 2014. Censuses in the Philippines record more than a hundred different ethnic groups, of which the largest are the Tagalog people, who live in metro Manila and the surrounding area and make up one-quarter of the population, followed by the Visayans and Cebuano, who inhabit an area encompassing Cebu and surrounding islands and northern parts of Mindanao, and the Ilocano of northern Luzon. In terms of religion, around 80 percent of the total population are Catholic. If Protestants and members of the Philippine Independent Church and other groups are included, Christians account for around 90 percent of the population, with Muslims making up just 5.6 percent.

Muslims provide the base of support for rebel groups such as the Moro National Liberation Front, the Moro Islamic Liberation Front, and Abu Sayyaf, but ethnically they are quite diverse. Another distinctive characteristic of the Philippines is that there were 1.5 million Filipinos working overseas, according to the 2015 census, equivalent to 1.6 percent of the total population. These numbers look small, since it is often said that some 10 percent of Filipinos work overseas. This discrepancy arises, according to Suzuki Yurika (2015), because censuses tend to underreport the number of overseas workers owing to the census method used. Nearly half of those workers who are included in the 10 percent foreign worker category live permanently overseas, while most of the rest have plans to return home at some undetermined time in the future. Most of them are not counted in population censuses. Some 43 percent of overseas workers have a college education or higher—an extremely high percentage—and in 2010, overseas workers accounted for 7.3 percent of all Filipinos (aged twenty or older) with a college degree or higher (see Suzuki 2015: 38–39).

Indonesia has a population of 284 million. In terms of religion, Muslims make up 87 percent of the population, followed by Protestants at 7 percent, Catholics at 2.9 percent, Hindus at 1.7 percent, and Buddhists at 0.7 percent. Indonesia is home to as many as 2,500 local and regional languages used in everyday life. At the same time, over a thirty-year period from 1980 to 2010, the proportion of people aged five and older who routinely use Indonesian as the language of everyday life increased by 8 percentage points, to 20 percent, while the percentage using Javanese, spoken mostly in central and eastern parts of Java, fell by 9 percentage points, to 32 percent of the total population. These trends show the steady progress in Indonesia toward national integration (see Masuhara 2015: 41–43).[2]

ECONOMIC DISCREPANCIES

Economic Diversity

Another important feature of Southeast Asia is its economic diversity. Table 3.1 shows the GDP for Southeast Asian countries in 2014 and 2020 and per capita GDP for 2014. The table shows the diversity that exists among the countries of Southeast Asia, both in terms of the scale of their economies and in per capita GDP. To put it bluntly, there are serious economic disparities across the region. It should also be said that in some countries, per capita gross national income (GNI), which includes remittances sent from overseas, might be a more appropriate indicator than per capita GDP when considering living standards. The largest economy in Southeast Asia is Indonesia, which in 2014 had a GDP of $888 billion, equivalent to 36 percent of the total economy of ASEAN, or around one-fifth of the Japanese economy. By contrast, countries like Brunei, Cambodia, and Laos have very small economies, worth just $17 billion, $16 billion, and $11 billion respectively. Between these two poles are medium-sized economies like Vietnam, the Philippines, Singapore, Malaysia, and Thailand. Myanmar is likely to join this group within the next ten to twenty years.

There are also large variations in per capita GDP. In 2014, Singapore had a per capita GDP of $56,286, higher than Japan or the United States. By contrast, Cambodia, Laos, and Myanmar had per capita GDP figures below $2,000: a differential of fifty to one compared to Singapore.

If we define middle-income countries as those with a per capita GDP of $4,000–12,000, Malaysia and Thailand already qualify, with Indonesia, the Philippines, and Vietnam likely to join them soon. This is

Table 3.1   Economic Size and per Capita GDP of ASEAN Countries, 2014 and 2020

	GDP ($ billions, current prices)		GDP per Capita ($, current prices)
	2014	2020	2014
China	10,356	17,100	7,571
India	2,051	3,443	1,607
Brunei	17	19	41,460
Cambodia	16	27	1,080
Indonesia	888	1,193	3,524
Laos	11	20	1,693
Malaysia	338	544	11,049
Myanmar	63	106	1,227
Philippines	284	507	2,862
Singapore	307	394	56,286
Thailand	404	473	5,896
Vietnam	185	287	2,051
ASEAN	2,513	3,570	n/a
United States	17,348	22,294	54,369
Japan	4,602	4,746	36,221

Source: International Monetary Fund, World Economic Outlook Database, October 2015, https://www.imf.org/external/pubs/ft/weo/2015/02/weodata/index.aspx.
Note: n/a = data not available.

why the middle-income trap is now seen as a serious challenge in these countries in recent years.

This economic diversity/disparity among the countries of Southeast Asia, as illustrated by the per capita GDP figures, has both positive and negative effects. Large variations in per capita GDP naturally lead to massive movements of workers, both within the region and from farther afield. This is shown by the presence of large numbers of legal and illegal workers in countries like Thailand and Malaysia, as well as by the many Filipinos working overseas. At the same time, differentials within the region also have a positive effect in terms of the integration of the ASEAN economy. Since the mid-1980s, many companies, including Japanese firms, have developed production networks across the region, based on the information and communication revolution and the liberalization of trade and investment. Companies divide the production process into segments, carrying out assembling and similar tasks in places with cheap labor costs and locating product development and research in places where highly skilled engineers, designers, and others are readily available. In this way, the production process has become fragmented, and factories and industrial centers have grown up in countries and regions specializing in certain types of tasks based on their comparative advantage. The production network has developed across borders, and this has led to substantial progress toward the economic integration that will provide the foundation for an ASEAN economic community. The economic disparities within the region have been fundamental to this process of integration.

Macroeconomic stability is of decisive importance for the running of the economy of any country. For the countries of Southeast Asia, the experience of the East Asian financial crisis of 1997–1998 continues to have a lingering effect on how they look to achieve this stability. In Indonesia, Malaysia, the Philippines, and Thailand, foreign currency reserves in 1996 (before the crisis) were equivalent to around four to six months of imports. This gradually increased after the crisis, and by 2010 these countries held foreign currency reserves equivalent to 8.5, 7.8, 12.4, and 11.2 months of imports respectively. The difference between these countries and Vietnam and Myanmar is striking.

Living Standards Improving in All Countries

Another important point to note is the long-term trend of economic performance in Indonesia, Malaysia, the Philippines, and Thailand. During the period from 1987 to 1996, shortly after the Plaza Accords of 1985 until just before the financial crisis of 1997–1998, Japanese companies, driven by the enormous appreciation of the yen to the US dollar, shifted their production bases to Southeast Asia through large-scale direct investment. Thailand and Malaysia were major beneficiaries of Japanese direct investment, and their economies grew accordingly: by an average of 9.5 percent annually in Thailand, and 9.1 percent annually in Malaysia. By comparison, the economic growth rate in Indonesia was slower, with an average growth of 7 percent. In the Philippines, where the lingering effects of the economic crisis of the Marcos era and the political instability that followed the 1986 People Power revolution were still being felt, average growth was just 3.7 percent. However, this trend has reversed since 2010, following the global financial crisis. As Table 3.2 shows, the Philippines has enjoyed the region's best economic growth, at an annual average of 6.3 percent, followed by Indonesia with 6.2 percent and Malaysia (5.7 percent), even though in 2014–2015, economic growth slowed from more than 5 percent to the 4 percent and 3 percent range respectively. Similarly, Thailand had an average growth rate of 4.3 percent for the period 2010–2012, but in 2014–2015 this fell to the 1 percent range. This is one of the reasons for growing concern that Malaysia and Thailand might be falling into the middle-income trap. What explains the dramatic turnabout in the economic performances of Thailand, Malaysia, Indonesia, and the Philippines before the East Asian financial crisis and after the global financial crisis? In simple terms, an important part of the explanation lies in what kind of political and economic reforms were carried out (or not) in Indonesia, Malaysia, and Thailand following the East Asian financial crisis of 1997–1998 and in the Philippines in the face the economic crisis of the 1980s under Marcos. I will have more to say on this subject later.

Table 3.2 Average Economic Growth Rates in Four ASEAN Countries, 1987–2012 (percentages)

	Before the East Asian Financial Crisis, 1987–1996	After the East Asian Financial Crisis, 2000–2006	After the Global Economic Crisis, 2010–2012
Indonesia	7.04	4.76	6.16
Malaysia	9.09	5.48	5.66
Philippines	3.71	4.66	6.34
Thailand	9.52	5.06	4.31

Source: Based on data from Asian Development Bank, "Key Indicators for Asia and the Pacific," various years, http://www.adb.org/statistics.

As a result of economic growth, standards of living have improved in all the countries of the region, although here too there is considerable variation in performance from one country to another. This can be seen in Table 3.3. In the thirty-year period from 1980 to 2010, the per capita GDP (constant prices, in local currency) increased considerably in all countries: by 442 percent in Vietnam, 360 percent in Thailand, 296 percent in Indonesia, and 129 percent in the Philippines. In the case of the Philippines, the importance of remittances sent home by overseas workers means that we need to look not at per capita GDP but at per capita GNI. I will return to this point later.

What I would like to say here for now is that in the space of thirty years, or one generation, income levels rose massively. As a result, people have come to expect that their lives will continue to improve, and that their children will enjoy a standard of living much better than their own. The governments in the region need to meet this "revolution of rising expectations" while also addressing the issues of income disparity and regional and urban-rural gaps, and ensure that these disparities do not foment identity politics. This is the biggest challenge for the politics of economic growth in all countries.

In this globalizing world, this means maintaining macroeconomic stability and encouraging investment to create jobs and tasks of greater added value in global value chains, while managing disparities through income redistribution and investing in human resources and productivity growth. The question is whether Southeast Asian states can address all these policy challenges and, if so, how.

Table 3.3   Increase in GDP per Capita, 1980–2010

	GDP per Capita (national currency, constant prices)		Increase in GDP per Capita (%)
	1980	2010	1980–2010
China	783	10,233	1,306
South Korea	4,277,252	25,608,148	599
Indonesia	9,769,377	28,884,425	296
Philippines	47,713	61,571	129
Singapore	18,146	63,497	350
Thailand	33,934	122,184	360
Vietnam	5,609,483	24,821,884	442
Japan	2,311,803	4,003,625	173
United States	28,338	47,726	168

Source: International Monetary Fund, World Economic Outlook Database, October 2014, https://www.imf.org/external/pubs/ft/weo/2015/02/weodata/index.aspx.

SOUTHEAST ASIA AND CHINA

A Region of Small and Middle Powers

In distinction to Northeast Asia and South Asia, Southeast Asia is a region of small and middle powers. Table 3.4 compares the countries in the region with China in terms of population and economic size. China is several times bigger than any of the countries in the region, both in its population and in the size of its economy. In 2015, I should add, China's economy was three times the size of Japan's, and in 2014 its population was ten times bigger. The table underlines the huge asymmetry between China and Southeast Asia in terms of population and economic size. Even Indonesia, which has the largest population and economy in Southeast Asia, is left far behind: China's population is five times bigger and its economy thirteen times bigger.

China dwarfs the Philippines and Vietnam, the countries with which it has territorial disputes in the South China Sea. China's population is

Table 3.4   Economic Imbalance in the Asia Pacific Region, 2014

	GDP ($ billions)	Per Capita GDP ($)	Population (millions)	Comparison with China (%)	
				GDP	Population
	2014	2014	2014	2014	2014
China	10,356	7,571	1,367	100	100
India	2,051	1,607	1,260	19.8	92.2
Brunei	17	41,460	0.4	0.2	0
Cambodia	16	1,080	16	0.2	1.2
Indonesia	888	3,524	255	8.5	18.7
Laos	11	1,693	7	0.1	0.5
Malaysia	338	11,049	31	3.3	2.3
Myanmar	63	1,227	52	0.6	3.8
Philippines	284	2,862	101	2.7	7.4
Singapore	307	56,286	5	3.0	0.4
Thailand	404	5,896	69	3.9	5.0
Vietnam	185	2,051	92	1.8	6.7
ASEAN	2,459	n/a	628	23.7	46.0
United States	17,348	54,369	319	167.5	23.3
Japan	4,602	36,221	127	44.4	9.3

Sources: International Monetary Fund, World Economic Outlook Database, October 2015, https://www.imf.org/external/pubs/ft/weo/2015/02/weodata/index.aspx; Asian Development Bank, "Key Indicators for Asia and the Pacific," 2015, http://www.adb.org/statistics.
Note: n/a = data not available.

thirteen and a half times larger than that of the Philippines and fifteen times larger than that of Vietnam. Its economy is thirty-six and fifty-six times bigger respectively. Even if we take the total figures for ASEAN as a whole, China is twice as big by population and four times as big by economy.

In this sense, the countries of Southeast Asia are small and middle powers, with Indonesia as a partial exception. At the same time, these countries' economies are growing rapidly, and like China, India, and Brazil, they are now called emerging economies. Unlike China, India, and Brazil, however, the countries of Southeast Asia are not major powers, and this can be seen in their patterns of behavior, where they look to strengthen their positions politically and economically by using ASEAN as a lever, rather than acting unilaterally in the way a bigger power might.

China's Increasing Importance as a Trading Partner

Until the end of the 1990s, Japan and the United States were the two most important trading partners for all the countries of Southeast Asia except Myanmar. Since the beginning of the twenty-first century, this has changed, as China has risen economically and become an important trade partner. As Tables 3.5 and 3.6 show, China has already overtaken Japan and the United States as an export market for Thailand and Malaysia. For Thailand, 21 percent of exports went to the United States in 2000, followed by Japan with 15 percent. China accounted for just 4 percent. By 2010, China was the largest export market, accounting for an 11 percent share. By 2013, this increased to 12 percent. In the case of Malaysia, the largest export destination was and remains Singapore. In 1996, the second biggest export market was the United States, followed by Japan. But since 2010, China has emerged as an important export market, rivaling Singapore.

For the Philippines (Table 3.7), the United States was overwhelmingly the most important export market in 1996 and 2000, but since 2010 Japan has taken over the number one position, and China's share is increasing rapidly too. In Vietnam (Table 3.8), Japan was the largest export market in 1996 and 2000, but since 2010 the United States has become the largest export market, though here too China is increasing its share in recent years. This is also the case with Indonesia (Table 3.9), where Japan was in the top position, followed by the United States until 2000, since China has increased its share in recent years.

Table 3.5 Thailand's International Trade, 1996–2013

	1996		2000		2010		2013	
	Trade Value ($ millions)	Percentage of Total	Trade Value ($ millions)	Percentage of Total	Trade Value ($ millions)	Percentage of Total	Trade Value ($ millions)	Percentage of Total
Total exports	56,451		68,963		193,366		224,888	
1. China	1,868	3.31	2,806	4.07	21,479	11.10	26,811	11.90
2. Japan	9,373	16.60	10,164	14.70	20,317	10.50	21,879	9.73
3. United States	10,026	17.80	14,706	21.30	20,243	10.50	22,650	10.10
4. Hong Kong	3,240	5.74	3,474	5.04	11,257	5.82	12,982	5.77
5. Malaysia	2,014	3.57	2,813	4.08	10,569	5.47	12,803	5.69
6. Singapore	6,749	12.00	5,997	8.70	9,003	4.66	11,056	4.92
7. Australia	840	1.49	1,615	2.34	9,372	4.85	10,179	4.53
8. Indonesia	846	1.50	1,338	1.94	7,347	3.80	10,702	4.76
9. Vietnam	478	0.85	838	1.21	5,846	3.02	7,065	3.14
10. India	242	0.43	566	0.82	4,395	2.27	5,102	2.27
Total imports	74,939		61,923		185,121		249,971	
1. Japan	20,449	27	15,315	25	38,320	21	40,978	16.40
2. China	1,953	3	3,377	5	24,526	13	37,595	15.00
3. United Arab Emirates	779	1	1,766	3	8,886	5	17,225	6.89
4. United States	9,240	12	7,291	12	10,885	6	14,660	5.86
5. Malaysia	3,606	5	3,344	5	10,857	6	13,204	5.28
6. South Korea	2,684	4	2,165	3	8,167	6	9,037	3.62
7. Singapore	4,004	5	3,416	6	6,368	4	8,179	3.27
8. Taiwan	2,950	4	2,895	5	6,898	4	7,571	3.03
9. Laos	842	1	692	1	5,231	3	9,205	3.68
10. Saudi Arabia	619	1	1,159	2	5,892	3	8,361	3.34

Source: Asian Development Bank, "Key Indicators for Asia and the Pacific," various years, http://www.adb.org/statistics.

Table 3.6 Malaysia's International Trade, 1996–2013

	1996		2000		2010		2013	
	Trade Value ($ millions)	Percentage of Total	Trade Value ($ millions)	Percentage of Total	Trade Value ($ millions)	Percentage of Total	Trade Value ($ millions)	Percentage of Total
Total exports	78,214		98,154		198,748		228,392	
1. Singapore	16,018	20	18,050	18	26,544	13	31,912	14.00
2. China	1,882	2	3,028	3	24,912	13	30,711	13.40
3. Japan	10,498	13	12,780	13	20,782	10	25,328	11.10
4. United States	14,251	18	20,162	21	18,987	10	18,474	8.09
5. Thailand	3,207	4	3,550	4	10,587	5	12,674	5.55
6. Hong Kong	4,607	6	3,330	5	10,088	5	9,898	4.33
7. Australia	1,217	2	2,426	2	7,472	4	9,238	4.04
8. South Korea	2,386	3	3,235	3	7,555	4	8,292	3.63
9. India	1,209	2	1,925	2	6,517	3	8,175	3.58
10. Indonesia	1,219	2	1,707	2	5,616	3	10,500	4.60
Total imports	78,458		82,205		164,735		206,118	
1. China	1,876	2	3,237	4	20,682	13	33,740	16.40
2. Singapore	10,475	13	11,763	14	18,761	11	25,504	12.40
3. Japan	19,241	25	17,331	21	20,726	13	17,809	8.68
4. United States	12,133	15	13,668	17	17,526	11	16,186	7.85
5. Thailand	2,594	3	3,176	4	10,263	6	12,281	5.96
6. Indonesia	1,426	2	2,269	3	9,151	6	8,879	4.31
7. South Korea	4,070	5	3,663	4	8,933	5	9,725	4.72
8. Germany	3,905	5	4,611	6	7,422	5	9,990	4.85
9. Hong Kong	3,351	4	2,441	3	6,648	4	7,278	3.53
10. Australia	2,210	3	1,593	2	3,184	2	5,242	2.54

Source: Asian Development Bank, "Key Indicators for Asia and the Pacific," various years, http://www.adb.org/statistics.

Table 3.7 International Trade in the Philippines, 1996–2013

	1996		2000		2010		2013	
	Trade Value ($ millions)	Percentage of Total	Trade Value ($ millions)	Percentage of Total	Trade Value ($ millions)	Percentage of Total	Trade Value ($ millions)	Percentage of Total
Total exports	20,562		38,216		51,432		53,978	
1. Japan	3,668	18	5,609	15	7,827	15	11,423	21.20
2. United States	6,966	34	11,406	30	7,568	15	7,832	14.50
3. China	328	2	663	2	5,702	11	6,583	12.20
4. Singapore	1,224	6	3,124	8	7,331	14	4,014	7.44
5. Hong Kong	868	4	1,907	5	4,334	8	4,418	8.18
6. South Korea	371	2	1,173	3	2,228	4	3,126	5.79
7. Netherlands	1,115	5	2,982	8	2,429	5	1,692	3.14
8. Germany	847	4	1,329	3	2,657	5	2,167	4.01
9. Thailand	780	4	1,206	3	1,784	3	1,936	3.59
10. Taiwan	661	3	2,861	7	1,752	3	1,801	3.34
Total imports	31,867		34,491		60,193		68,014	
1. United States	6,243	20	6,413	19	6,452	11	7,358	10.80
2. Japan	6,916	22	6,511	19	7,422	12	5,739	8.44
3. China	653	2	786	2	5,070	8	8,837	13.00
4. Singapore	1,689	5	2,325	7	5,703	9	4,650	6.84
5. Taiwan	1,582	5	2,255	7	4,045	7	5,367	7.89
6. South Korea	1,643	6	2,754	8	4,210	7	5,280	7.76
7. Thailand	575	2	879	3	4,253	7	3,719	5.47
8. Saudi Arabia	1,630	5	1,048	3	2,648	4	3,111	4.57
9. Indonesia	0	0	693	2	2,459	4	2,980	4.38
10. Malaysia	792	2	1,307	4	2,682	4	2,517	3.70

Source: Asian Development Bank, "Key Indicators for Asia and the Pacific," various years, http://www.adb.org/statistics.

Table 3.8 Vietnam's International Trade, 1996–2013

	1996		2000		2010		2013	
	Trade Value ($ millions)	Percentage of Total	Trade Value ($ millions)	Percentage of Total	Trade Value ($ millions)	Percentage of Total	Trade Value ($ millions)	Percentage of Total
Total exports	7,462		14,483		69,820		130,066	
1. United States	204	2.74	733	5.06	14,238	20.40	22,930	17.60
2. China	340	4.56	1,536	10.60	7,309	10.50	15,351	11.80
3. Japan	1,546	20.70	2,575	17.80	7,728	11.10	12,917	9.93
4. South Korea	558	7.48	353	2.43	3,092	4.43	6,534	5.02
5. Germany	228	3.06	730	5.04	2,373	3.40	5,683	4.37
6. Malaysia	78	1.04	414	2.86	2,093	3.00	5,482	4.22
7. Australia	65	0.87	1,272	8.79	2,704	3.87	3,660	2.81
8. Hong Kong	311	4.17	316	2.18	1,464	2.10	4,615	3.55
9. United Kingdom	125	1.68	479	3.31	1,682	2.41	3,643	2.80
10. Singapore	1,290	17.30	886	6.12	2,121	3.04	2,780	2.14
Total imports	11,285		15,637		83,365		167,440	
1. China	329	3	1,401	9	20,019	24	53,458	31.90
2. South Korea	1,781	16	1,754	11	9,761	12	23,196	13.90
3. Japan	1,260	11	2,301	15	9,016	11	11,575	6.91
4. Taiwan	1,263	11	1,880	12	6,977	8	9,819	5.86
5. Singapore	2,033	18	2,694	17	4,101	5	11,978	7.15
6. Thailand	495	4	811	5	5,602	7	7,771	4.64
7. United States	246	2	364	2	3,767	5	5,514	3.29
8. Malaysia	200	2	389	2	3,413	4	4,650	2.78
9. India	88	1	178	1	1,762	2	5,833	3.48
10. Hong Kong	759	7	598	4	860	1	8,315	4.97

Source: Asian Development Bank, "Key Indicators for Asia and the Pacific," various years, http://www.adb.org/statistics.

Table 3.9 Indonesia's International Trade, 1996–2013

	1996		2000		2010		2013	
	Trade Value ($ millions)	Percentage of Total	Trade Value ($ millions)	Percentage of Total	Trade Value ($ millions)	Percentage of Total	Trade Value ($ millions)	Percentage of Total
Total exports	49,890		62,124		157,778		182,551	
1. Japan	12,885	25.80	14,415	23.20	25,782	16.03	27,086	14.80
2. China	2,057	4.12	2,768	4.46	15,693	9.95	22,601	12.40
3. Singapore	4,565	9.15	6,562	10.60	13,723	8.70	16,686	9.14
4. United States	6,795	13.60	8,489	13.70	14,302	9.06	15,741	8.62
5. South Korea	3,281	6.58	4,318	6.95	12,575	7.97	11,422	6.26
6. India	531	1.06	1,151	1.85	9,915	6.28	13,031	7.14
7. Malaysia	1,110	2.22	1,972	3.17	9,362	5.93	10,667	5.84
8. Taiwan	1,609	3.23	2,378	3.83	4,838	3.07	5,862	3.21
9. Thailand	832	1.65	1,026	1.65	4,567	2.89	6,062	3.32
10. Australia	1,202	2.41	1,519	2.45	4,244	2.69	4,370	2.39
Total imports	42,902		33,515		135,663		186,628	
1. China	1,598	3	2,022	6	20,424	15	29,849	16.00
2. Singapore	2,875	7	3,789	11	20,241	15	25,582	13.70
3. Japan	8,504	20	5,397	16	16,966	13	19,285	10.30
4. Malaysia	823	2	1,131	3	8,649	6	13,323	7.14
5. South Korea	2,411	6	2,083	6	7,703	6	11,593	6.21
6. United States	5,060	12	3,393	10	9,416	7	9,082	4.87
7. Thailand	1,095	3	1,109	3	7,471	6	10,703	5.73
8. Saudi Arabia	665	2	1,598	5	4,361	3	6,526	3.50
9. Australia	2,535	6	1,694	5	4,099	3	5,038	2.70
10. Taiwan	1,664	4	1,270	4	3,242	2	4,480	2.40

Source: Asian Development Bank, "Key Indicators for Asia and the Pacific," various years, http://www.adb.org/statistics.

Last, Myanmar (Table 3.10), which is exceptional both because of the economic sanctions the United States and Europe imposed on the country for many years and because of the overwhelming importance to the economy of natural gas exports, sent more than 70 percent of its exports to Thailand, China, and India in 2013. This is expected to change as Myanmar becomes integrated into the global economy, and I believe this is one of the objectives of Thein Sein's policy of openness and liberalization since the shift to civilian government, as we shall see later.

Now let us look at imports. China is the largest source of imports for all countries except Thailand. China is particularly important for Vietnam and Myanmar. In Thailand, as of 2013, Japan is still the biggest source of imports, but this is due largely to imports of components to the industrial areas around Bangkok, where many Japanese companies have factories.

The same thing can be said of imports of components from China to Vietnam, and this is expected to become even more pronounced in the coming years as the Hanoi and Hai Phong region becomes increasingly integrated into the Guangzhou economic zone. As I will explain later, this represents something of a headache for Vietnam, and managing this asymmetry with China will be an important challenge for Vietnam in terms of national security.

China has rapidly increased its presence and importance for most of the countries in Southeast Asia in recent years both in imports and exports. Yet Southeast Asia is not a particularly large or important market for China, and this asymmetric interdependence works in China's favor. Additionally, Chinese economic cooperation has also become more important in recent years, particularly in infrastructure development projects.

As we have seen, the countries of maritime Southeast Asia and Vietnam have territorial disputes with China in the South China Sea. There is a vast difference in power between China and the countries of Southeast Asia. Dealing with this asymmetry will be an even more important challenge for Southeast Asian countries if trade with China continues to grow and economic cooperation with China continues to become more important, particularly in the field of building infrastructure. How to derive as much benefit as possible from China's economic rise while hedging against the national security risks posed by an increasingly assertive China? This will be a vital issue for many countries in Southeast Asia.

These are the general points to note about Southeast Asia. What strategies are Southeast Asian countries adopting to ensure their security

Table 3.10 Myanmar's International Trade, 1996–2013

	1996	2000		2010		2013	
	Trade Value ($ millions)	Trade Value ($ millions)	Percentage of Total	Trade Value ($ millions)	Percentage of Total	Trade Value ($ millions)	Percentage of Total
Total exports	1,183.0	1,980.3		6,454.8		10,443.3	
1. Thailand	n/a	233.0	11.8	2,590.3	40.1	3,655.4	35.00
2. China	125.0	113.5	5.7	873.6	13.5	2,554.2	24.50
3. India	134.9	162.9	8.2	1,019.1	15.8	1,246.7	11.90
4. Japan	93.9	108.4	5.5	353.4	5.5	688.0	6.59
5. South Korea	16.4	20.6	1.0	145.4	2.3	443.4	4.25
6. Malaysia	36.3	63.2	3.2	207.3	3.2	180.6	1.73
7. Singapore	190.7	99.8	5.0	74.8	1.2	162.6	1.56
8. Bangladesh	3.2	20.0	1.0	90.6	1.4	78.2	0.75
9. Vietnam	0.5	3.3	0.2	93.5	1.4	104.8	1.00
10. Taiwan	28.2	32.5	1.6	57.7	0.9	92.5	0.89
Total imports	2,677.8	3,039.9		9,945.2		20,302.8	
1. China	573.2	546.0	18.0	3,828.8	38.5	8,084.0	39.80
2. Thailand	n/a	544.7	18.3	2,280.2	22.9	4,103.7	20.20
3. Singapore	794.1	479.7	15.8	1,271.9	128.0	2,472.6	12.20
4. South Korea	143.9	318.2	10.5	526.7	5.3	775.6	3.82
5. Japan	279.4	215.6	7.1	290.5	2.9	1,161.5	5.72
6. Malaysia	242.8	254.1	8.4	402.1	4.0	784.7	3.87
7. India	50.5	52.9	1.7	300.6	3.0	737.0	3.63
8. Indonesia	85.8	71.2	2.3	312.6	3.1	612.0	3.01
9. Taiwan	41.5	219.5	7.2	118.0	1.2	197.8	0.97
10. Germany	50.8	44.7	1.5	33.4	0.3	179.1	0.88

Source: Asian Development Bank, "Key Indicators for Asia and the Pacific," various years, http://www.adb.org/statistics.
Note: n/a = data not available.

and economic development while maintaining political and economic stability? When I say "strategy," I mean grand strategy or national strategy. Unlike economic growth or national security policy, grand strategy is often not formally spelled out in a set of documents, but is taken for granted and can only be seen clearly in retrospect. We look back at a series of strategic decisions and understand that a certain way of thinking or set of ideas underlay these decisions. Policy is decided and resources are allocated in accordance with a certain way of thinking. In that sense, grand strategy is a kind of grand narrative, something that is shared and often taken for granted not only by the ruling elite but also by a majority of the population, who share a set of assumptions in regard to questions such as what the purpose of politics should be, who the state belongs to, what the state is there for, and what the main issues are that the government needs to address. Many countries have a set of shared assumptions on these questions. When these assumptions are lost, a country drifts, however stable it may appear.

What are the grand strategies that determine the ways in which Southeast Asian countries are run? How stable are their political systems? In the sections that follow I will address these questions by looking at a number of countries in turn, occasionally comparing them with one another, looking first at the countries of mainland Southeast Asia (Thailand, Myanmar, Vietnam), followed by the maritime states of Indonesia, Malaysia, and the Philippines.

THAILAND

Red Against Yellow and a Return to Military Rule

Let's start our discussion with Thailand. For nearly a decade since the coup d'état in 2006, Thai politics—more precisely, its political system and government—have been in a state of instability. The East Asian financial crisis of 1997–1998 had a severe impact on Thailand. The constitution was revised, and in 2001 a government headed by Thaksin Shinawatra came to power under the new constitution. Thaksin won major victories in the elections of 2001 and again in 2004, when he took two-thirds of the seats in the national parliament. Alarmed by these developments, the traditional elite, especially the military elite and its allies, with the blessing of the royal family, seized control of the government in a coup in 2006. The military junta disbanded Thaksin's Thai Rak Thai Party, banned 110 of its members from all political activities, froze Thaksin's assets, and promulgated a new constitution, under which elections were held in December 2007. Thaksin and his supporters won a majority again. In 2008, the Yellow Shirts (People's Alliance for Democracy), who had led opposition to Thaksin at the time of the 2006 coup, responded by occupying the office of the prime minister and international airports, and in September that year a constitutional court decision removed the prime minister from office on the grounds of conflict of interest. In December the court ordered disbanding the party.

Under pressure from the army, the ruling party handed control of the government to the opposition Democratic Party, in what amounted to a de facto coup. This prompted Thaksin's supporters to respond, and the Red Shirts (United Front for Democracy Against Dictatorship) took to the streets, demanding elections throughout 2009 and 2010. Eventually, in 2011, when the House of Representatives reached the end of its term, elections were held under a revised electoral code. Once again, Thaksin's coalition won a convincing victory. This gave new momentum to demonstrations by anti-Thaksin forces, who fomented further disorder and chaos in an attempt to force the military to intervene. This did not happen. In early 2013 the government, headed by Thaksin's younger sister Yingluck, proposed a constitutional amendment to convert the upper house to a popularly elected chamber. Opposition to this move and to a proposed general amnesty for political prisoners brought antigovernment forces back onto the streets. In November 2013, the two proposals were scrapped, but this only prompted the Yellow Shirts to shift their objectives. They were now determined to force the government from power. Even after the government dissolved parliament in December, protesters continued to demand the prime minister's resignation, and the Democratic Party boycotted the elections (Tamada 2014: 240). This brought electoral politics to a halt, and in May 2014 the military seized power under the leadership of Prayut Chan-o-cha, commander-in-chief of the army. As of August 2015, Thailand was under de facto military rule.

This is a general overview of Thai politics over the past decade and a half. The question is: What caused such a messy situation? A general consensus exists among scholars on this subject. The political system that has been in place in Thailand since 1973 is essentially a type of limited representative democracy in which the king can intervene in politics whenever needed. Tamada Yoshifumi says there are two main reasons why this democratic system with the king as head of state has become dysfunctional. The first is the tension between the old guard, who have seen their authority ebbing away as the democratic system has taken root—chief among them the royal family, the military, the bureaucratic elite, and capitalist groups allied with them—and the emerging forces that have taken control of the government through elections and the newly prosperous capitalist groups who support them. The other is the different outlooks and priorities of the Bangkok middle classes, the new middle classes in the provinces, and the "masses" made up of the lower-middle classes in Bangkok (Tamada 2014: 242–243, 247–248).

But these tensions between the military and bureaucratic elite and their capitalist allies on the one side, and the new money capitalists from the provinces on the other, is a predictable consequence of economic growth, better and broader access to education, and the social changes that have taken place as a result. Similar tensions have been seen around the world throughout history. In Thailand, too, things seemed to be going well until recently. The newly emergent social forces and the Bangkok establishment were gradually being integrated under the democratic system, with the king as head of state, that had prevailed since the student revolution of October 1973. As part of this process, a significant generational power shift took place among the political elite in the 1990s, starting with the establishment of the Chatichai Choonhavan government at the end of the 1980s and ending with the introduction of the 1997 constitution during the financial crisis. But developments in Thai politics since the coup in 2006 show that the expansion of political participation has not gone hand-in-hand with the integration of new political forces into the system. The question is why.

Income Disparities Between Bangkok and the North and Northeast

In simple terms, the reason is that the "masses" have been politically mobilized for the first time in Thai history and that the Bangkok-based middle classes have responded to this development with alarm. As a result, the question of how to integrate into the political system the different social forces now mobilizing and demanding participation has become an issue in itself. As we have seen, the Thai economy enjoyed a boom for a period from the 1980s onward. Per capita income increased nearly 3.5 times in the thirty years from 1980 to 2010, although this was hit hard by the crisis in the late 1990s. When income grows this much in a single generation, people naturally start to assume that their lives will be better tomorrow than they are today, and that their children will enjoy better lives than they have known themselves.

Over the past thirty years, together with this increase in income, new lifestyles have come to be shared in the regions. Consumption patterns have changed, and satellite television, internet access, and smart phones have become commonplace. Secondary education is the norm and growing numbers now have access to higher education as well. But there still exist huge income disparities between Bangkok and the growing metropolitan region around the capital on the one hand, and the rural areas in the north and northeast of the country on the other. On this subject, an article by Suehiro Akira, "Formation of a Greater Bangkok Metropolitan Region" (2015), is very useful. I summarize two of the points he makes.

One is that the Bangkok metropolitan region, which includes the capital and its five neighboring provinces, has long been regarded as the center of the nation's economy, education, and cultural activities. But the 2010 census showed that per capita income in the provinces east of Bangkok (440,000 baht) exceeded that in the capital metropolitan region (410,000 baht) for the first time. These six provinces east of the capital are home to a concentration of factories for the automotive industry and related component industries, and in 2010 the metropolitan region plus the six provinces (that is to say, twelve provinces in total) accounted for 66 percent of Thailand's total GDP. This greater metropolitan region has become a "mega-region" for Thailand.

Another point to note is the regional disparity that comes with this development. In the 2010 census, the output of the Bangkok metropolitan region was 3.142 trillion baht, while the figure for the greater metropolitan region was 7.157 trillion baht and that of the whole country 10.808 trillion baht. But the greater metropolitan region has a far smaller share of the population, at 30 percent. (Some 8.3 million people live in Bangkok, and 19.9 million in the greater metropolitan region—of whom 15.9 million were registered residents—out of a national population of 66 million.)

Per capita domestic income is 457,000 baht in Bangkok, and 449,000 baht in the greater metropolitan area. This compares to 161,000 baht nationwide, 45,000 baht in the northeast, and 68,000 baht in the north. According to the 1995 population census, per capita domestic income was 251,114 baht in Bangkok and 208,882 baht in the Bangkok metropolitan area, compared to a national average of 70,884 baht and just 18,866 baht in the northeast and 27,439 baht in the north. Taken together, Bangkok accounts for 12.6 percent of the total population and 29.1 percent of gross domestic product. Per capita domestic income in the capital is ten times what it is in northeastern Thailand. Given that the equivalent figure was thirteen times higher than the figure for the northeast in 1995, one could argue that the gap is shrinking somewhat, but significant regional disparities remain between Bangkok and the northeast and north.[3]

Thaksin was not blind to this fact. The 1997 constitution replaced multiple-seat electoral districts with an electoral system that combined single-seat districts (400 members) with seats elected by proportional representation (100 members). Thaksin understood that campaign pledges would be increasingly important under this system. Accordingly, he was the first to release a manifesto, promising to carry out reformist policies including universal healthcare, micro-credit, and agricultural subsidies, thereby securing support among the new middle classes of the northeast and north and the lower middle classes in Bangkok (Pasuk and Baker 2009: 2; Tamada 2013: 20).

In his article "The Yellow Shirts and Red Shirts in Thai Politics: Who, Why, and Where to Next?" (Tamada 2011: 143–159), Tamada Yoshifumi draws on work by Thai researchers to describe the Red Shirts as chiefly "lower middle class people," living in cities and villages, who are not poor, whose lives are closely linked with the market economy, and whose well-being is often unstable (Tamada 2011: 148). In the five-year period from 2005 to 2010, 31 percent of the Red Shirts took part in demonstrations or other mass gatherings (compared to 8 percent for the Yellow Shirts), 19 percent volunteered to help in election campaigns (8 percent for the Yellow Shirts), and 97 percent said they always voted at elections on a national level (compared to 88 percent for the Yellow Shirts), with 88 percent also voting in local elections (73 percent for the Yellow Shirts). This was the first time in Thai history that such large numbers of people had been politically mobilized. Clearly, these people form the basis of political support for Thaksin and his party (Tamada 2011: 149).

By contrast, it was members of the Bangkok middle classes who came onto the streets in support of the royalist Yellow Shirts, alarmed by the political mobilization of the "masses" under the Red Shirt banner. They feel threatened by the rise of the masses in electoral politics, particularly the emergence of new middle classes in the provinces. This concern is reinforced by the fact that the Democratic Party, which derives the bulk of its support from the Bangkok middle classes (and the south), has not been able to win an election for the past twenty years.

Bangkok middle-class reaction against the masses also has an element of a taxpayers' revolt. Back in the 1960s, more than 90 percent of the government budget was spent in Bangkok. Today, following the rise of Thaksin on the back of support from the masses and his "pork barrel" policies, more than 25 percent of the government budget is allocated to places outside the capital. To anyone familiar with Japan's income redistribution policies, it will be shocking to see that more than 70 percent of government spending still goes to the capital, even though Bangkok accounts for no more than 12.6 percent of the total population and 29.1 percent of GDP. But that is not how middle-class people in Bangkok see it. They find even this amount of redistribution intolerable. The way they see it, the government is taking "the money we pay in taxes" and handing it out to the lazy, ignorant, uneducated masses out in the provinces.

Another aspect involves identity politics. Many of the Bangkok middle classes are the descendants of immigrants who came from China two or three generations ago, and rose to their current middle-class status during the economic boom from the mid-1980s onward. They tend to think that their current position is the result of hard work—the hard work and sacrifices made by their grandparents and parents, continuing into the present. The masses are poor because they failed to work as hard. This widely held prejudice is expressed symbolically in their customary references to the masses as "water buffaloes." Also, although many of them have visited places like Hong Kong, Singapore, Tokyo, and Los Angeles, not very many of them have ever been to the rural areas of Thailand.

In this sense, they form part of the new urban middle classes that have emerged in East Asia since the 1990s, whose members enjoy a lifestyle that is very similar across the region. When Thaksin first came to power, the Bangkok middle classes supported him in large numbers. Their support was a factor in the victories he won in the elections of 2001 and 2004. But from 2005, he started to fall out with the traditional ruling elite, made up of the royal family and the military and bureaucratic elite, and began to emerge as the leader of the masses. From the perspective of the Bangkok middle classes, this made him a traitor, a turncoat, and a villain in chief (Pasuk and Baker 2009: 5–6).

Bangkok as a Hub of Mainland Southeast Asia

What is likely to happen next? We do not know the future, but we can surmise some of the trends likely to continue in Thailand in the years to come. The first thing to note is that Thailand enjoys a very benign international environment. As I noted in Chapter 2, Thailand is an ally of the United States and has built its security policy with the US-led hub-and-spokes system as given. It has no border, and no territorial disputes, with China. The Thai economy derives major benefits from Chinese economic growth, in rubber production, tourism, and other areas—but at the same time Bangkok and its surrounding region are home to a concentration of production facilities for Japanese companies and other multinationals, making it one of the major hubs of the East Asian production network. Economic cooperation with Japan and China is helping to build transnational regional infrastructure in the Greater Mekong Subregion, and Bangkok is becoming a major hub of mainland Southeast Asia—whether the Thai government does anything to support this. A cynic might take the view that it is precisely because they find themselves in such a benign international situation geopolitically and geo-economically that the Thai elite have been able to concentrate so much of their energies on internal squabbles for power, with the result that politics has drifted and stalled for so long.

But political instability has its own costs. Thaksin's attempt during his time as prime minister from 2001 to 2006 to transform Thailand into a hub was ineffectual, lost in the midst of political chaos and confusion. Yet the ruling elite still take the benign environment for granted and continue to maintain the overall direction of Thai diplomatic, security, and foreign economic policy without sufficiently considering the potential risks. One example is the plan to build a high-speed rail system. For now, the project looks likely to be given to either China or Japan, although how much demand there really is for such a system is a big question. Another example is the farce that arose over plans to buy submarines. In July 2015, the Thai navy announced that it would purchase three submarines from China at a cost of $355 million each. Two weeks later, this decision was withdrawn by the Thai government. This would have been the first export of the Yuan-class Chinese submarine, and China had apparently offered the submarines at a bargain price, prepared to take a loss on the deal. It is not immediately clear why the Thai navy would have a pressing need for submarines, but be that as it may, one of the reasons why it decided to acquire Chinese-made submarines (apart from the price) was apparently that unlike the United States, which had still not recognized the coup, China had given its full support to the military government, and was offering a wide variety of cooperation projects to Thailand, including military assistance. In the end, the United States expressed strong displeasure at the decision and the project was canceled after the Thai government withdrew its support. But the risk that political confusion can cause drift and confusion in national security and economic development policy is clear.

Second, there has been (and presumably will be) no change in the politics of economic growth. There is broad agreement that the chief objective of politics is to achieve economic growth. The question is whether it will be possible to formulate a strategy to achieve this in the medium to long term. Immediately after the coup, the military government instructed state-owned banks to pay 90 billion baht ($2.8 billion) to farmers who sold rice to the government. It also approved foreign direct investment projects worth $22 billion that had remained unapproved by the Board of Investment.

It also plans to implement 1.3 trillion baht out of a total of 2 trillion baht in planned infrastructure spending. This decision has helped to assuage most concerns that political chaos would lead to a delay in building infrastructure, creating a potential bottleneck to economic growth in the future. It is also clear that the government is trying to invigorate the economy through public works projects and by purchasing rice from farmers. In other words, even under the military government, the politics of economic development is taken for granted in policymaking.

A Grand Bargain? The Possible Road to Democratic Government

The pressing question is how to distribute the fruits of this growth, and how to combine investment in growth with income redistribution policies to address vast income disparities across classes and regions. As we have seen, a huge income gap exists between Bangkok and parts of northern and northeastern Thailand. Despite this, government spending tilts strongly toward the capital. This is the fundamental basis of the tensions between the Bangkok middle classes and the "masses." Is this antagonism likely to continue indefinitely? What is the likelihood that at some propitious moment in the future, a party or politician might promise to correct these disparities and respect electoral results, in return for the removal once and for all of Thaksin and his family from politics? Is a grand bargain along these lines a possibility?

Today, liberal democracy is more or less accepted as a norm around the world, and in these circumstances it will be quite difficult for a place like Thailand, with its open economy and past experience of a degree of democracy, to continue to exclude the masses from the political process and maintain an authoritarian government in the long term. Nevertheless, paradoxical as it may sound, a grand bargain such as the one I have just sketched will grow less likely if the Thai economy continues to grow, and more likely if the economy stagnates. The reasons for this are quite simple. As long as the economy continues on an even keel, the Bangkok middle classes will continue to enjoy prosperity. The living standards of the masses will also improve to a certain extent. Neither would have any special reason to accept a grand bargain that would involve major political compromises. However, if the economy starts to stagnate, giving rise to a sense of crisis that Thailand might be falling into the middle-income trap, this would raise the possibility of a grand bargain to put in place the conditions necessary to get the economy back on the right track. Immediately after the coup in May 2014, the London-based Economist Intelligence Unit predicted that although economic growth in Thailand would remain at around 2 percent for 2014, it would probably reach 5.2 percent in the period 2015–2018.

This was presumably one of the chief reasons why the Bangkok middle classes welcomed the coup. But as of August 2015, Thai economic growth remains at less than 2 percent, and the prospects for the future are hardly bright. In that sense, it may be that the economic conditions for a grand bargain, or a major political deal between the two sides, are starting to take shape.

But the political conditions for a grand bargain are still not in place. As Tamada Yoshifumi has argued, political instability in Thailand is at least partly due to an impasse in the democratic system with the king as head of state. This means that the system will have to undergo major changes when the reign of Bhumibol Adulyadej, who has been on the throne since 1950, finally comes to an end. As one era ends and another begins under a new king, the system will change drastically.

The monarchy is a strange institution. The person of the king and the institution of the monarchy are closely linked and difficult to separate, and the monarchy has to be reinvented each time a new king comes to the throne. Throughout the sixty-five years of his reign, King Bhumibol has intervened in politics whenever Thailand has fallen into serious political crisis and has won deep respect and trust from his subjects as a monarch. But the king was born in 1927, is already eighty-eight years old, and is not in good health. His era will inevitably come to an end, and there will be new developments in Thai politics once a new king takes the throne. It looks likely that the military government headed by Prayut Chan-o-cha is trying to carry out a massive cleanout of politics, stripping the Thaksin faction of its power and suppressing party politicians in general, in order to restore the old order based on a symbiotic relationship between the military and the royal family (Pongsudhirak 2015). But an overhaul of this nature, however ambitious in scale, will not be sufficient to silence the masses, who have given Thaksin and his political supporters a victory in every election held since 2001. In this sense, the attempt by the current government to restore the old order is perhaps better seen not as a long-term political project but as a measure designed to get through the end of the current era without massive chaos and unrest.[4]

In Thailand, generational changes in the political elite took place at the end of the 1980s and again in the wake of the 1997–1998 economic crisis, and we can expect another shift in the political elite at any time. It will be most likely to occur once people have understood how to play the game under the new reign. When that happens, what will the new game be like, and what kind of grand bargain will provide the basis for the new generation of the political elite? The answer to this question is likely to have a decisive impact on the prospects for Thai democracy and its political and economic future, and will also have a major impact on developments in mainland Southeast Asia as a whole.

MYANMAR

From the "Burmese Way to Socialism" to Reforms and Integration with the Global Economy

Next let's turn to Myanmar. The country has implemented a major shift in national strategy in recent years, transitioning to civilian government in January 2011. A new government headed by Thein Sein as president took office in March that year. But the chief reason for this dramatic change was not "democratization" per se. More important priorities included improving relations with developed countries, particularly the United States and Japan, and integrating Myanmar into the world economy through openness and liberalization. This was designed to put the economy on a growth trajectory, eradicate poverty, create jobs, and improve standards of living, in the hope that economic growth would stabilize and legitimize the new political system. But the question remains: Why did this major shift take place? Several reasons suggest themselves.[5]

The first thing to note is that the army, over the twenty-three years of military rule after 1988, built a political system with itself as the backbone (Kudō 2014a), and has become sufficiently confident in the stability of this system, based on the 2008 constitution. The constitution decrees that the army has the right to intervene systematically in national politics. One quarter of seats in the Union Assembly are set aside for appointment by the commander-in-chief of the armed forces, who also appoints the ministers of defense, home affairs, and border affairs. Additionally, the commander-in-chief has the right to take control in a state of national emergency. Since 2000, Myanmar has strengthened its relations with China, Thailand, India, and other neighboring states, and has secured reliable sources of foreign currency by developing gas fields and exporting natural resources. Under army leadership, the Union Solidarity and Development Party (USDP) was formed as a political party supporting the military. The USDP won an overwhelming "victory" in elections held in 2010.

But this system also brought massive costs. Many people were killed in the 1988 coup. Two years later, the junta ignored the convincing victory claimed by the National League for Democracy in the 1990 elections. The army held on to its position of power, repeatedly placed Aung San Suu Kyi under house arrest, and suppressed the National League for Democracy. These actions discredited the regime, at home and internationally. Advanced democratic countries imposed economic sanctions, and the United Nations passed annual resolutions criticizing the military regime. As a result, although Myanmar strengthened its economic relations through exports of natural resources to Thailand, China, and India, it became isolated from the United States, Japan, and other developed countries. The economic gap between Myanmar and neighboring countries grew larger, leading to concerns about the extent of the country's economic dependence on China (Kudō 2014a: 4).

This does not mean that the economy stagnated under the military regime. The junta did away with the "Burmese way to socialism" of the Ne Win period, liberalized trade, and allowed foreign direct investment. International trade expanded substantially from the 1990s into the 2000s. Even so, Myanmar was far less successful in achieving export-oriented economic growth than Vietnam, which also liberalized its economy and invited foreign direct investment at the same time. In 1990, the total value of Vietnam's exports was around two and a half times larger than Myanmar's. By 2012, it was seventeen times larger. In their analysis, Kudō Toshihiro and Kumagai Satoru (2014: 14–15) ascribe the scale of this gap between the two countries to the different levels of diversity of their exports. Myanmar started exporting natural gas to Thailand in 2000, and to China in 2013. The total value of gas exports increased from $186 million in 2000 to $3.4 billion in 2012, representing 41 percent of total exports. Other important exports include lumber (14 percent), clothing (12 percent), and fruits and vegetables (11 percent); together, these four items make up nearly 80 percent of all exports. Vietnam's exports are much more varied. In 2012, the biggest export item was smart phones and similar devices, which accounted for 19 percent of the total, followed by clothing (12 percent), shoes (9 percent), electrical equipment and components (7 percent), and crude oil (6 percent). In Myanmar, exports of crude oil fell from 33.4 percent of the total in 2000 to 6.2 percent in 2012. The reason is simple: in 2001, Vietnam signed a trade agreement with the United States, and gained access to the US market. Myanmar, by contrast, was subject to US trade sanctions, since 2003, and had lost the biggest market for its exports of clothing.

A Grand Bargain?

Aung San Suu Kyi and the NLD also had serious concerns that the situation might continue unchanged. Since their victory in the 1990 election, Aung San Suu Kyi and the NLD had demanded that the junta stand down and surrender control of the government. Instead, the army remained in power, placed Aung San Suu Kyi under house arrest, and suppressed the NLD. Aung San Suu Kyi was finally released in November 2010, when she was sixty-five years old, and the NLD was seriously weakened. The possibilities for democratization in Myanmar looked dim (Kudō 2014a: 4–5).

For all of these reasons, by the time the shift to civilian government took place in 2011, the conditions for a grand bargain were falling into place for both sides. Another factor was the generational shift among the ruling elite, already under way since the mid-2000s, even before the shift to civilian rule. Thein Sein became prime minister in 2007, and in 2008 announced elections for 2010. From that point on, to use Kudō Toshihiro's phrase, a precise date was inscribed onto Myanmar's political calendar. Gradually, members of the generation after Thein Sein's started to occupy central positions within the army. These were officers who had graduated from the Defense Services Academy in the second half of the 1970s; early in their military careers, many of them had fought against the guerrillas of the China-funded Burmese Communist Party along the border with China. It is no surprise that many of them felt apprehensive about their country's growing dependence on China.

Historically, Myanmar's great enemy was Thailand. This factor also played its role in focusing people's minds. During the 1990s and 2000s, middle-ranking and senior officers visited Thailand, where they saw for themselves the expanding economic gap between the two countries. Many were alarmed by the extent to which Myanmar was being left behind by its traditional rival. The idea that Myanmar needed to improve relations with the international community and persuade Western countries to lift economic sanctions became a consensus among the ruling elite, who realized that it was essential to reintegrate the country with the global economy. In this sense, a grand bargain with Aung San Suu Kyi was probably inevitable. In the middle of the 2000s, permission was granted for a private international school, which is now attended by the children of many senior officers and influential business people. It was a clear sign that the ruling elite was preparing their children and grandchildren for the globalizing world.

After Thein Sein assumed control of the government in March 2011, he immediately took steps toward the grand bargain. In April 2011, the Myanmar government put itself forward to assume the chairmanship of ASEAN for 2014. In the past, under pressure from other ASEAN countries apprehensive about criticism from the West, Myanmar had relinquished its turn to take the annual chairmanship of the organization. The fact that Myanmar had now volunteered to assume the chairmanship in 2014 indicated that the new government was willing to respond to international concerns about human rights and other matters, and was looking to improve its relations with the United States, the EU, and Japan. President Thein Sein met with Aung San Suu Kyi in August, and in a speech to the Union Assembly immediately after announced that the government would work toward national reconciliation and improving living standards through economic growth, and underlined his willingness to improve relations with the international community. Things moved quickly from then on. Political prisoners were amnestied, the rights to organize and strike were acknowledged, the law on registration of political parties was revised, and on 1 April 2012 by-elections were held to elect a total of forty-five seats: six in the upper house, thirty-seven in the lower, and two in regional assemblies. The NLD won a major victory, and Aung San Suu Kyi was elected to the Union Assembly. The government also reached a ceasefire agreement with six of the eleven ethnic minority groups that had been fighting an armed insurgency against the government. In economic policy, the law on foreign investment was revised for the first time in twenty-four years, and in April 2012 the multiple-currency practice was abolished and a managed floating exchange rate was introduced for the kyat currency.

The new government also started to take action on foreign policy. China had been Myanmar's most important partner since the time of military rule. Accordingly, when Jia Qinglin, member of the Politburo Standing Committee and chairman of the Chinese People's Political Consultative Conference, visited Myanmar, President Thein Sein declared that there would be no change in China policy, insisting that Myanmar would maintain its friendly relations with China, continue with economic and trade cooperation projects between the two countries, and stand alongside China on the international stage. In late May, Thein Sein visited China on his first official visit outside ASEAN for meetings with Hu Jintao, at which an agreement was reached to expand cooperation in energy, electricity, and transport infrastructure, and to promote the bilateral relationship to the level of a total comprehensive strategic partnership. Not long after this, however, something shocking happened: in September 2011, Thein Sein decided to cancel the Myitsone Dam project, work on which had already begun with Chinese assistance at a cost of $3.6 billion. The dam was being constructed along the Irrawaddy River in Kachin province in the north of the country, and the decision to cancel the project made it clear that the government had decided to prioritize reconciliation with the Kachin minority over economic cooperation with China (Shiraishi and Hau 2012: 79–81).

Thein Sein's New Regime and Relations with the United States, Japan, and China

By this time, Myanmar had begun to take steps to improve its relations with the United States, Japan, and other developed countries. In August 2011, the United States appointed a special representative and policy coordinator for Myanmar, and in September, Secretary of State Hillary Clinton welcomed the dialogue between the Myanmar government and Aung San Suu Kyi, and encouraged the government to "carry out true reforms and national reconciliation," and take concrete actions on human rights issues.

At the end of September, Myanmar's foreign minister, Wunna Maung Lwin, visited Washington, D.C., one day before the decision to cancel the Myitsone Dam project, where he had meetings with Kurt Campbell, assistant secretary of state for East Asian and Pacific affairs, and Derek Mitchell, the US government's special representative and policy coordinator for Myanmar. In November, Michael Posner, assistant secretary of state for democracy, human rights, and labor, noted favorably that reforms had begun, and endorsed the political and economic reforms under way in Myanmar.

That same month, President Obama met Thein Sein during his trip to Indonesia to attend the East Asia Summit, praising the Myanmar government's decision to release political prisoners and open dialogue with Aung San Suu Kyi. Endorsing the government's measures toward political reforms in the Union Assembly, Obama hinted at the possibility that US sanctions might be lifted, saying "if Burma continues to travel down the road of democratic reform, it can forge a new relationship with the United States." This was followed by a visit to Myanmar by Secretary of State Clinton in December, during which she expressed satisfaction that President Thein Sein had promised further steps toward broader reforms. Since then, the US government has successively lifted its sanctions on Myanmar, and relations between the two countries are returning to normal. In the field of defense, Myanmar took part in the US-led Cobra Gold multilateral military exercises as an observer in 2013 (Shiraishi and Hau 2012: 81–82; Tsumori 2014: 28).

The Japanese government too has been quick to respond to these moves by the new government. In October 2011, the Japanese government invited Myanmar's foreign minister, Wunna Maung Lwin, to Japan, where Minister of Foreign Affairs Genba Kōichirō informed him that Japan would resume official development aid for repairs to a hydroelectric plant, which had been suspended owing to the political situation in Myanmar. In December, Genba visited Myanmar for meetings with Thein Sein, following which he announced a plan to support democratization through economic cooperation, and with Wunna Maung Lwin on negotiations for an investment treaty. In April 2012, Thein Sein visited Japan for meetings with Prime Minister Noda Yoshihiko, at which Noda announced that Japan would write off 502 billion yen in debt and expressed Japan's willingness to take part in drawing up the Thilawa Masterplan for a special economic zone. Japan also played an important role at the Paris Club of major creditor nations, and in January 2013 the Asian Development Bank and the World Bank agreed, with Japanese assistance, to defer Myanmar's delinquent debt and to provide new financing (Umezaki 2014: 18).

Japanese companies also moved fast to start their operations in Myanmar. In January 2013, Deputy Prime Minister Asō Tarō visited the country, and a new yen-denominated loan worth 51 billion yen was announced in March. In May, Prime Minister Abe visited Myanmar and announced a further 40 billion yen as grant aid and technical assistance (Tsumori 2014: 29).

At a summit meeting of ASEAN foreign ministers in November 2011, a unanimous decision was taken to approve Myanmar for the chairmanship in 2014. This meant that President Thein Sein would attend a series of summit meetings such as the ASEAN Summit, the ASEAN+3 Summit, and the East Asia Summit, in a symbolic demonstration of Myanmar's return to the international community.

But these developments did not mean that Myanmar was tilting toward the United States, Japan, the EU, and India. At the end of November, immediately after the East Asia Summit, the Myanmar government dispatched Min Aung Hlaing, commander-in-chief of the armed forces, to China. Min Aung Hlaing met with then vice president (and deputy chairman of the Central Military Commission of the Communist Party of China) Xi Jinping, and they agreed to strengthen exchanges between their militaries as part of developing a strategic relationship of cooperation between the two countries. In addition, Xi Jinping hinted at enhanced economic cooperation, saying that "China will continue to support improvements to the living standard of the Myanmar people."

There is evidence that Myanmar maintains good working relations with China in the field of economic cooperation, too. The Chinese-operated Letpadaung copper mine continues to function, despite protests from the local population. Likewise, there has been no effect on the operations of the oil and gas pipeline from Kyaukpyu to Kunming, or on the development of gas fields in offshore areas of Rakhine.

As of August 2012, Chinese investment in Myanmar had reached a cumulative total of $14 billion, surpassing Thailand to become the top investor (Tsumori 2014: 27). Overall, we can characterize Thein Sein's diplomacy in the following terms. As president, Thein Sein has sought to correct Myanmar's excessive dependence on China alone, and has looked to develop a more balanced, rounded diplomacy, building what might be termed "normal" relationships with all countries (Tsumori 2014: 26).

From 2011 to 2012, then, under the leadership of President Thein Sein, Myanmar dramatically changed its national strategy. At the foundation of its approach was an agreement (or grand bargain) with Aung San Suu Kyi regarding the need to improve people's lives through national reconciliation and economic growth and to use this to build better relations with the international community.

Prospects for Power-Sharing
Between the Army, NLD, and USDP

So what is likely to happen next? I'd suggest three possible developments to look at. Let us start with the political outlook. Elections are scheduled for November 2015. Will the elections be free and fair, and what will the results be? It is generally expected that the NLD, led by Aung San Suu Kyi, will win. Will this happen? And if it does, what will the scale of the victory be? The Union Assembly has already decided that it will not revise the constitution, so that regardless of the size of the NLD's victory, Aung San Suu Kyi cannot become president. Who would become president if the NLD did win, and what would Aung San Suu Kyi's position be? How will "power-sharing" work between the military, the NLD, and the USDP? (Of course, this depends on how many seats the Union Solidarity and Development Party manages to gain.) What do we need to look at to answer these questions?

If the election turns out like the one held in 2010, which was neither free nor fair, and the USDP claims a victory, bringing the NLD out onto the streets in protest and prompting the army to suppress the demonstrations by force, it is not out of the question that the US Congress might move to reimpose sanctions on Myanmar. But I believe this is unlikely. If it did happen, the entire premise of Myanmar's national strategy since 2011 would collapse. Thein Sein and his government must be well aware of the risks involved in this line of action. It is much more likely the elections will be held in a reasonably fair and free manner under international observation—whatever the results may be.

This may be wishful thinking, but I wonder whether preparations for power-sharing may have already begun. Under the current system, the national government is under the control and leadership of the president, the commander-in-chief of the armed forces, and the speaker of the Union Assembly (Nakanishi 2014: 8). In August 2015, Schwe Mann, chairman of the USDP and speaker of the Union Assembly since 2011, was removed from his position as chairman of the USDP following a disagreement with Thein Sein about candidates for the election in November. It is unclear who will replace him, but an adviser close to the president has been appointed as secretary-general, and on August 12 it was reported that security forces had surrounded the headquarters of the ruling party in the capital, Naypyidaw.[6] It seems that with the support of the army, Thein Sein is taking control of the USDP in the run-up to the elections in November and that Thein Sein and the commander-in-chief of the armed forces will have an important say in who becomes the next president and the speaker following the elections under the collective leadership system.

Trade Liberalization and Reconciliation with Ethnic Minority Forces

Let us now look at the prospects for the economy. As I have mentioned, an ASEAN economic community is due to be formed at the end of 2015. The ASEAN countries have already made substantial progress on free trade, and by 2013 the average level of tariffs in the ASEAN-6 countries (Brunei, Indonesia, Malaysia, the Philippines, Singapore, and Thailand) will be zero. Even in Cambodia, Laos, Myanmar, and Vietnam, which joined ASEAN in the mid-1990s, the rate is just 1.4 percent. But Myanmar faces a difficult situation. Owing to the protectionist trade regime under the military and sanctions imposed by advanced democratic countries, the country failed to develop any industry capable of competing in international markets. Since Thein Sein started the openness and liberalization in 2011, the easing and lifting of Western economic sanctions, aid from developed countries and international bodies, and direct investment by foreign companies have helped trade to grow and Myanmar to benefit from free trade. But Myanmar will struggle to implement the measures required by an ASEAN economic community. For example, the plan for an ASEAN economic community positions the ASEAN "single window" at the center of measures to facilitate trade. This will involve online connections between single windows built by member countries. To make this happen, trade procedures within member states must be digitized and brought online. In Myanmar, little to no progress has been made to put this infrastructure in place. Another factor is the medium-to long-term effect of an ASEAN economic community on the industrial structure of the region, as countries divide tasks among themselves according to their comparative advantages. Myanmar is home to a number of inefficient state-owned enterprises and private companies, including state-run automobile factories, that will not be internationally competitive. It is likely that most of these companies will struggle to survive in a more competitive environment. The birth of an ASEAN economic community is likely to bring serious costs for Myanmar in terms of reorganizing its industrial structure. How the government responds to this challenge will be of vital importance in the medium to long term (Umezaki 2014: 19–20).

Yet another point concerns efforts toward national reconciliation with the armed ethnic minority groups. According to government sources, Myanmar is home to 135 ethnic groups, including the Burmans, who make up around 70 percent of the population. For more than sixty years since independence, conflict has been ongoing with armed insurgents belonging to ethnic minorities including the Karen National Union, Karenni National Progressive Party, New Mon State Party, and Kachin Independence Organization. In August 2011, Thein Sein announced a three-stage peace plan. In November 2013 a cease-fire was reached with thirteen armed groups, but negotiations failed to make progress with three others, including the Kachin Independence

Organization. Thein Sein is presumably hoping to achieve a ceasefire across all of Myanmar's territory, and then to achieve national reconciliation through political dialogue with the insurgents. At some stage in this process, it will probably prove necessary to revise the constitution and take steps toward some kind of federal system that will be acceptable to the ethnic minority groups (Igarashi 2014: 18–21).

VIETNAM

Doi Moi: In Search of Peace and Economic Development

As we have seen, Thailand has been stuck in political instability and drift, while Myanmar has radically shifted its national strategy in recent years. In Vietnam, a similar transformation in national strategy took place from the mid-1980s to the mid-1990s, designed to ensure the survival of its regime. Vietnam was reunited in 1975, after wars of liberation that had lasted since 1945. The following year, the Vietnamese Workers Party changed its name to the Communist Party, and a decision was taken to reconstruct the south along socialist lines, based on the ideal of "poverty-sharing socialism" (Furuta 2009). This decision drove ethnic Chinese to leave the country and aggravated the relationship between Vietnam and China, which had been tense since the rapprochement between United States and China in 1972. In the meantime, Pol Pot's Khmer Rouge seized power in Cambodia in 1975. The Pol Pot regime appealed to anti-Vietnamese nationalism to consolidate its rule within Cambodia, while killing their internal "enemies." From 1977 onward, conflict along the border intensified, prompting Vietnam to lend its support to anti–Khmer Rouge forces. At the end of 1978, Vietnam invaded Cambodia and toppled the Pol Pot regime. China reacted by sending troops to its border with Vietnam in February 1979 to "punish" Vietnam. The invasion of Cambodia led Vietnam to become increasingly dependent on the Soviet Union. At home, the ideals of "poverty-sharing socialism" were resisted by people in the south, while losing support in the north. The country fell into a serious economic and security crisis.

The reformist Doi Moi (Renovation) policy was born in response to this crisis. To overcome the crisis and maintain the party state system, Vietnam decided that its chief strategic objectives were to maintain peace and economic development. A decision was taken to make "economic strength," "appropriate defensive capability," and "wider international cooperation" the foundations of national strategy. This was the essential aim of the Doi Moi policy. The policy was proposed at the sixth National Congress of the Communist Party of Vietnam in December 1986 and implementation began in 1988.

The policy underlined the fact that introducing the principles of the market economy and adopting a mixed-economy model were crucial to rebuilding the Vietnamese economy. The government understood that getting the economy back on track was not something it could do alone and that economic development would require Vietnam to be an active participant in the international division of labor. Since then, economic development has become the main indicator of the stability and legitimacy of the party state system. The government has prioritized trade and encouraged direct investment. In foreign policy, it is vital to maintain a peaceful and stable international environment that will help economic development. The government has opened up Vietnam's economy, cultivated diplomatic relations with more countries, and begun playing a more active role in regional and international cooperation.

The government also decided to find peaceful solutions with the ASEAN countries regarding the conflict in Cambodia and with China on territorial disputes in the South China Sea. In line with this decision, Foreign Minister Nguyen Co Thach announced Vietnam's intention to join ASEAN in 1988, and Vietnam withdrew its troops from Cambodia in September 1989. At the seventh National Congress of the Communist Party of Vietnam in September 1991, the party changed its foreign policy from international socialist cooperation to a more multidirectional and international diplomatic strategy in the wake of the collapse of socialist regimes in the Soviet Union and Eastern Europe. In October 1991, the Paris Accords came into effect, and the conditions were in place for Vietnam to break out of its international diplomatic isolation. In November 1991, Vietnam normalized relations with China, and Japan resumed economic assistance in 1992. Vietnam became an official observer to ASEAN in 1992, and a full member in 1995.

In retrospect, it is clear that the period from the initial proposal of Doi Moi in 1986 to 1995 was a major turning point in Vietnam's economic development. From the second half of the 1980s, Vietnam was plunged into a serious crisis, facing rampant inflation, stagnant production, massive budget deficits, and a fall in the value of its currency. Vietnam responded by abandoning its policy of collectivization of agriculture in 1988. This immediately produced results, and in 1989 Vietnam became a net exporter of food for the first time in many years, becoming the world's third largest exporter of rice after Thailand and the United States. In 1989, it abolished food rationing and embarked on comprehensive liberalization of the command economy and scrapped state-controlled pricing. State-owned enterprises were granted autonomy and private-sector companies legalized. The state monopoly on international trade was scrapped, along with a shift to a fluctuating currency rate that matched market realities. All these vital policies were introduced during the same crucial period.

The Vietnamese economy grew nicely after these reforms. For the period 2000–2009, average economic growth was 7.3 percent per year, as per capita national income increased from $402 in 2000 to $1,174 in 2010. In 2001 Vietnam's trade dependency ratio exceeded 100 percent for the first time and reached 130 percent in 2005. Three ASEAN countries accounted for 10 percent of exports (Singapore, Malaysia, the Philippines) and three for 19 percent of imports (Singapore, Malaysia, Thailand), showing that Vietnam had started to integrate its economy into the transnational Southeast Asian production network and had to a certain extent successfully diversified its trading partners.

Shifting to an Omnidirectional Foreign Policy

Vietnam has taken special care in developing a new omnidirectional foreign policy strategy. This should be clear if we look at the actions of its leaders. At the National Congress of the Communist Party in 2006, Nong Duc Manh was elected as the general secretary of the Communist Party, and Nguyen Tan Dung appointed prime minister. Immediately after the congress, Manh visited China for talks with Hu Jintao and signed an agreement on economic and technological cooperation. Dung, meanwhile, visited Japan, where a joint statement was released on cooperation to build a strategic partnership for peace and prosperity in Asia. Party and government leaders' foreign visits repeatedly demonstrated this pattern in the years that followed. In 2008–2009, Manh visited Japan and China once each, while Prime Minister Dung visited China three times, Japan twice, and the United States once. Another leadership change took place in 2011. This time, Nguyen Phu Trong, number one in the party hierarchy, became secretary-general, number two Truong Tan Sang became president, and number three Nguyen Tan Dung became prime minister. That year, Truong visited China in October, and Prime Minister Dung visited Japan.

As this shows, Vietnam has worked hard in recent years to develop and nurture its relations with Japan and the United States. As a result, Vietnam has become the largest recipient of Japanese development assistance, and an important investment destination for Japanese companies.

The country has also signed a nuclear agreement with Japan, and an agreement for Japan to help build nuclear power stations in Vietnam. It has also greatly improved its relations with the United States since around 2000. Vietnam and the United States signed a bilateral trade agreement in 2001. In 2007, Vietnam joined the World Trade Organization. During a visit to the United States in 2008, Dung obtained the support of President George W. Bush for the sovereignty, safety, and territorial integrity of Vietnam. In the *Quadrennial Defense Review* in 2010, Vietnam was cited as a country with which the United States should look to build a "new strategic relationship." The same year, the first-ever defense dialogue took place between the US deputy assistant secretary of state for defense and Vietnam's deputy defense minister. In 2010, Vietnam announced that it would take part in the Trans-Pacific Partnership negotiations. In July 2013, it signed an agreement on a comprehensive partnership with the United States, followed by a nuclear treaty in May 2014. In July 2015 Secretary-General Nguyen Phu Trong visited the United States and met with President Obama.

Managing the Asymmetrical Relationship with China

The reason why Vietnam has put so much effort into strengthening its relations with Japan and the United States is China's ongoing attempts to change the status quo in the South China Sea by force. Historically, Vietnam bore the brunt of frequent invasions from China whenever a new empire arose there, and memories remain fresh of Deng Xiaoping's punitive expedition against Vietnam in 1979. Diplomatic relations between Vietnam and China were normalized after a summit meeting in 1990 and an agreement on a comprehensive political settlement to the conflict in Cambodia in 1991. But the relationship between the two countries is inevitably asymmetrical and unequal: as of 2014, China has a population that is fifteen times larger than Vietnam's, and an economy that is fifty-six times bigger.

For Vietnam, in the face of such an overwhelming asymmetry in all dimensions—population, land area, industry and technology, economic and military power—the best it can hope for in managing its relations with China is to make the best possible use of everything at its disposal as levers. During the Cold War, Vietnam's chief lever was the Soviet Union. In recent years, in addition to ASEAN and Russia, it has also taken to using Japan, the United States, and India as levers to help it stand up to China.

146 *Maritime Asia vs. Continental Asia*

How is Vietnam managing its relationship with China, particularly with regard to the territorial disputes over sovereignty in the South China Sea? Vietnam's position on the issue is quite clear. To use the words of Deputy Defense Minister Nguyen Chi Vinh in 2009, Vietnam's aim is to transform the "East Sea" (as the South China Sea is known in Vietnamese) into a "sea of peace and friendship and development." To that end, Vietnam calls on all concerned parties to exercise self-restraint, abide by their declarations, strengthen the code of conduct, and look to resolve disputes not by force but by peaceful means. But this emphasis on resolving issues through multilateral negotiations has come up against China's insistence on bilateral negotiations and its uncompromising strategy of steadily bringing areas of the South China Sea under its de facto control by force, increasing the activities of fisheries' observation vessels and other official shipping, and exploring for natural resources in disputed areas.

How can Vietnam respond to these challenges? Its answer has been to bolster its own naval capacity, and use ASEAN, as well as the United States and other countries, as levers. In 2010, Vietnam, with assistance from Russia, announced plans to construct a port at Cam Ranh Bay that would be capable of servicing naval ships from all countries, including submarines and aircraft carriers. In 2011, it decided to buy six Kilo-class submarines from Russia, three of which have already been deployed. The government has also granted India access to the military port at Nha Trang, north of Cam Ranh Bay, for its ships. The United States is not an ally of Vietnam. On the contrary, as the "National Defense White Paper" of 2009 makes clear, the United States is regarded as a potentially hostile power that has "abused" "democratic freedom, religious freedom, and human rights" to undermine Vietnamese solidarity. However, disputes over "sovereignty, sovereign rights and jurisdiction over the territories in the East Sea" have adversely affected national security and pose a serious threat to "the maritime economic development of Vietnam." The country must therefore respond to the threat from China by cooperating with Russia and India as well as the United States, Japan, and other countries. In national security, it works closely with Russia and India, and uses the United States and Japan as levers. Vietnam relies on cooperation with Japan to build important strategic infrastructure, including nuclear power stations, high-speed railways, and human resources training. It receives assistance from Russia for building and improving facilities in naval ports. It is fair to say that Vietnam is looking to use everything it can as levers to manage its asymmetry with China.

Economically speaking, the major challenges will be managing the creation of an ASEAN economic community and managing the asymmetrical relationship with China. As mentioned earlier, the integration of the industrial region around Hanoi and Hai Phuong with the supply-chain network centered on Guangzhou involves some tricky problems for Vietnam in terms of national security. However, simply trying to solve this problem by developing the industrial region around Ho Chi Minh City instead presents political problems of its own from the perspective of balanced regional development across the country. Another serious problem involves the costs involved in reorganizing the country's industrial structure when an ASEAN economic community comes into being, considering the inefficient state-owned enterprises that make up a large share of Vietnam's socialist market economy and its automotive, electronics, and electric appliance industries, which are not as competitive as those in Thailand and Malaysia.

How will Vietnam's party state attempt to deal with these challenges? The government, I believe, has not yet decided on a clear strategy. But my impression from talking to senior officials of the party's central committee is that however high the costs may be of adjusting the country's industrial structure, the government is determined to integrate Vietnam into the global economy and is looking to build up its industries by dealing with multinational companies such as Samsung Electronics on an individual basis.

According to recent reports, Samsung Display has invested 2.3 trillion Korean won in a factory in Vietnam producing organic EL display panels and has decided to increase the amount of its total investment to 370 billion yen by 2020. This investment is mostly in the production of small and medium-sized panels for smart phones. We may surmise that the government has decided on an alliance with Samsung to build a major production center for the electronics industry, capable of manufacturing core components. Vietnam is already an important production base for Samsung's smart phone components; in 2014, Vietnam's exports of mobile phones and smart phones were worth $24 billion, accounting for 16 percent of total exports. It is likely that exports of smart phones to the United States and other markets will increase once negotiations on the TPP are complete.[7]

In 2016, the National Congress of the Communist Party will be held and the National Assembly will convene to select the next party state leadership. Nevertheless, it is hard to imagine that there will be any major shift in national strategy. Vietnam and Thailand offer two contrasting cases in terms of the stability/instability of their politics and international environment. Thailand is blessed with a benign international environment, but its politics have been trapped for years in instability and drift. Nevertheless, the risks these pose to the survival of the country are small. By contrast, Vietnam faces an extremely challenging international environment, but the party state runs a stable political system and a consistent national strategy. Although it is not clear what Myanmar's political system will look like in the coming years, we can be reasonably sure that it will maintain the policy of openness it has followed since the shift to civilian government in 2011, at least if national reconciliation works out as hoped. In this light, it is probably fair to say that the future of mainland Southeast Asia depends greatly on how things develop in Thailand.

INDONESIA

From the New Order to Decentralized Democracy

What about the island nations of maritime Southeast Asia? Let's begin by looking at the situation in Indonesia. Following the collapse of Suharto's "New Order" in May 1998, Indonesia was ruled by a succession of relatively short-lived governments under B. J. Habibie (1998–1999), Abdurrahman Wahid (Gus Dur) (1999–2001), and Megawati Sukarnoputri (2001–2004). It was only during the presidency of Susilo Bambang Yudhoyono (2004–2014) that the country's politics finally became stable. Then, following peaceful legislative elections in April 2014, Joko "Jokowi" Widodo won a victory in the presidential election that July, becoming the first president to have risen to power from outside the ruling elite formed during the Suharto period and symbolizing the arrival of stable democratic rule in Indonesia.

Indonesia undertook major political reforms before it reached this point. Under Habibie, Wahid, and Megawati, freedom of speech, freedom of the press, and freedom of association and assembly were restored, and the constitution was extensively revised. Laws relating to political parties, elections, and the makeup of the national legislation were revised, along with laws defining the role of the armed forces, police, intelligence, regional governments, and other aspects of the political system. The political system changed from the centralized authoritarian system of government put in place under Suharto to a decentralized democratic system. The political stability achieved during Yudhoyono's presidency was built on the back of this.

The main characteristics of Indonesia's decentralized democratic system of government can be summarized as follows. The first thing to note is that the current system was the product of four years of constitutional reform. On the understanding that the 1945 constitution had made the prolonged period of dictatorship under Suharto possible, constitutional revisions were carried out every year for four years, based on restoring the fundamental sovereignty of the people, respect for basic human rights, and separation of powers. At the end of this period, after a process of trial and error, the country wound up with what was in effect a new constitution. The president was limited to two terms, for a total of ten years in office, and the president's right to dissolve the National Assembly was explicitly denied. The constitution gave the People's Representative Council the right to pass legislation, discuss and approve government regulations, and determine the national budget. Procedures for removing a president from office were changed, with the People's Representative Council alone given the right to petition the People's Consultative Assembly (comprising the People's Representative Council and the Regional Representative Council) to dismiss the president. The basic idea was to create a presidential democracy with a weak president and a strong representative assembly (on the reforms of the political system during this period, see Matsui and Kawamura 2005: 75–99).

Reflecting these constitutional changes and the amendments to laws relating to the political system that were carried out in tandem, elections took place in 1999, 2004, 2009, and 2014. The results for 2004, 2009, and 2014 are given in Table 3.11. As the table shows, seats were held by six national (or secular) parties and four Islamic parties. The secular parties are the Indonesian Democratic Party of Struggle, headed by former president Megawati Sukarnoputri; the Golkar Party, which was established as the government political organization under Suharto; the Great Indonesia Movement Party (Gerindra), led by Suharto's former son-in-law Prabowo Subianto; the National Democratic Party, which separated from Golkar; the People's Conscience Party (Hanura), led by Wiranto, former commander-in-chief of the armed forces; and the Democratic Party, led by former president Yudhoyono. The Islamic parties are the National Awakening Party, founded by former president Adburrahman Wahid, which derives its support from the Nahdlatul Ulama, a traditional Islamic organization; the National Mandate Party, founded by Amien Rais, which derives most of its support from the modernist Islamic Muhammadiyah organization; the Prosperous Justice Party; and the United Development Party. The president was chosen by direct vote in separate presidential elections in 2004, 2009, and 2014.

Table 3.11 Indonesian Elections: Seats Won and Share of Vote, 2004, 2009, 2014

	2004		2009		2014	
	Seats	Share of Vote (%)	Seats	Share of Vote (%)	Seats	Share of Vote (%)
Indonesian Democratic Party of Struggle (PDI-P)	109	18.53	94	14.03	109	18.95
Partai Golkar	127	21.58	106	14.45	91	14.75
Great Indonesia Movement Party (Gerindra)	—	—	26	4.46	73	11.81
Democratic Party (PD)	56	7.45	148	20.85	61	10.91
National Mandate Party (PAN)	53	6.44	46	6.01	49	7.59
National Awakening Party (PKB)	52	10.57	28	4.94	47	9.04
Prosperous Justice Party (PKS)	45	7.34	57	7.88	40	6.79
United Development Party (PPP)	58	8.15	38	5.32	39	6.53
National Democratic Party (Nasdem)	—	—	—	—	35	6.72
People's Conscience Party (Hanura)	—	—	17	3.77	16	5.26
Other	50	17.33	0	18.29	0	1.65
Total	550	100	560	100	560	100
Four major Islamic parties		32.5		29.09		29.95
Government coalition	391		423		246	
Opposition alliance	109		137		314	
Other	50		0		0	

Source: Institute of Developing Economies–Japan External Trade Organization (IDE-JETRO), *Ajia doko nenpo* [Yearbook of Asian affairs], 2005, 2010, 2015.

As Table 3.11 makes clear, the norm is that multiple parties have substantial representation in the National Assembly. Results in the 2004, 2009, and 2014 elections show a tendency toward a more even distribution between the parties both in terms of seats and in number of votes. Another factor is that under the Yudhoyono administration, the Prosperous Justice Party and other members of the ruling coalition frequently acted against the government in their own interests, in alliance with opposition parties. This means that negotiations with the leaders of both government and opposition parties are an extremely important part of the president's job in running the government.

Increasing Decentralization

Decentralization also progressed between the Habibie and Megawati Sukarnoputri administrations. In 1999, laws on local government and on the financial balance between the central and regional governments established provinces and cities as the basic units of local government, and decreed that at least 25 percent of state revenue should be allocated by the central government to local governments (10 percent of it to provinces, 90 percent to districts and cities). These laws decentralized political and economic powers away from the central government. In 2004, they were revised again, and direct elections were introduced for heads of local government—provincial governors, district heads, and mayors.

One of the characteristics of the system of local government in Indonesia is that setting up new local governments is quite easy. When a new province, district, or city is established, the number of official positions increases: the head of government and his or her deputy, together with civil servants, members of the regional assembly, and so on. There is also a guaranteed source of funding from the central government. For this reason, since 1999 numerous new local governments have been established. In 1998, there were 28 provinces and 314 districts and cities; by 2008, this number had increased to 41 provinces and 478 districts and cities. Allocations of funding from the central government to the regions increased from 19 percent in 2001 to 34 percent in 2007. Though I don't have the most recent figures, the general trend is clear: as decentralization has proceeded, so has the allocation of resources from the center to the regions. This has provided an incentive to establish more local governments and has made the positions of heads of local government more important.

In these circumstances, the introduction of direct elections for heads of local governments has brought unexpected political consequences. As new local governments have been established, it has become possible for ethnic and religious minority groups, even if they are quite small in absolute numbers, to make up a majority within a given local area, and as a result identity politics based on ethnicity has become confined to the level of local politics.

In this sense, one of the characteristics of Indonesia's political system is that in the center the country has a weak president and a strong National Assembly, while in the relationship between the center and the regions, the central government is weak and the local governments are strong. This can be seen clearly in funding for infrastructure development projects. For such projects implemented by the central government, the government needs the approval of the National Assembly for each individual project. Coordination with local governments is also required. The ratio of contributions to the funding for infrastructure projects varies from year to year, but in 2007 the central government, provincial government, and district and city governments contributed 43 percent, 21 percent, and 36 percent respectively to infrastructure projects.

Another area that reflects the characteristics of this decentralized democracy is the appointment of cabinet ministers. Even allowing for differences between different governments, in order to achieve a ruling coalition, governments have to assign a certain number of cabinet positions to the political parties. Also, in order to reflect and balance the ethnic and religious diversity of the country, cabinet positions also need to be allocated to representatives of the various ethnic groups.

Another characteristic of the system of decentralized democracy is that since identity politics based on ethnicity is largely contained at the regional level, economic issues—poverty reduction, employment, and prices in particular—have become major concerns in national politics, even though Islam-based identity politics has gained momentum more recently. This has led to a new consensus that the purpose of politics is economic growth, albeit in a different form from the consensus that prevailed under Suharto. Technocrats have historically played an important role in government, particularly in running the economy, and the proportion of technocrats in the cabinet serves as a useful indicator of the government's priorities in terms of balancing future productivity against wealth redistribution today.

In societies riven by ethnic, religious, or ideological divides, democratic systems based on a majority vote can tend to collapse because of opposition and protest from minority groups, and there is a school of thought that power-sharing and group autonomy are better ways of recognizing the rights of minorities than majoritarianism. Several countries employ what is known as consociational democracy of this kind (Tsunekawa 2006). As we will see, this model is useful when considering the political situation in Malaysia. However, despite the diversity of Indonesian society—ethnically, religiously, and ideologically—for historical reasons it has preferred a decentralized type of democracy to this kind of consociational democracy. In the mid-1960s, Indonesia underwent a catastrophe when Sukarno's revolutionary politics brought economic collapse and anticommunist purges that claimed perhaps 500,000 lives. The experience taught people that they wanted nothing more to do with ideological politics. In the name of Suharto's "stability and development," an authoritarian politics of economic development was introduced. For more than thirty years, the system worked well, and the legitimacy of this politics was widely accepted. But Suharto's politics of stability and development collapsed in the midst of the Asian financial crisis. By this time, the Suharto regime had gone on for too long, and his family politics had become synonymous with cronyism, corruption, and nepotism. The trial-and-error experiments with democratization and decentralization started as soon as Suharto was gone, and by the middle of the first decade of the 2000s a new decentralized democratic system was in place.

The terrorist attacks carried out by al-Qaeda-affiliated Jemaah Islamiyah, the sectarian conflicts in Maluku and Poso (Central Sulawesi), and the civil war in Aceh, as well as the arrival of identity politics into local government with the introduction of the new system of directly elected local government officials, led to a renewed national consensus that the most important issues facing national politics were economic growth and the survival of Indonesia as a unitary state.

As of this writing it is now seventeen years since the fall of Suharto, and four general elections and three presidential elections have been peacefully held without major problems. It is probably fair to say that democracy is now firmly established in Indonesia. Nevertheless, among people old enough to remember the Suharto years, a considerable number look back on those times with nostalgia and compare them favorably with today. This is one reason why Suharto's former son-in-law Prabowo Subianto, who was responsible for brutal clandestine warfare in the 1990s as commander of the army's special forces and chief of the Strategic Reserve Command, emerged as a leading candidate in the 2014 presidential election. He appealed to people by promising a kind of decisive politics. He also appealed to Islam to mobilize the support of pious Muslim voters. But in the end the Indonesian people opted for Jokowi and his promise of "clean politics." What will the new government look like? How is it promising to tackle the issues and challenges that today's Indonesia faces? I would like to address these questions briefly in the sections that follow.

The Middle-Income Trap and Management of Indonesia's Territorial Waters

Let us look at the economy first. The Indonesian economy faces a major turning point. Since the 2008 global financial crisis, Indonesia has enjoyed reasonably good economic growth on the back of the US policy of quantitative easing and an export boom for its primary resources like coal and palm oil. But the Federal Reserve Board's policy of quantitative easing is coming to an end, and the slowdown of the Chinese economy is lowering prices for Indonesia's natural resource exports. Meanwhile, Indonesia's per capita national income passed $3,500 in 2012, and how to avoid the middle-income trap will be a major challenge in the coming years. Indonesia will have to come up with a new growth model, by building infrastructure such as power plants, highways, ports, and airports; deregulating the economy and improving the investment climate; supporting SMEs; and investing in human resources development and social safety nets.

Another issue concerns foreign policy and national security. The balance of power in the Asia Pacific region is changing fast. During the years of Suharto's rule, the major challenge for national security was to maintain internal order. Today, however, the separatist movements are no longer an issue except in Indonesian Papua, and Islamist terrorist groups are largely contained—though we do not know what might happen when fighters who have joined ISIS return home. Indonesia also faces unilateral Chinese actions in the South China Sea and needs to find ways to assert control over its territorial waters.

Infrastructure, Maritime Strategy, and Industry

How is the new government tackling these challenges? Let's first consider infrastructure development. The government decided to cut spending on fuel subsidies, reducing government spending from 276 trillion to 81 trillion rupiah. At roughly 1,000 rupiah to the yen, this is equivalent to savings of around 2 trillion yen. The government has also announced that it will spend around three-quarters of these savings (around 1.5 trillion yen) on infrastructure and use the remainder (around 0.5 trillion yen) to build a social safety net. This decision will make it possible to direct more funding to infrastructure development than was possible during the Yudhoyono administration. This alone, however, will not be enough. It is estimated that Indonesia will require 50 trillion yen in infrastructure funding over the next five years, of which the government will be able to provide only 15 trillion. Another 35 trillion will have to be funded by other sources. There is no clear answer yet to this question, and this is why people are placing so much hope in the prospects for economic cooperation with China. Nevertheless, the decision to cut the fuel subsidy has improved the prospects for Indonesia's macroeconomic stability. What remains to be seen is what the government's priorities will be. Will the new investment go primarily to much-needed improvements in traffic infrastructure in Jakarta, to improving the infrastructure of daily life in major cities around the country, to industrial infrastructure around the capital and port facilities in Java or building highways in the "outer islands"? How much should be spent on what kind of projects and in which regions of the country? And what kind of framework should be put in place to make these decisions? These are crucial questions that will not be easy to answer. At the moment, the situation remains opaque.

There is no doubt that economic cooperation with China will play a vital role in funding infrastructure projects. Chinese fixers are already on the scene, and it would be no surprise if a major scandal broke out at any moment. National Democratic Party leader Surya Paloh, for example, is one of the country's major political bosses alongside Megawati Sukarnoputri. He has close associations with a Chinese businessman named Sam Pa and is involved in a wide range of business activities with him. According to media reports, Sam Pa has oil and mining interests in countries such as Zimbabwe, Venezuela, Argentina, Guinea, Tanzania, and Madagascar, and operates a joint venture company in Zimbabwe together with a member of President Mugabe's secret police. In Madagascar he is said to have signed an investment contract worth some $20 billion immediately after that country's coup d'état. Ahead of Prime Minister Li Keqiang's visit to Angola (in May 2014), Sam Pa was in the country to arrange economic cooperation projects including infrastructure building and natural resource deals.[8]

Now let us look at the president's idea of turning Indonesia into a global maritime fulcrum. This plan was already mooted during the presidency of Abdurraham Wahid (Gus Dur). As a major maritime state, Indonesia has a larger stretch of territorial waters than any other country. At present, however, Indonesian government sources claim that some 90 percent of the country's marine resources are being "stolen" by unlicensed fishing vessels from foreign countries—though it is uncertain how much evidence there is for these figures.[9] President Joko Widodo now says his government will make effective control over Indonesia's territorial waters a priority, as well as improving port facilities, increasing maritime traffic, and working to reenergize Indonesia's fisheries and shipbuilding industries and develop offshore resources.

The president has invested considerable energy and attention in this project, and recently appointed a new coordinating minister of maritime affairs, along with three other coordinating ministers in charge of political, legal, and security affairs; economic affairs; and public welfare. At the moment, however, this is acting as more of a negative than a positive. What happens if the responsibility for infrastructure development of port facilities is in the hands of the coordinating minister for maritime affairs, but the responsibility for roads and railways lies with the coordinating minister for economic affairs? At the moment, questions like this remain unanswered.

We also need to be aware that the president lacks any experience in diplomacy and national security policymaking and that without anyone serving as his permanent national security adviser, he may mishandle maritime affairs and create diplomatic tensions with neighboring states. What I have in mind is the way in which Indonesia has dealt with foreign-registered fishing boats caught carrying out unlicensed fishing. I will not go into details here, but in the first six months since the new government took office, unlicensed fishing boats from Vietnam, Thailand, Malaysia, and China were seized and sunk on the orders of the president. There are serious concerns about the destabilizing effect this might have on relations with other ASEAN countries, and the breakdown in trust that might result. For example, between May and July 2014, there were tensions between China and Vietnam when boats belonging to a Chinese state-owned enterprise were found to be exploring for offshore resources in the South China Sea. Vietnam's prime minister Nguyen Tan Dung visited President Yudhoyono in secret to ask him to intervene to help bring about a peaceful resolution to the crisis. This was possible because of the trust that existed between the two leaders. But a similar relationship of trust does not exist between Jokowi and Dung—and even worse, the new president may not even understand why such relationships are so important.

The third policy area we need to examine is the promotion of manufacturing industries and digital innovation, the downstreaming of resources industries, and human resources development. Indonesia made a start on this policy area under Yudhoyono, but in recent years Indonesia's economic growth has slowed to between 4 percent and 5 percent, and the country has a current account deficit. As the Chinese economy slows, the price of primary commodities has fallen. As exports of these commodities become sluggish, this leads to an unfavorable balance of trade. And since balance on services is negative, as trade deficit increases, this has a knock-on effect on the current account deficit, creating a vicious circle. The only way to deal with this is to implement policies that will stimulate manufacturing, promote innovation, and help to increase exports. This is why so much hope is placed on direct investment by Japanese companies, and also why the economy is attempting to move from the export of primary commodities to a new model built on processing natural resources at home and exporting finished products with greater value added. But this will depend on trading partners, and it is impossible to know at the moment whether or to what extent these strategies will go according to plan. As part of efforts to stimulate digital innovation and improve professional training, the

Department of Higher Education was recently separated from the Ministry of Education and incorporated into a new Ministry of Research, Technology, and Higher Education. It remains to be seen whether this reorganization will achieve its purpose in the years to come.

As we have seen, Indonesia's strategy under President Joko Widodo is informed by the politics of economic growth (infrastructure building, promotion of manufacturing and digital innovation, downstreaming of resource industries) and a vision for Indonesia's position as a maritime hub. But given the nature of the Indonesian political system, characterized by a weak presidency and strong National Assembly, together with a weak central government and strong regions, it is hard to imagine that everything will proceed according to the wishes of the president. Furthermore, the current president does not even have his own political party, and is merely, as former president Megawati Sukarnoputri has put it, a member of the Indonesian Democratic Party of Struggle. To what extent such a person will be able to overcome the systemic hurdles of the Indonesian political system and his own lack of political experience and demonstrate political leadership remains to be seen; even though the chance of a major change in national strategy is slight, there remains a real possibility that political drift will gradually erode the hopes and expectations that people have placed in the president.

MALAYSIA

Malays, Chinese, and Indians

Indonesia is a plural society, diverse both ethnically and religiously. In its attempts to manage these social divisions, the country has undergone a process of trial and error, from a parliamentary democracy in the 1950s and "guided democracy" under Sukarno, through the centralized authoritarian rule under Suharto, before arriving at today's decentralized democratic system, only to find identity politics becoming more pronounced in recent years. Malaysia has followed more or less the opposite path. Ahead of Malayan independence, three political parties representing the Malay, Chinese, and Indian communities reached a grand bargain between them, on the basis of which a system of "consociational democracy" was introduced. This system, and the "Bumiputera" policy of de facto favoritism for Malays practiced under it from the 1970s, both came under increasing pressure from around the time of the Asian financial crisis in 1997–1998.

To understand why this happened, we need to look back at the political history of Malaysia. Since the race riots of 1969, the Barisan Nasional (BN, National Front) has formed the chief plank in a ruling coalition, under the name of achieving "ethnic peace." In the 1970s and 1980s, before the financial crisis, the BN held a two-thirds majority in the National Assembly, necessary for amending the constitution. Further, two-thirds of the BN's seats were held by the United Malays National Organization (UMNO). In practice, UMNO controlled Malaysia. As the leading force in Malaysian politics, UMNO made the eradication of social and economic disparities between ethnic groups the top priority of national policy. Through its new economic policy and the national development policy that succeeded it, the party aimed to improve the social and economic position of Malays, and to create a Malay middle class through state-led economic and education policy. This was the basic policy (Khoo 2006: 178).

It is fair to say that these policies were successful to a considerable extent. The percentage of Malays owning company shares rose from 2.4 percent in 1970 to 19.3 percent in 1990, and Malay employees in manufacturing rose from 21.2 percent to 44.0 percent over the same period (Kaneko 2011: 77).

The Mahathir Years:
Industrialization and the Islamic Revival

Malaysia's political economy underwent major changes during the time of Mahathir Mohamad as prime minister (1981–2003). Under the rubric of "Malaysia Inc.," Mahathir encouraged joint ventures with Japanese and Korean companies and worked to develop heavy industries in Malaysia. Investment was liberalized, a policy that coincided nicely with the expansion of Japanese companies overseas following the Plaza Accord (1985), bringing industrialization to Malaysia from the second half of the 1980s into the late 1990s (Khoo 2006: 182–183). From around 1990, privatization of state-owned enterprises led to the creation of a Malay business elite.

The rise of a Malay middle class and the increasingly middle-class nature of Malaysian society as a whole brought major changes to Malaysian politics. One change was the increasing business orientation of UMNO. Originally, UMNO drew most of its support from farmers, elementary school teachers, and public servants. At the party convention in 1981, for example, some 40 percent of delegates were school teachers. By the end of the 1980s, however, business managers and entrepreneurs were the main source of the party's support.

In the late 1980s, business owners and executives made up around 1.4 percent of the Malay population, but came to make up 25 percent of UMNO delegates, while school teachers and public servants fell to 19 percent and 23 percent of the total respectively (Torii 2001). Mahathir's policy of privatizing state-owned enterprises and relying on private firms for public works and infrastructure development was instrumental in UMNO's shift to business. UMNO shared the benefits of this policy with its members to bolster the basis of its support in society. Malay business owners and executives joined UMNO in the hope of winning contracts for infrastructure projects using private businesses, threw their money around, and came to occupy important positions in the central and regional party. With time, UMNO grew into a huge machine for distributing largesse.

Another factor is the revival of Islam among the Malay community, particularly among middle-class Malays. Since the 1970s, the pious have been an increasingly important presence in Muslim populations around the world. The heightened visibility and importance of Islam in people's everyday lives is known as the Islamic Revival.

This is different from the Islamism that has also been an important political trend around the world over the same period. To use Ōtsuka Kazuo's terms (2000), we can describe Islamism as a political ideology that aims to establish an Islamic state. The Islamic Revival, by contrast, refers to a phenomenon in which symbols and actions widely acknowledged to be Islamic are given greater prominence in daily life, and come to exert an increasingly important influence on various aspects of Muslims' lives. The Islamic Revival is not only about extremist Islamic movements or societywide political activities, but also involves a growing role for religion on the personal level of individual salvation. This can be seen in the increasing number of women wearing headscarves.

Since the 1980s, the number of women wearing the hijab has increased across the Islamic world, whether in Egypt, Malaysia, or Indonesia. The trend is particularly noticeable among relatively young, urban women with a high level of education. Some of these women may well sympathize with Islamist ideas, but many others are eager to distance themselves from such movements. Nevertheless, the decision to wear a headscarf is not a simple return to the cultural practices of women of their mothers' or grandmothers' generation. In fact, it is an extremely contemporary phenomenon. Muslims today are well aware of the existence not only of other religions, but also of different types of Muslims. They know that some Muslims have beliefs that differ from their own. Through comparisons with such people, Muslims reflectively reconfirm their own faith and the faith of others around them, coming to consider their religion objectively and often deliberately and self-consciously choosing those aspects that they regard as "Islamic." This is at the heart of the Islamic Revival movement. In Malaysia, this movement has had an important impact not only on Muslims educated in Malay who have received an Islamic education, but also among Malays educated in English. To tap into this movement, UMNO welcomed Anwar Ibrahim, the head of the Muslim Youth Movement of Malaysia (ABIM), into the party. Anwar rapidly rose in the party hierarchy and in 1993 became deputy prime minister.

During the 1980s and 1990s, UMNO enhanced the legitimacy of its rule by positioning itself as the protector of the economic interests and Islamic identity of Malays. From 1993 to 1998, during what we can now see as the zenith of Mahathir's period in office, the combination of Mahathir as prime minister and Anwar Ibrahim as his deputy seemed to symbolize the success of Malaysian politics under UMNO rule. Partly aided by direct investment from Japanese corporations, the Malaysian economy grew steadily, and the international environment was also stable. Under the "Look East" policy, Mahathir strengthened Malaysia's relations with Japan and South Korea, and advocated the formation of an East Asian economic group. In 1991, the country published its "Vision 2020," and started on a policy of national development. The aim of the vision was to achieve average annual growth of 7 percent for the next twenty years, and make Malaysia into a developed country by 2020, at the same time constructing a unified nation-state rooted in the identity of the people of Malaysia.

This national development policy, like the new economic policy that preceded it, aimed to correct the social and economic disparities between ethnic groups, and to nurture Malay businesspeople as the advance guard of Malaysia Inc., while also liberalizing investment, and welcoming direct investment from multinational corporations and portfolio investment by institutional investors (Khoo 2006: 186). The government also liberalized university education, and from the mid-1990s also allowed private universities to be founded.

The East Asian Financial Crisis and Political Drift

It was in these circumstances that the East Asian financial crisis hit Malaysia. This triggered a systemic crisis in the rule of the BN coalition and its Bumiputera policy, which had originally been carried out in the name of correcting social and economic disparities between ethnic groups, but had long since become a de facto policy of privileging Malays and cultivating a Malay business elite. During the 1990s, Anwar Ibrahim and the ABIM activists, business owners, and entrepreneurs who supported him gradually became more powerful within UMNO. Nevertheless, Mahathir continued to have the final say over the distribution of interests and privileges. The tension that built up between these two groups was to a certain extent a generational conflict. It was in this context that Mahathir and Anwar fell out over their differing views of the East Asian financial crisis and the policy measures the government should take to respond to it. The crisis started in July 1997 in Thailand, soon spreading to South Korea and Indonesia, and then to Malaysia in 1998.

The Malaysia ringgit plunged in value against the dollar, and companies that had borrowed in dollars on the international markets faced a debt crisis. Asset prices fell and the stock market collapsed, plunging the entire economy into recession. Anwar's proposed response was to cooperate with the IMF, raise interest rates, liberalize the markets, and reform the financial sector and governance—in other words, to overcome the crisis by dismantling Mahathir's Malaysia Inc. (Khoo 2006: 187). In late 1997, as deputy prime minister and finance minister, Anwar advocated a policy of high interest rates and fiscal austerity, a policy that soon pushed Malay-run businesses to the brink of bankruptcy. Mahathir's response to the crisis was different. His view was that the best recipe for overcoming the crisis was to boost public spending, inflating the economy and saving Malay companies from collapse. In January 1998, this was adopted as official government policy by the National Economic Action Council, established in the prime minister's office.

The deep disagreement between Mahathir and Anwar Ibrahim threatened to split the government in the midst of a major financial crisis. Anwar challenged Mahathir at the 1998 UMNO general conference and ran against him in the election for UMNO president. But Anwar failed to defeat Mahathir, and in September 1998, Mahathir dismissed him from his positions as deputy prime minister and finance minister. The government introduced capital control and a fixed exchange rate system. The economy was inflated through fiscal easing and increased government spending. Malay-owned firms were rescued through capital injections and nationalization. The Japanese government also offered assistance in the form of the Miyazawa Initiative. By the second half of 1999, Malaysia had managed to accumulate sufficient reserves of foreign currency through a positive balance of trade, and the economy was on the road to recovery. Mahathir had succeeded in rescuing Malaysia

Inc. But the sacking, arrest, and incarceration of Anwar Ibrahim caused serious divisions within the Malay community (Khoo 2006: 189–190).

Malaysian politics began to drift and lose direction. UMNO split, and a new party, the People's Justice Party (Parti Keadilan Rakyat), was formed out of Anwar's support base in ABIM and the non-Malay NGOs founded around the country in the 1980s and 1990s. The People's Justice Party raised questions that had not previously been major topics for debate in the Malay community, including human rights, fairness, justice, and democracy, and organized demonstrations against the government. Malay NGOs that drew their members from the Malay middle class also became active around this time.

Moves began toward the formation of a nonracial, pan-Malaysian opposition alliance. In the run-up to the elections of December 1999, the Malay-based Pan-Malaysia Islamic Party (PAS), People's Justice Party, and Malaysian People's Party allied with the non-Malay Democratic Action Party (DAP) to form a multiethnic opposition alliance called the Barisan Alternative. Nevertheless, the 1999 elections were won by the ruling coalition. Although Malay voters moved in considerable numbers from UMNO to the People's Justice Party and the PAS, many Chinese and Indian citizens cast their votes for the ruling coalition out of concern about instability due to political fragmentation in the Malay community (Kaneko 2011: 82).

Following the shock of the al-Qaeda terrorist attacks of 11 September 2001, antagonism grew between the Islamic party PAS and the Chinese-dominated DAP, which advocated racial equality, and the opposition alliance disintegrated after two and a half years (Kaneko 2011: 83). Concluding that he was done with his job, Mahathir stepped down as prime minister in October 2003, and was succeeded by Abdullah Badawi. The new prime minister instituted an open and free style of politics, and during his time in office, non-Malay citizens began to call for equality among the different ethnic groups—openly calling for the abolition of preferential treatment for Malays. Following an intervention by Anwar to help mend the relationship between the PAS and the DAP, a new opposition coalition was formed between these two parties and Anwar's People's Justice Party (PKR).

At the 1999 election, the People's Justice Party was still an overwhelmingly Malay party. In 2008, however, it put up many non-Malay candidates and became a multiethnic party in name and reality. Since the election in 1999, many of the central figures in the NGOs that had supported the opposition forces put themselves forward as party candidates, and as Kaneko Yoshiki (2011) has noted, this maturation in civil society in Malaysia led to a shift to multiethnic party politics. The opposition coalition won a convincing victory in the 2008 elections, with the BN losing numerous seats in both the national council and the state assemblies. In the national council, the ruling party lost the two-thirds majority it needed in the lower house to revise the constitution. The opposition became the largest party in five of the thirteen states. At a stroke, Malaysian politics was transformed. The main reason was that Chinese and Indian Malaysians had transferred their support from the ruling coalition to the opposition (Kaneko 2011: 89).

Nevertheless, the UMNO-dominated ruling coalition could not simply drop the Bumiputera policy that favored Malays and Malay-owned businesses. As Mohamed Ariff (2012: 17–23), one of Malaysia's most respected economists, has argued, Malaysia has been searching for a new model since the East Asian financial crisis, struggling to decide what position it should occupy in a globalizing world. If correcting the social and economic disparities between ethnic groups was once the most pressing issue in Malaysia, today a more urgent concern is the problem of social and economic differences within ethnic groups. Malaysia's potential growth rate fell from 7.5 percent at the end of the 1980s to 5.5 percent in the 2010s, and the prospects of achieving its stated objective of becoming a developed country by 2020 now look remote. This is because inefficient Malay-run businesses are receiving preferential treatment. The technocrats in the Malaysian government are aware of this problem. But abolishing the Bumiputera policy would mean the collapse and destruction of UMNO and its BN coalition. The government continues to claim that, unlike Singapore, it is deliberately choosing to adopt a "second best" policy in the interests of "ethnic peace."

But it is obvious that the Bumiputera policy has hit a dead end. Direct investment from overseas has slowed, from an average annual increase of 9 percent from the years before the East Asian financial crisis, to just 4–5 percent today (Ariff 2012: 21). The frustrations of the Chinese and Indian populations are also increasing.

One sign of their resentment is the brain drain. Many young, ambitious, and gifted Chinese and Indian citizens go to study abroad and never come back. The Singaporean government knows this and offers scholarships to entice bright young Malaysians to the island state. Even so, the ruling coalition refuses to scrap the Bumiputera policy. The 2014 elections dramatically exposed the political dead end this had led to. The ruling coalition won a victory in the election, winning 222 seats to the opposition's 133. But the result was deceptive. The government won just 47 percent of the popular vote, compared to 51 percent for the opposition. The government had managed to win thanks to advantageous electoral zoning and a system of constituencies that worked to the advantage of the ruling coalition.

The Path to Developed-Nation Status

In 2014, Malaysia's per capita gross national income was $10,800, making it doubtful whether the government will achieve its goal of Malaysia becoming a developed nation by 2020. As the global "brain circulation" continues to gather pace, Malaysia is routinely losing gifted young Chinese and Indian citizens as a result of government policy. By contrast, many ethnic Malays have fallen into the habit of believing that they will find senior positions in government or companies without working particularly hard, thanks to the preferential treatment they receive. It is not easy for the ruling coalition to scrap the Bumiputera policy now that this culture of entitlement has taken root. UMNO itself long ago became a machine for distributing benefits and emoluments.

To see how corrupt the system has become, it is enough to consider the suspected embezzlement of as much as $700 million in public funds by Prime Minister Najib Razak.[10] The Bumiputera policy has hit a wall, even though I would not say the government is doing nothing. In fact, it has taken a number of steps: participating in the TPP and working to reform its industrial sector under external pressure, and developing the economy of Johor thanks to the cross-border expansion of the Singaporean economy. It is also working to turn Malaysia into a hub of Islamic finance. The problem is that the government cannot take the most important decision to ditch the Bumiputera policy—that is the reality in Malaysia in 2015.

THE PHILIPPINES

Corazón Aquino's Reforms and the People Power Revolution

What about the Philippines? In Indonesia and Malaysia, the 1997–1998 East Asian financial crisis marked a decisive turning point. In the Philippines, the major turning point in recent history came earlier, with the crisis of 1983–1986, in the final years of the Marcos regime. In retrospect, we can say that decisions taken in the 1980s by Marcos and his successor, Corazón Aquino, largely shaped the framework of the political economy of the Philippines.

During the 1970s, Marcos called for a revolution from the center and embarked on a state-led revolution from above with a developmentalist regime. During the 1970s, this project enjoyed a fair degree of success, with the economy seeing annual growth rates of 6.2 percent on average. By the end of the 1970s, however, the Philippine economy entered a serious crisis. The country's dollar-denominated debt had ballooned from $5 billion in 1976 to $15 billion in 1981. A change of monetary policy at the US Federal Reserve in 1979 saw the official discount rate shoot up, and many Filipino companies were plunged into a severe debt crisis.

The assassination of Senator Benigno "Ninoy" Aquino in 1983 transformed the economic crisis into a serious political crisis. The government attempted several times in the period 1983–1985 to salvage the situation by devaluing the peso and raising tariffs, as well as restricting imports and preventing capital outflow, but with no effect. Meanwhile, in the wake of the Aquino assassination, antigovernment demonstrations and protests spread among the Manila middle classes and upper classes. In the provinces, communist guerrillas gained ground and became an increasing threat to the regime (Shiraishi 2000: 169–171; Raquiza 2011: 40–41).

In many countries in the region, the ruling elite controls the state apparatus, especially using the armed forces as its power base. This was the case with the ruling elite of Indonesia under the Suharto regime, the old order in Thailand, and the junta in Myanmar. As a result, elite circulation has its own rhythm in these countries. Military officers and bureaucrats ascend the hierarchy with age, come to occupy important senior positions, and eventually retire from active service. A generational shift happens within the ruling elite according to this rhythm, as each generation of officers and officials accumulates power (and money) and then fades away from prominence when the next generation takes over. In the Philippines, however, the power base of the ruling elite exists outside the state apparatus, and the rhythm of elite circulation is different from that of the military and bureaucratic elite in other countries. This also means that the elite do not have automatic access to state resources. They have to assume an official position, as mayors, provincial governors, parliamentary members, and ministers, to gain access to state resources. Marcos mobilized and contained these locally entrenched politicians into his New Society Movement, while he relied on his trusted military officers for maintaining law and order and kept them in important positions within the military well past their retirement age and let technocrats and businesspeople closely associated with him manage the macro economy and run individual development projects. But the system he built started to crack as his health declined, and many of his development projects collapsed and the macro economy went into a crisis following the shift in US monetary policy. The political and economic crisis grew worse after the Aquino assassination, until eventually a coup attempt by a younger generation of officers associated with a faction of Marcos lieutenants triggered the People Power revolution of 1986 (Shiraishi 2000: 169–171).

Restoring Democracy and Dismantling the Developmentalist System

Corazón "Cory" Aquino, who came to power as president in the People Power revolution in 1986, faced two major challenges: restoring democracy and rebuilding the economy. Immediately after the revolution, Aquino set about dismantling the Marcos regime. Her government enacted a new constitution and restored the system that had been in place before martial law in 1973. After the revolution there was a rise of left-wing nationalism, and the Senate refused to ratify the military bases treaty with the United States, leading to the withdrawal of US forces from the Philippines. Aquino also set about ending the developmentalist system. Marcos had put his business associates, or "cronies," in charge of development projects. Aquino believed that this "crony capitalism," which had allowed the president's relatives and close friends to control the economy, caused the corruption and the economic crisis under Marcos, and set about dismantling it, confiscating companies under their control. She also reorganized the Department of Trade and Industry, abolishing the Bureau of Industrial Development in charge of industrial policy, and promoted liberalization of trade and tariff reduction (Raquiza 2011: 43–44). The Philippines thus made a major strategic turn by the early 1990s with the scrapping of US bases and liberalization of the economy.

Another point to note about the Philippine economy is the increasing importance of remittances from overseas. The educational expansion happened a generation earlier in the Philippines than in other Southeast Asian countries, and this together with Marcos's decision to encourage Filipinos to work overseas in the 1970s set the country on a different path of economic development from other Southeast Asian countries. In 1975, there were already 1,808 people in higher education for every 100,000 of the population in the Philippines; this rose to 2,641 per 100,000 in 1980, and to 2,760 in 1995. In Thailand, by contrast, there were only 316 people in higher education for every 100,000 of the population in 1975, and even in 1995 this had only risen to 2,096 (Hattori, Funatsi, and Torii 2002: 299). At the same time, the Philippine economy was in a deep crisis in the 1980s and was still struggling in the 1990s. As a result, many educated Filipino professionals looked for work overseas as engineers, business managers, doctors, and nurses. By 2002, their numbers had risen to 7.4 million, around 10 percent of the total population of the Philippines, and 21 percent of its working-age population. Remittances sent from overseas amounted to $7.5 billion, or 9 percent of the total GDP of the Philippines.

In 2011, some 9.5 million Filipinos (10 percent of the population) were working outside the country, and remittances were worth $23 billion. Between 22.5 and 35 million people in the Philippines depend on remittances for economic support, and this is the reason for the important role of consumption in economic growth in the Philippines (72 percent in 2010) compared with other Southeast Asian countries (Whaley 2012). This is also why it is more important to look at GNI rather than GDP in considering the Philippine economy. Philippine per capita GNI increased from $1,237 in 2000 to $2,829 in 2010. Although per capita GDP in 2014 was $2,865, Philippine per capita GNI exceeded $3,533, placing it on a par with Indonesian per capita GDP.

The Decline of Manufacturing and Growth of Service Sectors

Not a few scholars working on the Philippine political economy argue that the Philippines is an "anti-developmental state," pointing to the decline of the secondary industrial sectors (such as manufacturing, mining, and construction) in the Philippines (Bello, De Guzman, and Malig 2004; Raquiza 2011: 19). It is true that these sectors have shrunk as a share of the Philippine economy, from 26 percent in 1980 to 21 percent in 2009. The question is what this means for the Philippine political economy.

The expansion of education and remittances from overseas have helped service sectors such as retail, finance, and real estate to grow. At the same time, it has also brought an expansion in business process outsourcing in such areas as accounting, legal services support, advertising, computer programming, and market research. The call center business in the Philippines is worth $11 billion, and in

2010 this sector employed 683,000 people, with business process outsourcing not far behind (Whaley 2012).

This has led to a growing urban middle class in and around Manila and has also given rise to new movements in politics. To understand what this means, it is enough to look at how political alliances have been formed in recent years. These alliances form each time there is a presidential election. Traditional politicians, regional bosses, NGOs, and people's organizations form alliances around their candidate for president. If their candidate wins, all these various political forces and the people connected with them enter the government, place government ministries under their control, and implement their preferred policies. As a result, the government as a whole may not have any consistency and coherence in its policies. The president's political options also become limited. But some departments do continue to implement sensible and coherent policies, and the president allocates resources to fund these policies as a way of maintaining the support of the alliance. As a result, the government's performance tends to be uneven, varying wildly depending on which forces control which ministries, and what kinds of policies they look to implement there.

As the number of overseas workers has increased, remittances from overseas have come to play an ever more important role in the lives of the people, leading to an expansion of the services sector. These social and economic changes have had a huge significance for elite circulation. The 2010 presidential election came down to a contest between Benigno "Noynoy" Aquino III and Manuel "Manny" Vilar. Aquino, the son of former senator Benigno Aquino Jr., and former president Corazón Aquino, campaigned on a promise of "clean government." Vilar, who grew up in an area of Manila known for its slums, made his fortune in real estate development, particularly in housing development aimed at the lower middle classes.

In the world of real estate development in Manila, once you get beyond a certain level, the business is impossible without the involvement of politicians, from the president all the way down to mayors and councilors. In that sense, for Vilar, politics and business were two sides of the same coin, and as he built up his fortune he found himself naturally entering the inner circle of the political elite. Aquino came from "old money," from a family that had been prominent across three generations—but it would be an oversimplification to conclude because of this that Aquino is "clean" and Vilar "dirty." What is important is how they have made their fortunes. The Aquino family made their money as a farming family (sugar plantations) in an area that lost its international competitiveness decades ago. Vilar made his fortune on the back of the growing numbers of overseas workers, the increase in remittances, and the rise of the middle class. In the 2010 presidential election, Aquino won in part because Cory Aquino happened to die in 2009, bringing back memories of the 1986 revolution among the public.

Since coming to power as president, Aquino has enacted policies to meet the expectations of the Manila middle classes and overseas workers, while the macro economy has enjoyed stability thanks to the remittances from overseas, which now exceed 10 percent of GDP. He has worked to eradicate corruption, expand access to higher education, and improve infrastructure, and has become the most highly regarded president of the Philippines since independence. Socially, the Manila middle classes can now send their children to prestigious high schools and universities that would have been beyond their reach in the past. When scholars talk about politics in the Philippines, they often deploy the notion of "oligarchy," traditional politicians who dominate the government and local bosses who control their provinces. But a social revolution is quietly under way. Presidents in the Philippines serve a single term of six years. Looked at in the space of six or twelve years, every time a new president comes to office, the political alliances that support the administration change, and with them the people who occupy the important positions inside the various ministries. These shifts in personnel bring important changes to the Philippine political economy. The presidential election is approaching in 2016. At the moment, we do not know who the next president will be. The future of the Philippines will change considerably depending on who becomes the next president and on the nature of the political alliance that supports the winning candidate. But as a long-term trend, it is reasonably certain that we will continue to see a shift from old money to new, as the change in the ruling elite continues. The middle classes will continue to become more politically important as they become more prosperous on the back of remittances from overseas and the ongoing success of business process outsourcing.

SOUTHEAST ASIA: A SUMMARY VIEW

We can now summarize the overall state and prospects for Southeast Asia. In mainland Southeast Asia, the party state in Vietnam looks stable. In Myanmar too, if the country can manage the coming elections and a change of government without major unrest between 2015 and 2016, the country will probably enjoy political stability, and if national reconciliation stays on course, the transition to openness and democracy will continue. More worrying is the drift in Thai politics. In the long term, I still believe and hope that the country will move in the direction of liberal democracy and the market economy, but there is a growing risk that the political instability will continue until the current generation of the ruling elite is gone.

In maritime Southeast Asia, the Philippines looks to be on a stable economic growth trajectory, but in national security the question of how to manage relations with China is likely to become increasingly difficult in the years to come. The new government in Indonesia is still learning, and if the president is slow to learn, there is a risk that it may start losing its momentum and the trust of the people. In Malaysia, the ruling BN coalition and the Bumiputera policy have lost any useful purpose, but any dramatic change in the system looks unlikely in the near future.

NOTES

1. For an introduction to the Thai population census of 2015, see Suehiro 2015: 25.

2. I would note that Indonesia's religious, ethnic, and linguistic diversity varies considerably on a regional level. The 2015 census lumped together by region all the ethnic groups with a population of under 1 million and did not provide figures on regional ethnic and religious diversity. But the 2000 census tells us that there were more than a thousand ethnic groups in Indonesia. In the 2000 census, the population of the province of North Sumatra was 11.51 million. By ethnicity, this comprised 3.75 million Javanese (32.6 percent), 1.83 million Tapanuli Batak (15.9 percent), 1.12 million Toba Batak (9.7 percent), 910,000 Mandailang Batak (7.9 percent), 730,000 Nias (6.3 percent), 590,000 Karo Batak (5.1 percent), 570,000 Malays (5.0 percent), 390,000 Angkola Batak (3.4 percent), and 1.63 million people belonging to other ethnic groups. In terms of religion, there were 7.53 million Muslims (65.4 percent), 550,000 Catholics (4.8 percent), 3.06 million Protestants (26.6 percent), 20,000 Hindus, 320,000 Buddhists (2.8 percent), and 20,000 followers of other miscellaneous faiths. By contrast, Central Java and the special administrative region of Yogyakarta had a population of 34.04 million, made up of an ethnic majority of 33.31 million Javanese (97.9 percent), with the rest of the population made up of 340,000 Sundanese, 180,000 ethnic Chinese, 30,000 Tapanuli Batak, 20,000 Malays, 20,000 Madurese, and 140,000 from other ethnic groups. In terms of religion, there were 32.8 million Muslims (96.4 percent), 540,000 Catholics, 580,000 Protestants, and 110,000 "others." The population was much more homogeneous in Central Java than in North Sumatra.

3. In the Bangkok metropolitan region, the population recorded in the census (14.63 million) was 3 million higher than the number of registered residents (11.56 million). There was also a difference of 590,000 between the census

population and registered population in the six eastern provinces. In the northeast, by contrast, the census population was 3.91 million less than the registered population. Similar discrepancies were found in the north (520,000 lower on the census than registered) and south (510,000) of the country. This shows that many people have moved from the northeast to Bangkok and the industrial areas of the east of the country without changing their registration. The per capita regional income (or income per province) published by the National Economic and Social Development Board is calculated according to registered population. If we calculate the figures based on the actual population (as reported in the census), then the per capita GDP for the Bangkok metropolitan region in 2010 was not 413,000 baht but 326,000 baht, while the equivalent figure for the northeast was not 44,500 baht but 52,700 baht. In other words, the income discrepancies are probably not as wide in reality as the figures suggest.

4. On 6 September 2015, the National Reform Committee voted down a draft for a new constitution, postponing until 2017 the return to civilian rule previously planned for August–September 2016. "'Gun no kyōken' yōnin ga sōten ni, Tai kenpō sōan hiketsu," *Nihon Keizai Shimbun*, 7 September 2015.

5. Unless otherwise noted, my analysis of the current political and economic situation in Myanmar draws on the following studies: Kudō 2014a and 2014b: 2–5; Kudō and Kumagai 2014: 14–17; and Umezaki 2014: 18–21.

6. "Myanmā yotō Shue Man-tōshu kainin," *Reuters*, 13 August 2015.

7. "Samusun, Betonamu tōshi o 2400-oku-en tsumimashi, sumaho-yō yūki EL kōjō ni," *Nihon Keizai Shimbun*, 12 August 2015.

8. See "Sam Pa," https://en.wikipedia.org/wiki/Sam_Pa.

9. "Indonesia's Marine Policy: Fishing Trips—For the New Administration, the Path to Prosperity Is a Watery One," *The Economist*, 3 January 2015, https://www.economist.com/news/asia/21637451-new-administration-path -prosperity-watery-one-fishing-trips.

10. "Marēshia, Najibu-shushō ni kōkin ōryō giwaku, fujin nimo giwaku fujō, kokugai tōbō no kanōsei mo," 13 July 2015, https://jbpress.ismedia.jp/articles /-/44270.

4

Japan's Place in the Asia Pacific/East Asia/ Indo-Pacific Region

In the preceding three chapters I have looked at some of the long-term trends in the Asia Pacific/East Asia/Indo-Pacific region, discussed the region's geopolitical structure and political economy, and examined the national strategies of several Southeast Asian countries. By way of conclusion, this final chapter will consider Japan's place in the region.

THE STATE OF JAPAN IN 2015

Japan's Security Strategy

Let me begin with a review of recent developments in Japan, as of August 2015. It is nearly three years since Abe Shinzō began his second term as prime minister in December 2012. During that time, the government has pursued a vigorous foreign and security policy, as the following will suffice to show.

In November 2013, the Diet enacted legislation to establish the National Security Council to serve as a coordinating command center for foreign and security policy. The NSC duly opened in December that year. The activities of the new council focus on meetings between the prime minister, the chief cabinet secretary, and the foreign and defense ministers. A National Security Secretariat with a staff of sixty was established within the Cabinet Secretariat to serve the NSC's administrative needs.

Then, on 17 December, the government officially adopted a new national security strategy—the first time Japan had formulated a national security strategy in this way. Since it is readily accessible on the Cabinet

Secretariat's website, I will here merely provide a summary of the main elements of this document, which is central to an understanding of Japan's national security strategy.

The strategy declares that Japan will maintain its commitment to making a "'Proactive Contribution to Peace' based on the principle of international cooperation," by expanding and deepening cooperative relationships with partner countries, with "the Japan-US Alliance as the cornerstone." It underlines the importance of "building a comprehensive defense architecture" by implementing "joint operations" and "operations with flexibility and readiness." To deal with "gray-zone" situations, it states that Japan will "enhance the capabilities of the law enforcement agencies responsible for territorial patrol activities and reinforce its maritime surveillance capabilities" and "strengthen coordination among relevant ministries and agencies to be able to respond seamlessly to a variety of unexpected situations." In maritime security, it stresses Japan's role in maintaining and developing "Open and Stable Seas" upheld by a "maritime order based upon such fundamental principles as the rule of law, ensuring the freedom and safety of navigation and overflight, and peaceful settlement of disputes in accordance with relevant international law."

Mutual assistance is the other main element of the strategy. With respect to the Japan–United States alliance, the strategy emphasizes that Japan will look to strengthen cooperation with the United States in a broad range of areas, including ballistic missile defense, maritime security, space, cyberspace, and response to major natural disasters, by revising the Guidelines for Japan–United States Defense Cooperation. On cooperation with other partners, particularly countries in the Asia Pacific region "with which [Japan] shares universal values and strategic interests," the strategy says that Japan will enhance its strategic partnerships with Australia and further deepen and develop "cooperative relations with the ASEAN countries in all sectors." It also refers to the Strategic and Global Partnership with India, citing relations "in a broad range of areas, including maritime security." On relations with China, the document says that Japan will take a broad, long-term perspective, working to establish a "mutually beneficial relationship based on common strategic interests" and encouraging China to "play a responsible and constructive role" for the sake of regional peace, stability, and prosperity. Should China attempt to change the status quo by force, Japan will respond "firmly but in a calm manner."[1]

On 17 December, the government also adopted new guidelines for its national defense program and a program for medium-term defense (fiscal years 2014–2018). The new guidelines replace the concept of a "dynamic defense force" with the new idea of a "dynamic joint defense force," prioritizing the ability to respond flexibly to a wide range of situations and the capacity of the land, sea, and air forces to operate seamlessly together. The guidelines also say that a new amphibious rapid deployment brigade will be formed to defend remote islands and that intelligence, surveillance, and reconnaissance capabilities will be strengthened in the East China Sea and elsewhere.[2]

Following this, in April 2014 the cabinet adopted the "Three Principles on Transfer of Defense Equipment and Technology." These replaced the "Three Principles on Arms Exports," clarifying the conditions under which Japanese defense equipment may be transferred overseas. As well as facilitating security cooperation with other countries and enabling Japan to contribute to international peace efforts, the new policy seeks to maintain and strengthen the Japanese defense industry. It is worth noting that transfers to countries embargoed under previous principles remain prohibited under the new ones; the most substantial change is that under the new principles, transfers previously allowed on an exceptional basis are formally recognized as "cases where transfers may be permitted."

This new policy has brought even greater benefits than expected to Japan's security and defense cooperation. In June 2015, following the new policy's adoption, the Diet enacted the revised Act for Establishment of the Ministry of Defense, mandating the establishment of the Acquisition, Technology, and Logistics Agency. This agency is responsible for centrally managing the development, acquisition, and maintenance of defense equipment and controlling defense procurement costs, as well as promoting exports and joint development and production of defense equipment with other countries based on the "Three Principles on Transfer of Defense Equipment and Technology."[3]

Reinterpreting Article 9 of the Constitution While Preserving Its Basic Logic

On 1 July 2014, another cabinet decision committed the government to enacting security legislation and revising the interpretation of Article 9 of the constitution, the legal foundation of Japan's security policy, with regard to the right of collective self-defense. The cabinet decision aimed to adapt interpretations of the war-renouncing Article 9 to suit it to the present security environment without scrapping the basic logic underlying previous interpretations.[4] The reinterpretation still does not allow Japan to exercise the right of collective self-defense as generally understood in international law.

The constitution permits the right of self-defense only to the minimum extent: essentially, where the use of force is necessary to defend Japan from an "imminent and unlawful attack." The previous interpretation was that collective self-defense was prohibited on the grounds that it exceeded "the minimum extent necessary." The recent change modifies that interpretation slightly by recognizing collective self-defense as a means with which Japan may exercise force to "the minimum extent necessary" for defending itself. As of August 2015, the Diet is still debating the government's security package. This draft legislation concerns the very foundations of Japan's security policy, and the ultimate outcome of this debate will be of huge significance both for Japan's security and for the peace, stability, and prosperity of the vast region stretching from the Pacific to the Indian Ocean.

The Guidelines for Japan–United States Defense Cooperation were revised before the security package was put before the Diet. In December 2012, Prime Minister Abe instructed his defense minister, Onodera Itsunori, to look into possible revisions to the guidelines. In October 2013, the Japan–United States Security Consultative Committee (made up of the Japanese defense and foreign ministers and the US secretaries of defense and state) set to work on revisions, which were agreed by the two governments in April 2015. The guidelines define the general parameters and direction of Japan–United States cooperation, including bilateral action in the event of an attack against Japan (in accordance with the Japan–United States Security Treaty, and based on the 2013 national defense guidelines). As such, they expand Japan–United States defense cooperation in both geographical range and scope—encompassing threats in the new fields of space and cyberspace—in order to promote a peaceful and prosperous Asia Pacific and beyond.

The Prehistory of the New Security Policy

Of course, the Abe government deserves credit for formulating this series of important foreign and security policies and putting them into practice. But in fact, most of them had long been on the political agenda. Take "proactive pacifism," for example—Japan's commitment to making a proactive contribution to peace. This concept was first put forward in the 1980s. The issue of collective defense was already a major bone of contention at the time of the 1990–1991 Gulf War. And quite a few of the recently adopted policies were initially suggested by the Democratic Party government, particularly under Prime Minister Noda Yoshihiko. In the area of security as elsewhere, the Democratic Party was relatively free to put forward new policies, as long as they did not split the party, since it was not subject to the constraints on security policy imposed by successive Liberal Democratic Party governments since the Cold War through ministers' answers to questions in the Diet. One example of Democratic Party innovations was the idea of a "dynamic defense force" put forward in the 2011 national defense guidelines.[5] Formulated to replace the idea of a "basic defense force," this was the first attempt to address changes in Japan's security environment directly since the end of the Cold War. The "dynamic defense force" was replaced in the 2013 national defense guidelines by the idea of a "dynamic joint defense force," but in their essentials the two ideas are closely related. In June 2012 the Study Group on Defense Production and Technological Bases submitted a report to the minister of defense that laid the groundwork for the reformulation of the "Three Principles on Arms Exports," renamed the "Three Principles on Transfer of Defense Equipment and Technology." The report stressed the importance to Japan's defense industry and technology strategy of participating in joint international projects to develop and produce defense equipment.[6]

Cooperation in the Asia Pacific and Indian Ocean Region

Prime Minister Abe has also been a busy traveler since he took office, and has energetically engaged in summit diplomacy. In East Asia, South Asia, and Oceania alone, over the course of 2013 he visited Vietnam, Thailand, and Indonesia in January; Myanmar in May; Malaysia, Singapore, and the Philippines in July; Brunei in October; and Cambodia and Laos in November; and in December hosted the ASEAN-Japan commemorative summit meeting in Tokyo. In 2014 he visited India in January; Australia and New Zealand in July; and Bangladesh and Sri Lanka in September. He welcomed Australian prime minister Tony Abbott to Japan in April, followed by Indian prime minister Narendra Modi in August.

As we have seen, the East Asia regional cooperation framework has steadily expanded since the East Asian financial crisis of 1997–1998. The ASEAN+3 (Japan, China, and South Korea) summit has met since 1997. In 2005, the ASEAN+6 (comprising the ASEAN+3 countries plus India, Australia, and New Zealand) established the East Asia Summit. During

Vietnam's year as chair of ASEAN in 2010, the ASEAN Defense Ministers Meeting+8 was launched, providing for regular meetings involving
the ASEAN+6 countries as well as the United States and Russia. In 2011,
the East Asia Summit was further enlarged to become the ASEAN+8
Summit, with the inclusion of the United States and Russia. During the
1990s, the Asia Pacific region, dominated by the United States, was the
most important framework for regional cooperation, as represented by
APEC. This has changed since the East Asian financial crisis of 1997–
1998, as the focus of cooperation has shifted to the ASEAN+3 countries
of East Asia, which have looked to exclude the United States and build an
East Asian community. Since 2005, the term "East Asia" has started to
assume a broader meaning, and since around 2010 the "Indo-Pacific,"
referring to the vast region from Asia Pacific to the Indian Ocean, has
come to form the framework of regional cooperation.

Key players in this vast region include Japan, the United States,
China, South Korea, ASEAN, India, and Australia. As a glance at a map
reveals, the region consists of two axes forming a T: the horizontal axis
extending from Japan through Taiwan, the Philippines, and Indonesia to
India; and the vertical axis extending from Indonesia to Australia. To the
north lies continental Asia, stretching southwest from China to Vietnam,
Laos, and Cambodia through Thailand, Myanmar, and Bangladesh to
India. Abe has visited all these countries since becoming prime minister.

Not a Counterstrategy to China's "String of Pearls"

What is the significance of all this? Many argue that it is designed to
contain China and counter its "String of Pearls" strategy. China certainly believes so, and this view is not entirely mistaken. China's emergence as a military power and its attempts to change the regional status
quo by force in the East China and South China Seas have alarmed
neighboring countries, Japan included.

But these developments are better seen as one manifestation of a
broader, systemic change. Japan, the United States, the archipelagic island
nations of maritime Southeast Asia, Vietnam, India, and Australia have
all responded variously to China's military rise. Extensive regional partnerships have formed without any one country guiding the process. This
is exemplified by the East Asia Summit, involving the ASEAN+8 countries. Another example is the region's changing security arrangements.
In the 1950s a hub-and-spokes system began to emerge, consisting of a
series of bilateral alliances between the United States and individual

countries—chiefly Japan, South Korea, and Australia. For many years, this system underpinned the stability of the region. In recent years, however, it has gradually evolved into a network of alliances, as the allies and partners of the United States have strengthened security cooperation among themselves: Japan and Australia, Australia and India, India and Japan, Japan and Indonesia, as well as multilateral relationships involving three or more of these countries. The reason this has happened is simple: the balance of power in the region is shifting rapidly.

Working for International Peace and Stability by Strengthening the Japan–United States Alliance

What should Japan do for the sake of stability, peace, and prosperity in the region? The national security strategy gives a very clear answer: strengthen the Japan–United States alliance, and enhance diplomacy and security cooperation with Japan's partners, the partners cited being South Korea, Australia, the ASEAN countries, and India. Prime Minister Abe's summit diplomacy shows that he is concentrating on ties with partner countries at the core of the Indo-Pacific. Australia and India are already moving in that direction under the Abbott and Modi governments, and Vietnam and the Philippines are likely to do so in the near future. The new Indonesian government envisages turning the country into a "maritime axis," although it is not yet clear how that vision will be translated into policy. Such geopolitical partnerships are extremely important for stability and cooperation in the Indo-Pacific; coupled with the US rebalancing toward Asia, it is possible that they could induce China to change its maritime strategy in the medium to long term. I should emphasize that none of this means that the Korean Peninsula is unimportant for Japan's security. North Korea's nuclear weapons and missile programs are a grave menace, and instability on the Korean Peninsula has always been perceived as a security threat to Japan. But the South Koreans appear to have made a grand decision, almost as a matter of popular sentiment, that their country can guarantee its security and economic prosperity by skillfully managing its bilateral relations with the United States and China. This was strikingly illustrated by President Park Geun-hye's decision to attend the Chinese parade commemorating victory in World War II, despite objections by the United States. It takes two to engage in diplomacy and security cooperation. This is no doubt part of the reason why Japan's geopolitical focus has started to shift away from Asia Pacific and toward the Indian Ocean.

Join the TPP, Stay Out of the AIIB

In terms of its external economic policies, Abe's government concluded a free trade agreement with Australia in July 2014 (which took effect in January 2015) and joined the Trans-Pacific Partnership negotiations in July 2013. Earlier, in March 2013, it formally agreed to commence negotiations on an economic partnership agreement with the EU. The TPP and the Japan–European Union Economic Partnership Agreement will form the backbone of the global trading system in the twenty-first century, together with the Transatlantic Trade and Investment Partnership between the United States and the EU. In June 2015, Japan decided— for various reasons, I suspect—not to join the Chinese-led Asian Infrastructure Investment Bank, at least for the time being. Nevertheless, the Japanese government will allow the Asian Development Bank to co-finance loans with the AIIB on some projects. In a sense, Japan is taking a wait-and-see attitude, and evidently wants to see what the AIIB is capable of before committing itself.

Taken together, what do these national security and economic policies mean for Japan's national strategy? How have they altered that strategy and the thinking that underlies it?

COMPARATIVE HISTORICAL ANALYSIS

A Country Grown Too Big for Itself

Here I want to take a comparative historical approach to answering that question. After World War II, Japan regained its sovereignty with the San Francisco Peace Treaty and signed the Japan–United States Security Treaty. During the 1950s and 1960s, what became known as the Yoshida Doctrine was institutionalized as Japan's national strategy. This remained the de facto national consensus until the 1980s and 1990s, when it began to be reexamined by the governments of Nakasone Yasuhiro (1982–1987) and Miyazawa Kiichi (1991–1993). From a historical perspective, the regional framework has changed greatly in the years since, as the focus has shifted from Asia Pacific to East Asia to the Indo-Pacific. Japan's position within that framework has changed too.

In the 1980s and 1990s, at the height of Japan's prosperity and influence, commentators were already speculating about the national strategic challenges that lay ahead. For example, Gyōten Toyoo, who served as vice minister of finance for international affairs (June 1986– July 1989) under Finance Minister Miyazawa Kiichi in the Nakasone government, describes Japan in those days as follows in his book *Rise and Fall of the Yen: Confessions of a Currency Mobster*.

> Japan had become in a sense a monster. It had reached the peak of its postwar recovery, and that elicited both favorable and unfavorable reactions. Japan was at a turning point; it was time, I believe, for a fundamental change in the way it operated as a country and in its global strategy. Frankly, I do not think the country can be given full marks for having negotiated this historic turning point wisely, unerringly, and with courage. Too few people in Japan were aware that the country was at a turning point. (2013: 142)

Gyōten's characterization of Japan as a "monster" is evocative. It brings to mind the image of a country that had grown so huge it did not know what to do with its bulk: having outgrown its comfort zone, it lumbered along monster-like without any sense of direction, oblivious of the nuisance it was causing. Japan was at a turning point and needed to reshape its global and national strategy. If it could not be given full marks for the way it responded, does it at least deserve a passing grade? That is a delicate question.

Janus-Like Japan: Country with Two Faces

Another example is Kenneth Pyle's book *The Japanese Question: Power and Purpose in a New Era*. This was published in 1992, so the manuscript was presumably written around 1990–1991. Pyle, a historian at the University of Washington in Seattle and a leading Japan specialist, is an even-handed scholar a generation older than myself, being around the same age as Japanese intellectuals like Murakami Yasusuke, Satō Seizaburō, Amaya Naohiro, and Yamazaki Masakazu. His book describes Japan circa 1990 as having two faces, like the Roman god Janus:

> One face looks forward to the new century: it is fresh, young; its features are still not fully formed. It is a Japan still in the making, preparing for the future, impelled by a robust and sometimes naive optimism; above all a self-confident Japan, open to the world, assessing new policies, intent on reordering its society and government to meet new challenges. The face of the other Japan is strong, with clear though weather-worn features, looking back over a century-long struggle to achieve world power. It is a Japan still insecure, inward looking, satisfied in its proven ways, a Japan clinging to the order and discipline of its national life, less hospitable to reform, less tolerant of new ways, reluctant to part with the values and institutions that have brought success. (1992: 118)

The word choice in the subtitle of Pyle's book is noteworthy: "power and purpose." Essentially, what he is discussing here is political purpose. Since the Meiji period, Japan had ceaselessly striven to catch up with and overtake the West. But now it was at a turning point, as Gyōten too argued with regard to "global strategy." It was torn between the past and the future. What direction would it take now? Having drawn level with the West, what did it want to use its hard-won power for? The question remained unanswered, Pyle implied—and that was the problem.

I was living in the United States at the time, teaching at Cornell University in the small town of Ithaca (population 50,000) in upstate New York. I observed Japan from afar. I recall the need to revise the Yoshida Doctrine being debated in terms of Japan's role as an "international state," the "new internationalism," "neoconservatism," "proactive pacifism," and "internationalization." How was Japan's national strategy articulated at the time, and how was it translated into policy?

Institutionalizing the Yoshida Doctrine

It all began with the Yoshida Doctrine. This doctrine began to take shape from the end of the 1940s—as the Cold War commenced in Asia and before Japan regained full sovereignty—in negotiations between Prime Minister Yoshida Shigeru and Special Ambassador John Foster Dulles. It had three main tenets. First, Japan's national goal should be economic rehabilitation. For this, it would need to cooperate politically and economically with the United States. Second, Japan should remain lightly armed and not become embroiled in international political-strategic issues. It should concentrate on industrial development and avoid aggravating internal conflicts that could split the nation—what Yoshida termed a "thirty-eighth parallel in the hearts of the Japanese people." Third, to guarantee its own security, it should provide the US military with bases on Japanese soil (Pyle 1992: 25).

It is well known that Yoshida himself came to have doubts about this doctrine in the 1960s. He later wrote about the prolonged failure of an independent Japan that had joined the front ranks of the global community to wean itself from dependence on another country for its self-defense, and lamented its refusal to lend a hand to the peacekeeping mechanisms of the United Nations as a member while expecting to enjoy its benefits—something he described as "sheer selfishness, a have-your-cake-and-eat-it approach to life."

Yet the Yoshida Doctrine became increasingly institutionalized in the 1960s. Prime Minister Satō Eisaku articulated the "Three Non-Nuclear Principles" in 1967. The same year, his government adopted the "Three Principles on Arms Exports," which banned arms exports to communist-bloc countries, as well as to countries subject to an arms embargo under a UN resolution and belligerents or potential belligerents in an armed conflict. Under the Miki Takeo government (1974–1976), the ban on arms exports was extended to all countries, and the definition of "armaments" was expanded to encompass not only weapons and military equipment but also weapons parts and components. It was during the 1960s that the established practice began of keeping defense spending within 1 percent of gross national product, a ceiling enshrined in the 1976 national defense guidelines. There were murmurings of possible moves in a different direction. Japan's role in collective security in Asia became a topic of debate under US president Richard Nixon (1969–1974), particularly in connection with the return of Okinawa to Japanese sovereignty and the Nixon Doctrine, but Japan declined to participate directly in the region's security mechanisms. During the 1960s and 1970s, therefore, successive governments, by institutionalizing the Yoshida Doctrine, maintained the national consensus about putting the economy first. Japanese security and defense policy was couched in terms of "comprehensive security," "an exclusively defense-oriented policy," and "a basic defense force." This was presented as part of a comprehensive policy of putting the economy first and consolidating Japan's strengths as a trading nation.

Rethinking the Yoshida Doctrine

What approaches were taken to rethinking this doctrine in the 1980s? Perhaps the most incisive was proposed by Amaya Naohiro, when he asserted that Japan should become "a nation of merchants." This astute description of Japan showed pride in Japan's chosen course as a trading nation; Amaya was also shrewd enough to see Japan at arm's length, with a touch of irony, while suggesting how this view of the country could help to reshape its national strategy. As Amaya put it: "To prosper in a warrior society, a merchant requires outstanding information-gathering and planning skills, intuition, and diplomatic ability; on occasion he also needs to be able to grovel." At the time, Japan had finally achieved its goal of catching up with the West, and Prime Minister Nakasone was calling for a "total reassessment of postwar politics"—a phrase that nicely encapsulates his sense of the times. Japan had recovered from the war and caught up with the West; it was a major power, and it was time to start acting like one.

For the United States, the 1980s was an era dominated by high interest rates under Federal Reserve Board chairman Paul Volcker and, internationally, by the new Cold War politics of President Reagan. The Federal Reserve Board hiked the discount rate to above 16 percent to stamp out the rampant inflationary expectations of the 1970s, the dollar "hit the stratosphere" (in Volcker's words) against the mark and the yen, and US companies struggled to compete with their Japanese and German rivals on international markets. That led to trade disputes between Japan and the United States in one industry after another, including steel, televisions, automobiles, and semiconductors (Volcker and Gyōten 1992: 264).

What were the aims of Japan's prime ministers at the time: men like Nakasone Yasuhiro, Takeshita Noboru, and Miyazawa Kiichi? Nakasone sought to turn Japan into an "international state"—a somewhat bizarre term. To speak of the Japanese "nation-state" makes perfect sense, but it is unclear what a Japanese "international state" might mean. Rereading Nakasone's pronouncements, it appears to boil down to a matter of Japan becoming involved in international political issues and exercising proactive leadership on the global stage. As prime minister, Nakasone actively engaged in summit diplomacy, strengthened ties with the United States—as epitomized by his strong personal relationship with Ronald Reagan—and played the part of a major power at G7 summits. But in terms of security policy, he never managed to do more than tinker with the Yoshida Doctrine, making a few revisions to the "Three Principles on Arms Exports" and raising the ceiling on defense spending. The doctrine's institutional underpinnings were left virtually intact. The consequence was that Japan's international role in the Nakasone era was mostly restricted to financial matters and science and technology. In this regard, the most important manifestation of Japan's international role at the time was the 1985 Plaza Accord and the role that Japan played in providing monetary and financial support to President Reagan's new Cold War.

In part, this was a consequence of the fact that monetary and financial policies were less restricted by domestic conditions than other areas of policy such as security, trade and industry, and agriculture. Even in the areas of monetary policy and financial policy, it was financial policy that bore the brunt domestically, as a survey of developments between the Plaza and Louvre Accords and between Black Monday and the bubble economy reveals; on the fiscal policy front, Japan failed to meet the US government's expectations. But for all the talk of making Japan an "international state," building a political consensus at home was a formidable task. The quickest way to meet international expectations, particularly those of the US government, was to act in areas where a consensus could be achieved. Under the Nakasone government, that meant the Plaza Accord; under Takeshita, it meant official development assistance. Regarding the interface between foreign relations and domestic politics, Prime Minister Nakasone reportedly told Takeshita, on naming him as his successor, "Domestic politics is now going to be of vital importance. Developing our foreign relations will require political support within the country. You're a great domestic consensus-builder, which is why I've asked you to do the job." It was certainly a judicious choice (Hasegawa 2014: 321).

Manifestations of Japan's Economic Confidence

What was it that limited Japan's ability to act at the time? The answer, I believe, was closely linked to the difficulty of its position as a major economic power. Despite having become the world's second largest economy, Japan was still only economically half the size of the United States and the European Community. If it wanted to engage in great power politics on the international stage, it needed to punch above its weight. Most Japanese wondered why the United States was pressing Japan to increase its defense spending when there were no serious threats on the horizon. They argued that the reason for the constant trade disputes with the United States was simply that Japanese companies made better and less expensive products. Japan could hardly be blamed for that. In Asia, Japan was like Gulliver among the Lilliputians. For China and the other Asian countries to grow, all Japan needed to do was to help by providing economic aid and expertise. If East Asia was going to become economically integrated anyway, as direct investment by Japanese companies built a cross-border production network that spanned the region, why not simply leave things to the logic of the market? Japan would be wiser to avoid getting bogged down in regional cooperation and rulemaking if it was just going to end up tying its own hands and rousing US suspicions. These views were shared by much of the Japanese public.

It was a way of thinking that was grounded in an assumption that the balance of wealth and power would continue to shift in Japan's favor. Murakami Yasusuke, for instance, an outstanding all-round social scientist, wrote an essay in the November 1985 issue of the magazine *Chūō Kōron* titled "Afutā hegemonī" [After hegemony]. The article postulated that the age of overwhelming US military and economic dominance had already ended. The world had changed, and the Pax Americana, the dollar-based international monetary system, and the free trade system that had underpinned the twentieth-century global order could no longer be maintained simply by depending on the United States. This view was a typical demonstration of confidence in Japan's future and its technological and economic prowess.

Similar confidence is evident in a global economic forecast released by the Japan Center for Economic Research in 1992. According to the report, as of 1990 the Americas accounted for 29.0 percent of nominal global GDP (North America 26.1 percent, Central and South America 2.9 percent); Europe 32.9 percent (Western Europe 30.4 percent, Eastern Europe 2.5 percent); and Asia and Oceania 20.9 percent (Japan 12.8 percent, China 1.6 percent, the rest of Asia 5.0 percent, and Oceania 1.5 percent). The economies of Asia and Oceania, in other words, were only two-thirds as big as the economies of the Americas and Europe. But by 2010, the report predicted, Asia and Oceania would account for 29.4 percent (Japan 17.5 percent, China 2.6 percent, the rest of Asia 8.0 percent, and Oceania 1.3 percent) versus 26.0 percent for the Americas (North America 23.0 percent, Central and South America 3.0 percent) and 28.7 percent for Europe (Western Europe 26.7 percent, Eastern Europe 2.0 percent). Growth in Asia and Oceania would "needless to say" be driven by the East Asian economies, the report said: Japan (increasing from 12.8 percent to 17.5 percent); the Asian newly industrializing economies (increasing from 2.2 percent to 4.1 percent); ASEAN (increasing from 1.2 percent to 2.2 percent); and China (increasing from 1.6 percent to 2.6 percent). That led Suzuki Yoshio, who once served as an executive director of the Bank of Japan, to write that "East Asia is for the first time stepping into the limelight of modern global economic history" (1992: 109–110).

An Alliance Anchored in
Cooperation on Security and Finance

It is the nature of forecasts to be wrong, of course. Regardless of its accuracy, this forecast is of interest for what it reveals about the confidence with which the Japanese looked ahead to the future in those days.

Most people who read or heard about forecasts like this in 1992 no doubt found them convincing and envisaged the future of Japan, Asia, and the world accordingly. This optimism about the future helps to explain why the Japan–United States alliance was considered a vital good not only for Japan's security but also for the peace, security, and prosperity of Asia. It explains why the alliance was redefined in the second half of the 1990s, as for example in the Clinton-Hashimoto agreement. It helps to explain too why Japan ended up footing much of the bill for the "gardening" aspects involved in maintaining US security policy in Asia. A case in point can be seen in what happened in the Philippines after the 1986 revolution. The US government intervened in the final stages of the revolution, when President Marcos and his wife fled to Hawaii, and Corazón Aquino formed a new government. Subsequently the Japanese and US governments worked together at the bureaucratic level to support the new government. Japan increased its offical development assistance to the Philippines, and when the new regime was threatened by a coup, the United States dispatched fighter jets from Clark Air Base as a clear signal of intent and foiled the coup. The division of roles between the two partners was clear.[7]

Despite the frequent trade disputes, therefore, during the 1980s and 1990s the US-Japanese alliance remained anchored in cooperation on security and defense and on monetary and financial policy. Within this framework, Japan acted as a major economic power on the global stage. In Asia, meanwhile, it focused on furthering de facto economic integration by direct investment backed up by infrastructure investment and technical assistance.

This was expressly articulated as a strategy in a report submitted to Prime Minister Miyazawa Kiichi in 1994 by the Advisory Committee on Asia, the Pacific, and Japan in the Twenty-First Century. The essence of the report was as follows. The expanding production network being developed by Japanese companies in Southeast Asia would in and of itself accelerate Asia's de facto economic integration. This in turn would be advantageous in "managing" trade disputes with the United States. The growth of the newly industrializing economies of East Asia (South Korea, Taiwan, Hong Kong, and Singapore); other ASEAN countries (Thailand, Malaysia, Indonesia, and the Philippines); and the coastal regions of China, together with the larger markets that would follow, would likewise be advantageous to the Japanese economy. Economic development would also make these countries politically stable. The political model followed in Japan since the end of World War II was one built around achieving productivity and economic growth—creating jobs, reducing poverty, and improving living standards. If, as seemed likely, this model proved successful in other Asian countries, they would become politically stable, and the Japanese political model would spread throughout Asia. This was the basic thinking behind Japan's Asia strategy as part of its national strategy. Inevitably, the increasing prevalence of such thinking was viewed warily in the United States. Japan was accused of attempting to build a second Greater East Asian Co-Prosperity Sphere, and of being a neomercantilist state. People began to argue that Japan differed from the United States both in the nature of its capitalism and in its character as a nation. Trying to negotiate trade disputes was pointless; the Japanese politico-economic system itself needed replacing.

The Rise of Asia Pacific and the US Rebalance

So what happened? The first thing was that the balance of power shifted dramatically. Look again at Table 1.1 (see page 10). Let me reiterate what I said earlier: at least two things can be read from this. One is the erosion of the economic power of the G7 and the rise of the emerging economies since the beginning of the twenty-first century. The other is the erosion of North American and European economic power and the rise of Asia Pacific—although it is not Japan but China that has been responsible for most of this growth. As a whole, the world today does not look radically different from the future envisaged by Japanese forecasters in 1990, but in Asia Pacific the distribution of wealth and power has shifted in a way quite contrary to Japanese expectations.

The second major event was the East Asian financial crisis of 1997–1998. This precipitated the successive collapse of the developmental states, and the Japanese model based on a politics of economic growth foundered in many countries. This brought an era to an end. Countries that instituted bold reforms and established new institutions soon resumed growth, but countries where reforms were halfhearted or abortive saw their economies stagnate, as illustrated by the differing economic destinies of the Philippines and Indonesia, and of Thailand and Malaysia. From the Japanese standpoint, Japan's economic sclerosis and the East Asian financial crisis dashed optimistic expectations that Japan's politics of economic growth would spread through East and Southeast Asia and turn the region into Japan's "backyard" through the power of the market, even without institution-building. Instead, elites throughout the region tended to turn to the Anglo-American model and became increasingly globalized. Meanwhile, Chinese economic aid had an immense and growing influence in the areas of trade and infrastructure development.

Third, Japan's geopolitical position changed. During the Cold War, Germany was still a divided nation, with East and West facing off across the front lines of the Berlin Wall. Japan was not on the front lines of the Cold War, despite what Yoshida called the "thirty-eighth parallel in the hearts of the Japanese people." By the early twenty-first century, the rise of China and its attempts to change the status quo in the East China Sea by force had turned Japan into a frontline state. This was in stark contrast to Germany, now safely embedded deep within NATO and the EU owing to the eastward expansion of these organizations since the end of the Cold War.

Japan's foreign and security policies in recent years mark a rational response to these external changes. The alliance with the United States naturally remains the cornerstone of Japanese foreign and security policy, and Japan has accordingly coordinated its actions with the US rebalancing strategy. The establishment of the National Security Council, the government's national security policies, the 2013 national defense guidelines, the adoption of the "Three Principles on Transfer of Defense Equipment and Technology," the reinterpretation of the constitution with regard to the right of collective self-defense, the enactment of security legislation, the formulation of the revised Japan–United States defense cooperation guidelines, Prime Minister Abe's summit diplomacy, the evolution of the US-centered hub-and-spoke security system into a network of alliances[8]—all these moves indicate that the rethink of the Yoshida Doctrine, which began in the 1980s and 1990s, is finally reaching a conclusion.

A Global Japan: The Shifting Balance of Power

Why was Japan able to do in the 2010s what it could not in the 1980s and 1990s? There are many factors, among them the shifting balance of power, the failure of Japan's Asia strategy, and the country's changing geopolitical position. In addition, what Yoshida called the "thirty-eighth parallel in the hearts of the Japanese people" has gradually faded as a new generation has come of age. But psychological walls, unlike the Berlin Wall, do not crumble physically and then cease to have any effect. As the opposition to the security legislation shows, Japan's evolution into a "normal country" in terms of its foreign relations and security policy is still impeded by what Yoshida described as a "have-your-cake-and-eat-it approach." This mindset, rooted in the desire never to experience the horrors of war again, leads to a readiness to avoid peril at all costs.

More broadly, the advent of a new generation has altered Japanese perceptions of "internationalization." In a 1986 survey by the Economic Planning Agency, some 70 percent of respondents described themselves as positive about some of the most commonplace forms of contact with the rest of the world, such as "news from abroad," "technology from overseas," and "overseas telephone calls and mail." Today, these things would not even be considered as "internationalization"—they are simply the norm. There was similar support for short-term human exchanges with foreign tourists and students. But less than 30 percent approved of anything that could result in the "internationalization" of Japanese society itself, such as admitting more foreign employees or greater numbers of international marriages (Pyle 1992: 113).

That was three decades ago. What is the situation today? As of 2005, one in ten marriages contracted in Japan involved at least one non-Japanese partner. For Tokyo, the figure was one in eight. Go to a school sports day at any primary school these days, and you are bound to see at least one or two children in every class from an obviously mixed ethnic background. The percentage of non-Japanese working at Japanese universities, research institutions, and companies has also risen as brains circulate, and Japan begins to tap into the global talent pool. And the number of foreign visitors has increased dramatically over the past few years, to the extent that spending by foreign tourists now has an impact on the stock market. Observing the debate over the Abe government's social and economic policies, particularly the discussion about special economic zones, I have come to believe that generational affiliation is now a more important consideration than ideology for Japanese political leaders. The rise of a new generation has changed how Japan responds to phenomena like internationalization and globalization and facilitates external economic policies that would have been almost unthinkable ten or fifteen years ago. The TPP is a prime example of this.

Japan's Grand Strategy: Come to Terms with History and Help Build a Twenty-First-Century Order

What course should Japan follow in the twenty-first century? As I have said, no written document exists that officially outlines Japan's "national strategy." Instead, the strategy takes the form of a national consensus on what the country should do in today's world. It centers on a number of key terms: pacifism, international cooperation, the Japan–United States alliance, globalization, a globally competent work force, brain circulation, female empowerment, and economic partnership, to list a few that come to mind. Interestingly, references to Japan as a "major power," and in particular to it as a "great economic power," are heard much less frequently today than they used to be in the 1980s and 1990s, when these were the most important keywords of all. Another key idea is the need to come to terms with history. A national strategy is inevitably also a grand narrative to some extent. At some point, Japan's national strategy must somehow come to terms with the country's militaristic past. Prime Minister Abe's statement on the seventieth anniversary of the end of World War II appears to have put that matter largely to rest. The statement treated Japan's imperial past and its postwar history as essentially separate, acknowledging that the country had taken the wrong course (or adopted the wrong national strategy, to use Japanese terms) in the 1930s and 1940s. That, I think, is as it should be.

What should be Japan's national strategy in the future? I have said that references to the country as a "major economic power" are less commonly used than in previous decades. I think this is highly significant. For there should be no room for doubt: Japan is a major power. It is the world's third largest economy and has the world's sixth largest defense budget. But it is not a superpower, and it needs to be realistic about this point. What is the difference between a superpower and other major powers? A superpower is a state that can set the international rules, either on its own or by taking leadership. A merely great or major power is one that can play a substantial role in the international rule-making process by negotiating with the superpower and helping to set the rules. The TPP negotiations could never have been launched under Japan's leadership, even if it had faced no domestic obstacles. They started only once the United States assumed leadership. But in view of the TPP's goal of establishing a trading order for Asia Pacific in the twenty-first century, there would be little point in a TPP without Japan. China has enacted domestic legislation on its territorial waters and is now attempting to force these on its neighbors. Were Japan to cave in, that would be the end of the game. That is what it means to be a great power. Japan needs to accept that it is a major power but not a superpower. In foreign relations and security, it should engage in the politics of power and balancing with the fundamental goal of transforming the US-centered hub-and-spokes system into a network of alliances. On international economic policy, it should play an active role in setting the rules of economic cooperation and free trade based on market liberalization. And it should help to strengthen the global financial order. These are the basic elements of a Japanese national strategy.

Establishing a Liberal International Order

The question remains: Why bother? And for what purpose? What Yoshida described as a selfish attitude, being inward-looking and only caring about yourself, is a common enough attitude. It is certainly not confined to Japan. This brings us back to the question I raised earlier in this chapter, regarding power and purpose. Japan is not a superpower; nor does it wish to be. Nonetheless, as one of the major powers, Japan possesses various capabilities: economic and military might, scientific and technological prowess, and a remarkably strong sense of social solidarity, as demonstrated by the people of the Tōhoku region following the 2011 earthquake and tsunami. What is Japan going to use those capabilities for? What do we expect of it as a nation-state? What is the right thing to do?

As a way of getting to grips with the question of power and purpose, let us return to what I said in the preface. The twentieth-century system was built on four institutional foundations: internationally, the Pax Americana and a liberal trade system centered on the dollar standard and the WTO; and within Japan, the liberal democratic state and the market economy. Today, the world is changing rapidly—Asia in particular. When China accounted for less than 5 percent of the global economy, it was able to free-ride on the dollar standard and the WTO trading system, accepting US hegemony while maintaining its own very different political and economic institutions at home in the form of a one-party state and a socialist market economy. But when China's share of the world economy exceeds 15 percent, it will find it increasingly difficult to continue its free ride on the dollar standard and the WTO trading system while preserving its socialist market economy. And if it challenges the Pax Americana head-on, as seems to be the almost inevitable logical outcome of its "rich country, strong army" policy, Japan will have no choice but to respond. So what should Japan do? What kind of world do we want to build? Do we want to build a freer, fairer world on the foundations of the present order? Or will we only care about ourselves and stick to the "have-your-cake-and-eat-it approach" to life? That is the question that now confronts us. I believe that a consensus is gradually emerging. While coming to terms with Japan's imperialistic past, we should defend and enhance the liberal international order under which postwar Japan has enjoyed peace, stability, and prosperity. In the wake of the disastrous political leadership of Prime Ministers Hatoyama Yukio and Kan Naoto, this approach has slowly but surely been spreading since the days of the Noda government with the advent of a new generation, and has gained new momentum under the Abe government.

NOTES

1. See Government of Japan, "National Security Strategy of Japan," December 2013, https://www.cas.go.jp/jp/siryou/131217anzenhoshou/pamphlet_en.pdf.
2. See "National Defense Program Guidelines for FY 2014 and Beyond" (provisional translation), 17 December 2013, https://www.mod.go.jp/j/approach/agenda/guideline/2014/pdf/20131217_e2.pdf.
3. "Three Principles on Transfer of Defense Equipment and Technology" (provisional translation), https://www.mofa.go.jp/files/000034953.pdf.
4. "Cabinet Decision on Development of Seamless Security Legislation to Ensure Japan's Survival and Protect Its People, July 1, 2014" (provisional translation), http://japan.kantei.go.jp/96_abe/decisions/2014/__icsFiles/afieldfile/2014/07/03/anpohosei_eng.pdf.
5. See "National Defense Program Guidelines for FY 2011 and Beyond" (provisional translation), 17 December 2010, https://www.mod.go.jp/e/d_act/d_policy/pdf/guidelinesFY2011.pdf.
6. See "The Three Principles on Transfer of Defense Equipment and Technology," 1 April 2014, https://www.mofa.go.jp/press/release/press22e_000010.html.
7. For one example of US intervention during the coup crisis in the Philippines, see Powell and Persico 1996: 520–523.
8. But transforming the current hub-and-spokes system of regional security into a network of alliances will require considerable effort on Japan's part. One means of assessing how the US-centered hub-and-spokes security system actually functions is to observe the overall pattern of joint military exercises. According to Hirose Ritsuko (2013), in the 1980s (1981–1990), during the Cold War era, a total of 405 joint exercises were held in East Asia, of which 329, or 81 percent, were between the United States and the following countries: Japan (225), Australia (51), South Korea (30), Thailand (17), and the Philippines (6). These figures plainly testify to US leadership in the hub-and-spokes security system and the importance of the Japan–United States alliance as its cornerstone. In the 2000s (2001–2009), the number of joint exercises increased to 996. Of these, a total of 433, or 43 percent, were between the United States and

an ally: Japan (201), Australia (89), the Philippines (86), South Korea (31), and Thailand (26). In addition, joint exercises involving other combinations also increased, such as the United States and India (44), Australia and New Zealand (43), Australia and Thailand (39), Australia and Singapore (28), and Singapore and Indonesia (30). Thus Australia has emerged as a second hub alongside the United States as the hub-and-spokes security system in East Asia evolves into a network of alliances.

References

REFERENCES IN ENGLISH

Ariff, Mohamed. 2012. Preface to *Malaysia's Development Challenges: Graduating from the Middle*, edited by H. Hill, T. S. Yean, and R. H. M. Zin, 17–23. London: Routledge.

Baldwin, Richard. 2013. "Misthinking Globalization." Keynote speech, International Symposium on Global Value Chains: Quo Vadis? GRIPS, Tokyo, 5 July.

Baldwin, Richard, Itō Tadashi, and Satō Hitoshi. 2014. "Portrait of Factory Asia: Production Network in Asia and Its Implications for Growth—The Smile Curve." Vol. 159 of Joint Research Program Series. Chiba: Institute of Developing Economies. https://www.ide.go.jp/library/English/Publish/Download/Jrp/pdf/159.pdf.

Bello, W. F., M. De Guzman, and M. L. Malig. 2004. *The Anti-Development State: The Political Economy of Permanent Crisis in the Philippines.* London: Zed.

Brands, Hal. 2014. *What Good Is Grand Strategy? Power and Purpose in American Statecraft from Harry S. Truman to George W. Bush.* Ithaca: Cornell University Press.

Bremmer, Ian. 2012. *Every Nation for Itself: Winners and Losers in a G-Zero World.* New York: Portfolio. (Consulted in the Japanese translation by Kitazawa Itaru, published by Nikkei in 2012.)

Brzezinski, Zbigniew. 2007. *Second Chance: Three Presidents and the Crisis of American Superpower.* New York: Basic.

Chen, Zhiwu. 2015. "China's Dangerous Debt: Why the Economy Could Be Headed for Trouble." *Foreign Affairs*, June: 13–18.

"China's Lending Hits New Heights." 2011. *Financial Times*, 17 January. https://www.ft.com/intl/cms/s/0/488c60f4-2281-11e0-b6a2-00144feab49a.html#axzz1euurZLQp.

Hagel, Chuck. 2014. "Reagan National Defense Forum Keynote." Ronald Reagan Presidential Library, Simi Valley, California, 15 November. https://www.defense.gov/Speeches/Speech.aspx?SpeechID=1903.

Halberstam, David. 2001. *War in a Time of Peace: Bush, Clinton, and the Generals*. New York: Scribner. (Consulted in the Japanese translation by Ogura Yoshirō, published by PHP Institute in 2003.)

Hau, Caroline S. 2004. *On the Subject of the Nation: Filipino Writing from 1981 to 2003*. Manila: Ateneo de Manila University Press.

Hill, Hal, and Shiraishi Takashi. 2007. "Indonesia After the Asian Crisis." *Asian Economic Policy Review* 2(1): 123–141.

Ikenberry, G. John. 2011. *Liberal Leviathan: The Origins, Crisis, and Transformation of the American World Order*. Princeton: Princeton University Press.

Khoo, Boo Teik. 2006. "Malaysia: Balancing Development and Power." In *The Political Economy of South-East Asia: Markets, Power, and Contestation*, edited by Garry Rodan, Kevin Hewison, and Richard Robison, 170–196. Melbourne: Oxford University Press.

Kissinger, Henry A. 2011. *On China*. New York: Penguin. (Consulted in the Japanese translation by Tsukagoshi Toshihiko et al., published by Iwanami Shoten in 2013.)

Luttwak, Edward. 2012. *The Rise of China vs. the Logic of Strategy*. Cambridge: Belknap. (Consulted in the Japanese translation by Okuyama Masashi, published by Fuyo Shobō in 2013.)

Mann, James. 1999. *About Face: A History of America's Curious Relationship with China from Nixon to Clinton*. New York: Knopf. (Consulted in the Japanese translation by Suzuki Chikara, published by Kyōdō News in 1999.)

McCoy, Alfred W. 2015. "The Geopolitics of American Global Decline: Washington Versus China in the Twenty-First Century." In Alfred McCoy, "Washington's Great Game and Why It's Failing." *Tomgram*, 7 June 2015.

McGregor, Richard. 2010. *The Party: The Secret World of China's Communist Rulers*. New York: Harper. (Consulted in the Japanese translation by Kotani Masayo, published by Sōshisha Publishing in 2014.)

McKinsey Global Institute. 2012. *The Archipelago Economy: Unleashing Indonesia's Potential*. New York.

Obama, Barack. 2011. "Remarks by President Obama to the Australian Parliament." 17 November. https://www.whitehouse.gov/the-press-office/2011/11/17/remarks-president-obama-australian-parliament.

Panetta, Leon. 2012. "The US Rebalance Towards the Asia Pacific." First Plenary Session, Shangri-La Dialogue 2012.

Pasuk Phongpaichit and Christopher J. Baker. 2008. Conclusion to *Thai Capital: After the 1997 Crisis*, edited by Pasuk Phongpaichit and Christopher J. Baker. Chiang Mai: Silkworm.

———. 2009. *Thaksin*. Chiang Mai: Silkworm.

Pillsbury, Michael. 2015. *The Hundred-Year Marathon: China's Secret Strategy to Replace America as the Global Superpower*. New York: Holt.

Polanyi, Karl. 2001 (1957). *The Great Transformation: The Political and Economic Origins of Our Time*. Boston: Beacon. (Consulted in the Japanese translation by Yoshizawa Hidenari et al., published by Tōyō Keizai in 1975.)

Powell, Colin, and Joseph E. Persico. 1996. *My American Journey*. New York: Ballantine. (Consulted in the Japanese translation by Suzuki Chikara, published by Kadokawa Shoten in 1995.)

Pyle, Kenneth B. 1992. *The Japanese Question: Power and Purpose in a New Era*. Washington, D.C.: AEI. (Consulted in the Japanese translation by Katō Mikio, published by Simul in 1995.)

Raquiza, Antoinette R. 2011. *State Structure, Policy Formation, and Economic Development in Southeast Asia: The Political Economy of Thailand and the Philippines*. New York: Routledge.

Shambaugh, David. 2013. *China Goes Global: The Partial Power*. Oxford University Press. (Consulted in the Japanese translation by Katō Yūko, published by Asahi Shimbun in 2015.)

Shiraishi Takashi. 2005. "The Asian Crisis Reconsidered." In *Dislocating Nation-States: Globalization in Asia and Africa*, edited by Patricio N. Abinales, Ishikawa Noboru, and Tanabe Akio, 17–40. Kyoto: Kyoto University Press.

———. 2008. "Introduction: The Rise of Middle Classes in Southeast Asia." In *The Rise of Middle Classes in Southeast Asia*, edited by Shiraishi Takashi and Pasuk Phongpaichit, 1–23. Kyoto: Kyoto University Press.

Shultz, George P. 1993. *Turmoil and Triumph: My Years As Secretary of State*. New York: Scribner.

Spence, Michael. 2011. *The Next Convergence: The Future of Economic Growth in a Multispeed World*. New York: Farrar, Straus, and Giroux. (Consulted in the Japanese translation by Hijikata Nami, published by Hayakawa in 2011.)

Suehiro Akira. 2014. "Technocracy and Thaksinocracy in Thailand: Reforms of the Public Sector and the Budget System Under the Thaksin Government." *Southeast Asian Studies* 3(2).

Summers, Lawrence. 2015a. "A Global Wake-Up Call for the U.S.?" *Washington Post*, 5 April.

———. 2015b. "Time US Leadership Woke Up to New Economic Era." *Financial Times*, 5 April.

Swaine, Michael D. 2015. "Xi Jinping's Address to the Central Conference on Work Relating to Foreign Affairs: Assessing and Advancing Major-Power Diplomacy with Chinese Characteristics." http://carnegieendowment.org/files/Michael_Swaine_CLM_46.pdf.

Tamada Yoshifumi. 2008. "Democracy and the Middle Class in Thailand: The Uprising of May 1992." In *The Rise of Middle Classes in Southeast Asia,* edited by Shiraishi Takashi and Pasuk Phongpaichit, 40–82. Kyoto: Kyoto University Press.

Thitinan Pongsudhirak. 2015. "Thailand's Stunted Transition." https://www.project-syndicate.org/commentary/thailand-military-junta-shinawatra-by-thitinan-pongsudhirak-2015-05.

"Understanding the Major Social Changes in East Asia Based on Population Censuses." *Aji-Ken Wārudo Torendo*, special issue. IDE World Trends, August 2015.

US Department of Defense. 2012. *Sustaining U.S. Global Leadership: Priorities for 21st Century Defense*. January 4.

Whaley, F. 2012. "A Youthful Populace Helps Make the Philippines an Economic Bright Spot in Asia." *New York Times*, 27 August. https://www.nytimes.com/2012/08/28/business/global/philippine-economy-set-to-become-asias-newest-bright-spot.html?_r=2&pagewanted=all.

White, Hugh. 2013. *The China Choice: Why We Should Share Power.* New York: Oxford University Press. (Consulted in the Japanese translation by Tokugawa Iehiro, published by Keisō Shobō in 2014.)

World Trade Organization and IDE-JETRO. 2012. *Trade Patterns and Global Value Chains in East Asia: From Trade in Goods to Trade in Tasks.*

Youwei. 2015. "The End of Reform in China: Authoritarian Adaptation Hits a Wall." *Foreign Affairs,* June: 2–7.

REFERENCES IN JAPANESE

Aoyama Rumi. 2013. *Chūgoku no Ajia gaikō* [China's foreign policy in Asia]. Tokyo: Tokyo University Press.

Endō Homare. 2012. *Chaina jajji: Mō Takutō ni narenakatta otoko* [China judge: The man who could not be Mao Zedong]. Tokyo: Asahi Shimbun.

Furuta Motoo. 2009. *Doimoi no tanjō: Betonamu ni okeru kaikaku rosen no keisei katei* [The birth of Doi Moi: The formation of a reform track in Vietnam]. Tokyo: Aoki Shoten.

Gyōten Toyoo. 2013. *En no kōbō: "Tsūka mafia" no dokuhaku* [Rise and fall of the yen: Confessions of a currency mobster]. Tokyo: Asahi Shimbun.

Hasegawa Kazutoshi. 2014. *Shushō hishokan ga kataru Nakasone gaikō no butai ura: Bei-Chū-Kan to no sōgo shinrai wa ikani kōchiku sareta ka* [Behind the scenes of Nakasone's diplomacy, according to the prime minister's secretary: How trust was built between the United States, China, and Korea]. Tokyo: Asahi Shimbun.

Hattori Tamio, Funatsu Tsuruyo, and Torii Takashi, eds. 2002. *Ajia chūkansō no seisei to tokushitsu* [Formation and characteristics of the Asian middle class]. Tokyo: Institute of Developing Economies.

Hirose Ritsuko. 2013. "Higashi-Ajia ni okeru kyōdō gunji enshū no henyō: Habu supōkusu kara nettowāku e" [Changes in joint military exercises in East Asia: From hub and spokes to networks]. PhD dissertation. Tokyo: National Graduate Institute for Policy Studies.

Igarashi Makoto. 2014. "Shōsū minzoku mondai" [Ethnic minority problems]. *Aji-Ken Wārudo Torendo,* February.

Japan Institute of International Affairs, The. 2013 *Saikin no Chūgoku jōsei to wagakuni no taiō* [The current situation in China and Japan's response]. 3 December. Tokyo.

Kamo Motoki. 2015. "Shū Kinpei seiken no 'han-fukai' towa nani ka" [What is the meaning of Xi Jinping's "anti-corruption" purge?]. *Chūō Kōron,* May.

Kaneko Yoshiki. 2011. "Marēshia, Singapōru: Gurōbaruka ni yureru taminzoku kokka" [Malaysia and Singapore: Multiethnic states shaken by globalization]. In *Nanbu Ajia* [South Asia], edited by Yamakage Susumu and Hirose Takako. Kyoto: Minerva Shobō.

Kawamura Kōichi. 2005. "Seiji seido kara miru 2004-nen sōsenkyo" [The 2004 general elections, from the perspective of political systems]. In *Megawachi kara Yudoyono e, Indoneshia sōsenkyo to shin-seiken no shidō* [From Megawati to Yudhoyono: Indonesia's election and the start of the new administration], edited by Matsui Kazuhisa and Kawamura Kōichi. Tokyo: Akashi Shoten.

Kudō Toshihiro. 2014a. "Tokushū ni atatte: Tein Sein seiken to kaikaku (1): 'Posuto gunsei' makuake no haikei" [Special report: The Thein Sein government and reforms (1): The background to the beginning of the post-military age]. *Aji-Ken Wārudo Torendo*, February.

———. 2014b. "Tokushū ni atatte: Tein Sein seiken to kaikaku (2): 'Posuto 2015-nen' o tenbō suru" [Special report: The Thein Sein government and reforms (2): Looking ahead to the post-2015 era]. *Aji-Ken Wārudo Torendo*, March.

Kudō Toshihiro and Kumagai Satoru. 2014. "Myanmā no yushutsu shikō, gaika dōnyū no seichō senryaku" [Myanmar's growth strategy: Exports and foreign capital]. *Aji-Ken Wārudo Torendo*, March.

Masuhara Ayako. 2015. "Indoneshia, bōdai na kazu no shima kara naru taminzoku kokka no jinkō haaku" [Ascertaining the population in Indonesia, multi-ethnic nation made up of a huge number of islands]. *Aji-Ken Wārudo Torendo*, August.

Matsui Kazuhisa and Kawamura Kōichi, eds. 2005. *Megawachi kara Yudoyono e, Indoneshia sōsenkyo to shin-seiken no shidō* [From Megawati to Yudhoyono: Indonesia's election and the start of the new administration]. Tokyo: Akashi Shoten.

Ministry of Defense, The (Japan). 2014. *Bōei hakusho* [Defense of Japan]. Annual white paper. Tokyo.

Murakami Yasusuke. 1992. *Han koten no seiji keizai gaku: Shinpo shikan no tasogare* [Anticlassical political economics: The twilight of the progress view of history]. Vol. 1. Tokyo: Chūō Kōron Shinsha.

Nakanishi Yoshihiro. 2014. "Tein Sein no tsuyomi to yowami" [Strengths and weaknesses of Thein Sein]. *Aji-Ken Wārudo Torendo*, March.

National Institute for Defense Studies, ed. 2015. *Higashi Ajia senryaku gaikan 2015* [East Asian strategic review 2015]. Tokyo.

Ōizumi Keiichirō. 2008. "Dai-Mekon-ken (GMS) kaihatsu puroguramu to CLMV no hatten: Keizai kairō seibi de hirogaru kanōsei to Nihon no yakuwari" [Progress of the Greater Mekong Subregion development program and CLMV: Expanding potential by building economic infrastructure, and Japan's role]. In *Kan-Taiheiyō bijinesu jōhō RIM* [Pacific rim business information: RIM]. http://www.jri.co.jp/MediaLibrary/file/report/rim/pdf/2716.pdf.

———. 2011. *Shōhi suru Ajia* [Consumer Asia]. Tokyo: Chūō Kōron Shinsha.

Ōtsuka Kazuo. 2000. *Isurāmu-teki: Sekaika jidai no naka de* ["Islamic" in an era of globalization]. Tokyo: NHK Publishing.

Shiraishi Takashi. 2000. *Umi no teikoku* [Empires of the sea]. Tokyo: Chūō Kōron Shinsha.

———. 2010. "Indoneshia ni oite keizai seichō no seiji wa ikani shite fukkatsu shita ka" [How the politics of economic growth were revived in Indonesia]. In *Kokka to keizai hatten* [States and economic development], edited by Ōtsuka Keijirō and Shiraishi Takashi. Tokyo: Tōyō Keizai.

Shiraishi Takashi and Caroline Hau. 2012. *Chūgoku wa higashi Ajia o dō kaeru ka: 21-seiki no shin chiiki shisutemu* [How China will change East Asia: New regional systems in the twenty-first century]. Tokyo: Chūō Kōron Shinsha.

Suehiro Akira. 2015. "Tai, kakudai Bankoku shutoken no keisei" [Thailand: Formation of a Greater Bangkok metropolitan region]. *Aji-Ken Wārudo Torendo*, August.

Suzuki Yoshio. 1992. *Nihon keizai no saisei: Baburu keizai o koete* [Rebirth of the Japanese economy: Overcoming the economic bubble]. Tokyo: Tōyō Keizai.

Suzuki Yurika. 2015. "Firipin, jinkō bōnasu wa shibaraku tsuzuku" [Philippines: Demographic bonus likely to continue for some time]. *Aji-Ken Wārudo Torendo*, August.

Tamada Yoshifumi. 2011. "Tai seiji ni okeru ki-shatsu to aka-shatsu: Dare, naze, doko e" [The Yellow Shirts and Red Shirts in Thai politics: Who, why, and where to next?]. *Kokusai Jōsei Kiyō*, February.

———. 2013. "Minshuka to teikō: Shin kyokumen ni haitta Tai no seiji" [Democratization and resistance: A new phase in Thai politics]. *Kokusai Mondai*, October.

———. 2014. "10-gatsu 14-ka seihen kara 40-nen: Tai seiji no genchiten" [Forty years since the 14 October uprising: Thai politics in the present moment]. *Kokusai Jōsei Kiyō*, February.

Tanaka Takeo. 2012. *Wakō: Umi no rekishi* [Wako pirates: A maritime history]. Tokyo: Kōdansha.

Torii Takashi. 2001. "Marēshia no kaihatsu senryaku to seiji hendō" [Malaysia's development strategy and political changes]. In *Ajia Seijikeizairon: Ajia no naka no Nihon o mezashite* [Political economics in Asia: Toward a "Japan in Asia"], edited by Yamakage Susumu and Suehiro Akira. Tokyo: NTT Publishing.

———. 2015. "'Mienai'? soretomo 'kakusareta'? minzoku mondai" [Ethnic issues: Invisible or deliberately concealed?]. *Aji-Ken Wārudo Torendo*, August.

Tsugami Toshiya. 2015a. "Ajia infura tōshi ginkō o shikaketa Chūgoku no omowaku" [China's intentions in launching the Asian Infrastructure Investment Bank]. *Chūō Kōron*, May.

———. 2015b. *Kyoryū no kutō: Chūgoku, GDP sekai ichii no gensō* [The struggles of the giant dragon: China's illusions of becoming the world's largest economy by GDP]. Tokyo: Kadokawa Shoten.

———. 2015c. "2015-nen no Chūgoku; Shū Kinpei seiken no yukue" [China in 2015: Where is Xi Jinping's government headed?]. Presentation to the seventy-ninth study session at China Research and Sakura Science Center, Japan Science and Technology Agency, Tokyo, 15 January.

Tsumori Shigeru. 2014. "Myanmā no gaikō" [Myanmar's foreign policy]. *Aji-Ken Wārudo Torendo*, February.

Tsunekawa Keiichi. 2006. "Minshushugi taisei no chōkiteki jizoku no jōken: Minshuka no funsō riron ni mukete" [Condition for the long-term sustainability of democratic systems: Toward a conflict theory of democratization]. In *Minshushugi ideorogī* [Ideology of democracy], edited by Keiichi Tsunekawa. Tokyo: Waseda University Press.

Umezaki Sō. 2014. "Myanmā to chiiki kyōryoku: Ajia no atarashii kessetsuten e" [Myanmar and regional cooperation: Asia's new hub]. *Aji-Ken Wārudo Torendo*, March.

Volcker, Paul, and Gyōten Toyoo. 1992. *Tomi no kōbō: En to doru no rekishi* [Rise and fall of riches: A history of the yen and the dollar]. Tokyo: Tōyō Keizai.

Wakatsuki Hidekazu. 2006. *"Zenhōi gaikō" no jidai: Reisen hen'yō ki no Nihon to Ajia 1971–80-nen* [The age of omnidirectional diplomacy: Japan and Asia in the Cold War transitional period, 1971–80]. Tokyo: Nihon Keizai Hyōronsha.

Index

Abbott, Tony, 177, 179
Abe Shinzō, 71, 98, 103, 138, 173, 176–177, 179, 180, 189, 191
Abu Sayyaf, 110
Acquisition, Technology, and Logistics Agency, 175
Act for Establishment of the Ministry of Defense, 175
affluence, 13, 35–36, 38, 91
Afghanistan, US intervention in, 3, 47, 49–50, 73
Amaya Naohiro, 181, 183
Anglo-Americanization, 88, 188
antiaccess/area denial (A2/AD) capability, 55
Apple iPod, 30, 31
Aquino, Benigno "Ninoy," 165–166, 168
Aquino, Benigno "Noynoy," III, 168
Aquino, Corazón, 165–166, 168–169, 187
Armed Forces of the Philippines Modernization Act, 80
arms exports, Japan's, 183
ASEAN, 4–5, 29, 35–36, 41, 43, 76–78, 80–82, 93–94, 97, 99–103, 107, 109, 111–113, 115–116, 136–138, 140–141, 144–147, 156, 174, 178–179, 186–187
ASEAN defense' ministers meeting, 79, 101
ASEAN economic community, 101–102

ASEAN foreign ministers' meeting, 77–78, 80
ASEAN Regional Forum (ARF), 52, 76, 80, 89
ASEAN Summit, 138
ASEAN+3, 78, 100, 138, 177–178
ASEAN+3 Summit, 138
ASEAN-5, 10(table), 35
ASEAN+6, 29(table), 76, 93, 141, 177–178
ASEAN-7, 17, 17(table), 18, 44(n3)
ASEAN+8, 77–78, 93, 178
ASEAN+10, 101
ASEAN+China, 29(table)
ASEAN-China Summit, 82
ASEAN+India, 29(table)
ASEAN+Japan, 29(table)
ASEAN-Japan summit, 177
ASEAN-plus free trade agreement, 93
ASEAN+South Korea, 29(table)
Asia Pacific Economic Cooperation (APEC), 29(table), 71, 178
Asia Pacific framework, 100, 180
Asian currency crisis (1997), 14
Asian Development Bank, 39, 82, 138, 180
Asian financial crisis (1997–1998), 21, 27, 39, 43(n2), 93, 100, 112–113, 124, 153, 157, 160–161, 163–164, 177–178, 188
Asian Infrastructure Investment Bank (AIIB), 21, 43(n2), 71, 180
Asian Monetary Fund, 21

cyber-defense system, 55
Czech Republic, 21

Dawei, Myanmar, 84, 103
decentralized democratic system, 148,
  152–153, 157
defense spending, 47, 183–185
Democratic Action Party (DAP;
  Malaysia), 162
Democratic Party (Japan), 177
Democratic Party (Thailand), 125, 128
democratic systems, 7, 125–126, 132,
  148, 152–153, 157
democratization, 7–8(n1), 11, 97–98,
  133, 135, 138, 153
Deng Xiaoping, 58, 65, 145
denuclearization of the Korean
  Peninsula, 96
Department of Defense, US, 48, 52–
  53, 55–56
developed countries, 13, 23, 133–134,
  137, 141
developed economies, 9
developing economies, 9, 10, 30, 101
Development Assistance Committee
  (DAC) of the OECD, 5, 15
diplomacy, 56, 66–68, 71, 81, 89, 99,
  105–106, 139, 156, 177, 179, 184,
  189
Doha Round WTO negotiations, 23
Doi Moi (Renovation) policy, Vietnam,
  57, 142–143
Dulles, John Foster, 182
dynamic defense force (Japan), 177

East Asia framework, 100, 180
East Asia Summit, 76, 78, 85, 93, 137–
  138, 178
East Asian financial crisis. *See* Asian
  financial crisis
East China Sea, 24, 66, 69–70, 74, 76,
  93, 102, 175, 189
East-West Economic Corridor, 82,
  83(fig.)
eclecticism, 7
economic development, 2, 5, 32, 37,
  58, 65, 73, 97, 103, 107, 124, 130–
  131, 142–143, 146, 152, 166,
  187

economic disparities, 110, 112,
  115(table), 158, 160, 163
economic diversity, 110, 112
economic growth, 124; ASEAN
  economic community, 101, 114;
  China, 52, 57–58, 62–63, 73, 91–
  92; four ASEAN countries,
  113(table); global, 17; Indonesia,
  37, 152–153, 156–157; Japan, 19,
  187–188; Korea, 95; middle-
  income trap, 40, 41; Myanmar, 85,
  133–134, 136, 139; Philippines,
  167, 170; the politics of, 41, 43;
  revolution of rising expectations,
  38; Thailand, 126, 130–132;
  Ukraine, 22; urbanization and
  affluence, 36; Vietnam, 144
economic integration, 67, 112, 187
economic partnership agreements, 29,
  45, 100, 180, 191
economic stimulus package (China),
  61, 90
education, 6, 18, 33, 40–42, 80, 109–
  110, 126–127, 157–160, 166–167,
  169
Eight-Character Dictum (Deng
  Xiaoping), 65
11 September 2001, 3, 50, 73, 162
emerging countries, 23, 27
emerging economies, 3, 10–16, 23, 25–
  27, 39, 44(nn4,5), 116, 188
emerging powers, 46
energy, 15, 71–72, 75, 82, 86–87, 137
Estonia, 21
ethnic minorities, 85, 108, 136, 140–
  142
European Community, 101
European Union (EU), 4, 10, 16, 23,
  29, 100–101, 180
European Union Free Trade
  Agreement, 23
Europe/North Atlantic region, 21
*Every Nation for Itself: Winners and
  Losers in a G-Zero World*
  (Bremmer), 14
exchange rate, 2, 19, 20, 85, 136, 161

Federal Reserve, US, 27, 43, 44(n5),
  153, 165, 184

state-owned enterprises (Malaysia), 158
state-owned enterprises (SOEs, China), 20, 62, 64, 73, 75, 104(n4)
Straits of Malacca, 5, 74–75, 103
Strategic and Global Partnership, 174
Striking Black *(Dahei)* movement, 92
"String of Pearls" strategy (China), 86, 178
The Struggles of the Giant Dragon (Tsugami), 62
submarines, 130, 146
Suehiro Akira, 127
Suharto, 148–149, 152–153, 157, 165
Sukarno, 157
Summers, Lawrence, 43(n2)
Surabaya, Indonesia, 37
Surakiart Sathirathai, 14
Surya Paloh, 155
Suzuki Yoshio, 186
Suzuki Yurika, 110
Syria, 16, 50

Tagalog people, 109
Taiwan, 8(n1), 33, 36, 55, 70, 94, 97, 117, 119–121, 123, 178, 187
Tajikistan, 68, 72
Takeshita Noboru, 184–185
Tamada Yoshifumi, 125, 128, 132
taoguang yaohui (building up strength) policy, 58
technocrats, 40, 152, 163, 165
Territorial Waters Act (1992), 76
terrorist attacks, 3, 50, 73, 153, 162
Thai Rak Thai Party, 124–125
Thailand, 14, 33, 68, 70, 72, 97, 101, 141–144, 147–148, 178, 187–188, 193–194(n8); Asian financial crisis, 28, 161; Bangkok hub, 129–130; China's importance as trading partner, 116; democratization, 131–133; economic development zone, 103; economic growth, 36, 113(table); economic imbalance, 115(table); economy, 111–113; education, 167; elite rule, 165; foreign policy and national security, 98–99; GDP, 17(table); Greater Mekong Subregion development,

82–84; income disparities, 126–127, 129; increase in GDP per capita, 114(table); Indonesian territorial waters, 156; international trade, 117–123; Japan's economic growth, 188; Japan's investment, 113; middle-income trap, 42; Myanmar's relationship with, 134–135, 139; regional cooperation, 177; religion and ethnicity, 107–109; return to military rule, 124–126; South China Sea dispute, 81; urban populations, 35; US foreign and security policy, 57; US hub-and-spokes security system, 22; US military presence, 48; US policy in Asia Pacific, 47
Thailand+1, 102
Thaksin Shinawatra, 124–125, 128–132
Thein Sein, 85, 122, 133, 135–142
Thilawa Masterplan, 138
"Three Principles on Arms Exports," 175, 177, 184
"Three Principles on Transfer of Defense Equipment and Technology," 177, 189
Tiananmen Square massacre, 51, 57
Tianjin, China, 36
tianxia (all under heaven) order, 87–89
tourism, 32, 34
Toyotomi Hideyoshi, 88
trade disputes, 184–185, 187
trade liberalization, 23
Trans-Atlantic Trade and Investment Partnership (TTIP), 23
transnational production networks, 45, 101
Trans-Pacific Partnership (TPP), 23–24, 29(table), 45, 48–49, 93, 100, 145, 147, 164, 190–191
Treasury, US, 52–53
Truong Tan Sang, 144
Tsugami Toshiya, 62, 89–91, 104(n4)
Turkey, 27, 68
Turkmenistan, 72
Twenty-First Century Maritime Silk Road, 67–68, 71

Ukraine crisis, 22, 44(n5), 50, 87

About the Book

Shiraishi Takashi reflects on the diplomatic challenges facing the countries of Asia in today's geopolitical order, exploring historical context, long-term trends, and current strategies.

The tectonic shifts in the global order are having a particularly dramatic impact in Asia, with its combined economy now larger than that of either North America or Europe. As he explores the nature of that impact, Shiraishi highlights the diversity of Asia (focusing on the ASEAN countries, China, and Japan) and the national strategies that have resulted from these differences. One key question that he addresses: What accounts for the divide between the maritime states and the countries of mainland Asia?

Shiraishi's incisive analysis, combining a discussion of international relations with a consideration of Asia's varying political cultures, sheds light on current affairs in the vast region from the Pacific to the Indian Ocean and beyond.

Shiraishi Takashi is chancellor of the Prefectural University of Kumamoto and also professor emeritus at Japan's National Graduate Institute for Policy Studies (GRIPS). He previously served as president of GRIPS and president of the Institute of Developing Economies (IDE-JETRO), among many other senior posts.